WHERE THE MOON STANDS STILL

WHERE THE MOON STANDS STILL

Revealing the Cosmic Genius of Ohio's Indigenous Earthworks

JAMES W. GRAHAM

Trillium, an imprint of
The Ohio State University Press
Columbus

Library of Congress Cataloging-in-Publication Data

Names: Graham, James W. author

Title: Where the moon stands still : revealing the cosmic genius of Ohio's Indigenous earthworks / James W. Graham.

Description: Columbus : Trillium, an imprint of The Ohio State University Press, [2026] | Includes bibliographical references. | Summary: "Tells the story of the discovery of Ohio's earthworks and the Indigenous achievement behind this UNESCO World Heritage site"— Provided by publisher.

Identifiers: LCCN 2026015610 | ISBN 9780814259917 paperback | ISBN 9780814285053 ebook

Subjects: LCSH: Fort Ancient culture—Ohio | Hopewell culture—Ohio | Newark Earthworks (Newark, Ohio) | Hopewell Site (Ohio)

Classification: LCC E99.H69 G73 2026 | DDC 977.1/01—dc23/eng/20260508

LC record available at https://lccn.loc.gov/2026015610

Cover design by Susan Zucker

Text design by Juliet Williams

Type set in Palatino Linotype

♾ The paper used in this publication meets the minimum requirements of the American National Standard for Information Sciences—Permanence of Paper for Printed Library Materials. ANSI Z39.48-1992

In memory of my mother
Virginia P. Graham
1927–2025

CONTENTS

ILLUSTRATIONS

AUTHOR'S NOTE

I was privileged to enjoy many hours of interviews with Robert Horn, Professor Emeritus of Philosophy, and Ray Hively, Professor Emeritus of Astronomy and Physics, who both spent most of their careers at Earlham College in Richmond, Indiana. Unless otherwise noted, quotations attributed to them are from conversations or emails between 2021 and 2025. If there are errors made in the book, they are the author's responsibility. Opinions expressed are not necessarily those of people about whom I have written.

When referring to the First People of the Americas, modern writers and tribal authorities sometimes differ in their opinions about the best words to describe them. Tribal names are generally preferred when they are known. The word "Indian" is problematic for well-known reasons. When tribal identity is not an option, I will use "Indigenous," mostly, but will sometimes refer to "Native people," "Native Americans," and "Indians," depending on context. References to harmful stereotypes and pejorative words can be hurtful to read but are sometimes needed to understand the violence historically inflicted on Indigenous people and their culture. No disrespect is intended.

CHAPTER 1

Moundbuilders Country Club

> A friend in Brooklyn told me that his little son had gone out to watch workmen breaking up a sidewalk. He was fascinated to see earth under the cement. He had never seen it before.
>
> —N. Scott Momaday, Kiowa, from *Earth Keeper: Reflections on the American Land*[1]

To the women of the club came the call to arms. "It's that time of year again," the Facebook post declared one morning in May 2021. "We are looking for help to plant a few flats of flowers around the clubhouse and the patio. The men have spread the mulch around the golf course and the clubhouse, and the hanging baskets for the pool and patio have been purchased and are being hung next week as well. As they say, 'many hands make for light work.'"[2]

They should know. The work of many ancient hands gave the Moundbuilders Country Club the exceptional topography—the vast geometric mounds—that some two thousand years later would host golf, a swimming pool, Tuesday Rotary Club meetings, and pretty flowers. As country clubs go, this one's landscape architecture was like none in the world.

Their president called it a "blue-collar country club."[3] For more than five generations members brought their children there to swing a golf club, swim the seventy-five-foot-long pool, and, upon coming of age, quaff a beer or two after eighteen holes. Growing up like that, day after day, who wouldn't take such exclusive surroundings for granted? If every day you swept the steps of the Lincoln Memorial, you'd be forgiven if you did not pause each day

1. Momaday, *Earth Keeper*, 39.

2. Moundbuilders Country Club (@Moundbuilders-Country-Club-100063650346075), "Good morning women of MCC."

3. Bahr, "Push to Move."

to view its perfect, majestic alignment with the Washington Monument and the squinting-white glare of the Capitol dome two miles away. So golfers of the Moundbuilders Country Club might be forgiven for asking, "What's so special about piles of dirt?" Likewise, the homeowners whose backyards end at high berm-like mounds might be forgiven for paying them little mind as they tend to their barbeques. It's a bit like that time the world-class violinist Joshua Bell played his Stradivarius in a subway for three-quarters of an hour, case open for donations, and went all but unnoticed. Genius hiding in plain sight.

Certainly there were golf courses better designed for the game. Instead of the typical gentle hills, here perfectly flat expanses of turf were interrupted by monotonously straight, level earthen walls, like levies, some in sweeping arcs, others straight as railroad elevations, unnatural in their symmetry, appearing mechanically constructed but long predating the mechanistic age. The mounds rarely vary in their height of between five and six feet. When it was still open, the president of the club showed me around one summer day and said a big challenge was the golf ball that hits the mound and rolls down to its base. "We often call it the 'crotch,'" he said. "When it collects down there, that's the hardest place for the mower to get, so it's often the longest grass."[4] Other golfers gave one of the larger mounds the nickname "Big Chief."[5]

Today, most Americans know nothing of this place. Many Ohioans do not know it. Among those who do are nonlocals who travel to see the Newark Earthworks, not to chase a ball, but to gaze into a little-known Indigenous past that predated European contact by more than a millennium. Native people came to see for themselves the awesome and mysterious sculpted shapes that surrounded golfers in their cleats and carts. They used their imaginations to blot out the fairways that meandered into, around and across two enormous earthworks so geometrically precise you would think the builders had laser surveying instruments. On the southwest side of the property is a near-perfect earthen circle, more than three football fields across. It connects by a short pair of parallel walls to a larger octagon on the northeast half of the golf course, sculpted with equal mathematical precision, enclosing an area 40 percent larger than the footprint of the Pentagon in Washington. Being airborne gives a good perspective, but the experience on foot is jaw-dropping

4. Dave Kratoville, president, Moundbuilders Country Club, interview by author, July 26, 2021.

5. Bahr, "Push to Move."

FIGURE 1.1. Known as the Newark Octagon, it is actually an octagon connected to a circle, known as the "Observatory Circle." Here the Moundbuilders Country Club played golf for more than a century. Photo by Timothy E. Black / Newark Earthworks Center.

too once you wrap your head around it. Draw an imaginary axis down the center of the aligned circle and octagon, bisecting them lengthwise, and the resulting line is a half mile long. One mile southeast of those earthworks is the Great Circle earthwork, even larger than the circle that's mated to the Octagon, and relatively well preserved as a state park. The Great Circle has a geometric area ten times that of the baseball playing field that is home to the team formerly known as the Cleveland Indians.[6]

Visiting the golf course in 2022, as I did, a student of Indigenous "prehistory" would need to concentrate her gaze, erase the golf carts and the facing homes with their J. D. Vance-for-Senate yard signs, mentally chop down the overgrowth of trees, and go back in time, back as far, perhaps, as Jesus's time.

6. Cleveland's Progressive Field, like all ballparks, has a playing field that is a quarter circle in shape, in this case with an area of about 107,000 square feet, not including foul territory. The Great Circle has an area of about 1,130,400 square feet.

Uncluttered by distractions and focused on the ancient construction, she might ask, what people built this? Why? Indigenous people today see it as a grand and sacred place. But they too ask, what purpose did this abstract land art serve? How did these monuments speak to the pilgrims who traveled to them from across the continent two millennia ago?

The larger four-square-mile Newark Earthworks complex, of which the country club site was a major part, required Native people to move seven million cubic feet of earth. That would take more than 175,000 Jeep Comanche pickup trucks—a five-hundred-mile-long caravan.[7] Without wheelbarrows or metal tools, the builders loosened dirt with sharpened sticks and hoes made by affixing the shoulder blades of deer to wooden shafts. The soil came from different sources, including adjacent trenches that were later filled with water to create parallel or concentric "moats" or pools. Additional material had to be brought to the site. Clays and gravel were transported, perhaps sometimes by canoe or raft, or hauled from nearby riverbanks.[8] They filled woven baskets with earth and hand-carried them to reshape the flat plain. The layering and soil engineering itself was a clever invention that made the structures last to this day. The enormity of the labor is impressive enough without even considering the big mystery of their social organization and purpose. Nowhere on earth is there a collection of geometric earthworks as large as this.

When Europeans arrived, they saw great human-sculpted earthen monuments all across the present-day United States east of the Rockies. At first glance they resembled natural topography, but then pattern recognition sets in: the mounds are too perfectly formed. They had to be products of educated minds. A lot of educated minds. The mounds numbered in the many tens of thousands, baffling white people. Many were conical or flat-topped, some as high as eighty or ninety feet, but mostly smaller. Some were for burials, some for apparent ceremonial uses, still others had unknown purposes.

7. Ohio History Connection estimates the earthworks consist of seven million cubic feet of soil over four square miles. Seven million cu. ft. = 259,259 cu. yds. Comanche pickups carry 1.5 cubic yards of soil in their cargo box. 259,259 ÷ 1.5 = 172,839 trucks. Pickup length of fifteen feet x 172,839 = 2.6 million feet, or 492 miles. For hauling soil today, it would of course make more sense to use dump trucks. The dump truck caravan for seven million cubic feet of soil would be more than 90 miles long (259,259 ÷ 13 x 24.5 = 488,603 feet or 92 miles). Chrysler stopped making Comanche pickup trucks in 1992 but continues production of the Jeep Cherokee SUV. In 2021, the Cherokee Nation asked Chrysler to drop the brand name. The company declined to do so.

8. Wimble and Powers, "Hopewell Earthwork Mounds."

FIGURE 1.2. The Great Circle in Newark, Ohio. Photo by Bradley T. Lepper. © Ohio History Connection.

Those in areas around the Great Lakes were often elegantly shaped effigies—giant birds, serpents, mammals, and some human forms. All the major waterways were lined with them. The greatest concentration was in the Midwest, in places now known as Illinois, Indiana, Missouri. And Ohio. The most extraordinary were Ohio's, especially along the Scioto River and other nearby waterways.

In the 1500s, their builders were long gone. Asked by European colonizers, Indigenous people could not explain their origin, at least not with consistency.[9] Absent a written history, cultural memory can cross only so many generations. For centuries, as Europeans pushed westward across the Appalachians and more people saw the mounds with their own eyes, they formed bizarre theories about their builders. Being mostly Christian, they leaned toward Biblical interpretations, deploying exceptional mental gymnastics to fit the evidence into their Bible-story frame of reference.

9. Lepper, "Early Historic American," 8.

By the late nineteenth century, an archaeologist discovered distinctive artifacts associated with mound builders centered around Ohio and attributed them and their landscape architecture to a culture distinct from others that came to be known as "Hopewell," a name taken from the owner of a farm where some of the earliest, most important finds were unearthed. In the years that followed, European colonizers plowed through, vandalized, bulldozed, and grave-robbed most of the earthworks they found. But not all, and in recent years, using what little was preserved, attitudes are changing and glimmers of greater intellectual honesty flicker among the now dominant culture. Since the 1970s, a small group of archaeologists and other scholars have discovered new meaning encoded in these works. Native people are teaching the rest of America how to look at these ancient sculptures the way they see them. Modern artists are taking inspiration from them. Wild-eyed theories and outright indifference persist and sometimes smother the reawakening. But, thanks to a few curious scholars, the Newark Earthworks saw their decades as a country club end and their two-millennia-long historical value rediscovered, their sacred purpose better honored. The journey to this awakening was long, with odd twists and much damage along the way. It isn't over. But it's not too late to rescue more of this Indigenous legacy. Thanks in no small measure to little-known efforts of two people in particular, we may still wrench from the damaged earthworks an understanding of their heritage.

CHAPTER 2

The Humanist and the Astrophysicist

> I've always believed that the role of serendipity in science is vastly underestimated.
> —Bradley Lepper

Richmond, Indiana, was a small college town of 33,000, just over the Ohio border, when Bob Horn was born there in 1930. The city's size hasn't changed much since. Some country roads were hardly more than cart paths then, but Bob's father loved to explore them on Sunday afternoon drives. For him, losing one's way was the point.

"Getting lost was difficult because he knew the region from long experience," Bob said. "But he was good at it."

On one drive they found their path dead end at a river ford. Pondering the water's depth and their wheels' height, his mother asked, "Now where are we?"

"I think we're lost," he said, gleefully. "I hope we are."

In mock horror, she said, "What will the boy think?"

"Well, you *do* want him to *think,* don't you?"

If a life of the mind was what they wished for young Bob, the future Kierkegaard scholar would not disappoint. Indeed, teaching college students how to think would be Bob's lifework. As a boy, those trips across the Indiana and Ohio countryside exposed him to one particular set of curiosities he would never erase from his mind.

"The region, and nearby Ohio, were dotted in many counties with so-called Indian mounds, with local names and stories which I found fascinating," said Bob. "By fourth grade I was trying to discover all I could about them. This led me eventually to archaeological reports (Depression-era Works Progress Administration projects) in the local public library and to some meager comprehension of the local pre-Columbian past."

When he was eight or nine his parents took him to New Castle and Anderson, two nearby Indiana towns that had circular Native mounds similar to, but much smaller than, the ones he would later explore at Newark. The earthworks in Anderson were contained in an area that at that time had just become a state park. Its surviving archaeological features remained intact because the land's previous owners found a creative way to preserve them. In the 1920s they turned the area into an amusement park and let the mounds serve as an added attraction. By 1930, however, the Depression robbed the amusement park of customers, it closed, and the Mounds State Park was born.

"Later, in the mid-1940s, I got interested in the archaeological work on the Indiana mounds and earthworks of the local Whitewater Valley. I visited most of the mapped ones, trying to understand their situation and environment," Bob said.

One thing that put Bob's hometown of Richmond on the map was highly regarded Earlham College. Founded by Quakers in 1847, it retains that affiliation and culture of governance today, favoring consensus and frowning on the contentiousness of other academic settings. Bob was accepted for admission there and became one of about 1,000 students in all.

"I thought of making a career in archaeology," Bob recalled in a 2005 talk at Newark. "Instead I chose to study philosophy and to concentrate on the history and philosophy of religions as an avenue into the ancient world."

In 1953 he traveled to Denmark to pursue his interest in that country's nineteenth-century theologian and philosopher Søren Kierkegaard, who at that time was just being discovered by American academics. Kierkegaard's works weren't even translated into English until the mid-twentieth century. As Bob said, "In 1953 Earlham had no college-sponsored foreign study program. I was determined to understand Kierkegaard, the first thinker I had encountered who both demanded my attention and baffled all my attempts to interpret him." He found a way to go to Denmark, aided by a small grant from a Quaker educational fund but mostly paying his own way.

The local paper currency was his "first and strongest impression of Denmark," specifically the fifty kroner note. "On the face of the note was an etching of what the Danes call a 'dysse,' a dolmen or burial mound, perhaps five thousand years old." These prehistoric stone burial chambers featured enormous granite capstones hoisted impossibly atop a pair of similarly heavy upright slabs. Sometimes the structures were then buried by builders under mounds of earth and stone.

"Danish rural churches often were built close to them," said Bob. "There were still rural families who made annual food offerings to them. My thoughts returned to the many mounds and earthworks in my own country, most neglected and unnoticed. . . . At worst they were looted and destroyed."

After his time abroad, Bob finished up at Earlham and then moved on to graduate studies in philosophy at Union Theological Seminary in New York City. His first teaching job was at another Quaker institution, Haverford College, a highly regarded all-male liberal arts school outside Philadelphia. Then followed an invitation from Union to join their faculty in New York. In time, his undergraduate alma mater gave him a chance to return home to Richmond, to a teaching position back at Earlham.

"It was tempting because it was an opportunity to come back to an area where I was fascinated with the archaeology." Moreover, Earlham offered him an opportunity to help design a new philosophy curriculum.

The Danish kroner note that so caught Bob's attention had on its opposite side an image of Danish astronomer and physicist Ole Christensen Rømer, discoverer of the speed of light. It was an omen of sorts, for Bob would one day come to meet an astrophysicist at Earlham, in some ways his opposite too, destined to form with him a partnership of more than forty years: two sides of the same scholarly krone.

⊕

As a child living in Muskogee, Oklahoma, in the 1950s, Ray Hively's family had a small house with a backyard overlooking a "pasture with one calf."

"Behind me there were no lights and as a child I would spend a lot of time lying down on my back in the backyard looking at the Milky Way and the stars. And I could see those things in a way you can't see them now. I've never seen them as well since . . . I could see the majesty of the sky the way the ancients did. I wasn't thinking about it in those terms then, but I was awestruck by the sky and I always had the sense, even as a child, that whatever meaning there was for life in the universe was out there somewhere. It wasn't down here. The stuff down here was too small. The 'out there' was so much larger, so grand, that I really decided I wanted to do astronomy."

Ray's pursuit of a career in astrophysics could not be better timed. He majored in physics at the University of Oklahoma and in the summer of 1965, his final year there, he landed a summer internship at NASA's Manned Spaceflight Center in Houston just as they were working out the problems of landing a man on the moon. Ray went on to Harvard for his PhD in astronomy, spending two more summers at NASA, a dual path sure to lead to great things in the dawning space age. He helped draft crew instructions for a Gemini spaceflight and helped plot descent trajectories that would keep Apollo lunar landers from crashing into craters.

"I remember as a summer intern I sat in on an astronauts' meeting where they were discussing the possibility of a serious fire in a spacecraft that had an all-oxygen atmosphere . . . people recognized the danger of that. But the counterargument, well, there were two counterarguments. One, they had extensive space flight experience with an oxygen atmosphere without any problem. And they needed to beat the Russians and if they tried to reengineer the interior with nitrogen-oxygen it would set them far back, so far that they might not beat the Russians. Those considerations caused them to take what they knew would be a risk. I'll never forget that. It was a good example of risk assessment that turned bad.

"Of course, it was not more than a year or two years after that the first three astronauts were burned to death in an Apollo spacecraft on the pad in an oxygen fire."

Ray's faculty advisor at Harvard was David Layzer, a leading proponent of the "Cold Big Bang Theory," which held that during the time leading up to the Bang, matter was absolute-zero cold. With Layzer's encouragement, Ray tackled the subject in his thesis, which he titled "Cosmology of a Cold Universe," and they collaborated on other published works. An essay they coauthored shows up on the Gravity Research Foundation's twenty best of 1971, a list topped by an article called "Black Holes," by Stephen Hawking.[1] A member of Ray's thesis committee was one of the great theoretical physicists of his day, Philip Morrison, a former Manhattan Project scientist who was said to have "helped assemble the first atomic bomb with his own hands."[2]

With experience, connections, and academic credentials like that, Ray was ready to reach for the stars in more ways than one. He pictured himself back at NASA or at a prestigious research institution. Two things went wrong. 1972 was the year of the sixth and final Apollo lunar landing. The gusher of US space funding dried up. Meanwhile, with ink on his thesis barely dry, new data was being collected about something called the cosmic microwave background, the radiation left behind by the Big Bang, still measurable in tiny traces.

---

1. Gravity Research Foundation, "Abstracts of Award Winning."
2. Overbye, "Philip Morrison, 89, builder."

"People proved that the microwave background had a black-body spectrum, which meant that it almost certainly came from a beginning that was very hot," said Ray. That was cold water on the Layzer-Hively school of cosmology. Their theory of the universe was universally dropped.[3] Well, not entirely. Curiously, years later, in 2013, Ray's Harvard thesis was cited in a paper published in *The Proceedings of the International Conference on Creationism*. The author, whose qualifications consisted of a master's degree in education, used Ray's thesis as one of many pieces of scholarly "evidence" of a universe arisen from a cold abyss, which the author wrote, "easily accommodates the rapid cosmological formation timeframes of the six day Genesis account."[4] Probably not the kind of citation Ray was looking for.

By 1972, his work at Harvard behind him, Ray knew his career fallback could always be teaching. An offer from a small liberal arts college in Indiana came, and he took it.

"I took the job at Earlham largely as a kind of way station," Ray said. "I was attracted earlier in particular because it combined a rigorous liberal arts curriculum with historical Quaker values which I always respected. I'm not a religious person myself, I'm not a Quaker, but I always respected their concern for the values of social justice and simplicity, and they tended to be very nonjudgmental about people who didn't share their theological convictions. All of that appealed to me and that was the primary reason I thought it would be a good thing for me initially although at the time I never expected to stay there for a very long time. I ended up staying for forty-two years."

Ray welcomed the opportunity to teach classes in astronomy and cosmology, although the adjustment could not have been easy. From the vast resources of Harvard and NASA, Ray found himself at a college with a telescope and observatory so old it would soon be on the National Register of Historic Places. Its copper-sheathed dome protected a telescope with a six-and-a-half-inch diameter lens; innovative in its day, perhaps, but its date of manufacture was 1856.[5] A charming relic.

Nonetheless, his first two years went well. Settled and comfortable, he was in for a surprise. Earlham's academic dean, Joe Elmore, had a new idea about how Ray could contribute to the curriculum. Elmore was a former professor of religion and a strong admirer of the intellect of the college's philosophy professor, a man some years older than Ray. Elmore had hired

3. Davies, "Counting Back to Zero."
4. Davies, "Counting Back to Zero."
5. National Park Service, "National Register of Historic Places."

them both, and now he told Ray he wanted to pair them up to co-teach an extended curriculum. The class would cover the history of cosmology from multiple academic perspectives.

"The main thing I remember about Elmore is his commitment to critical thinking across the disciplines," Ray recalled.

But, Ray thought, a philosophy professor? He'll have no grasp of astrophysics.

Though Ray found the idea interesting, he and Bob Horn had the same reaction. They hated it.

Bob recalled, "I was faced with teaching a course with a physicist I didn't know, and Ray was faced with teaching a course with a humanist he didn't know. So we were both disturbed to say the least." Ray remembers it the same way.

"We got together on the phone," said Bob, and then met face-to-face. "We found we had so much fun arguing with each other we decided we would do the course. I would put forth a proposition; he would blow it out of the water. He'd put forth something else and I would do the same. And we so much enjoyed it and actually made some headway in the discussion we were having that we looked forward to doing the course."

Elmore's "challenge to me and Ray, putting us together in a cosmology course which neither of us would have imagined, catches much about him. I think he must have chuckled over our likely consternation when confronted with the idea, seeing things about both of us that we learned only by working together. He was a rare spirit, my idea of an educator."

Dean Elmore had acquired grant funding to introduce a concept called PIE, or Program for Integral Education. The two would lead the class but also bring in other members of the faculty. The class would be called "Cosmology: from Stonehenge to the Big Bang."

As Bob explained it, "The idea was to develop courses, oftentimes with a number of faculty members, not just two, maybe three, four or five in different fields, all of which were pertinent to answering a question that the course itself posed.

"We involved a historian, a professor from the religion [department] whose primary field was Old Testament studies and archaeology, a geologist who had been one of my teachers when I was a student at Earlham. And they were all pertinent to answering questions about what a work like Stonehenge was."

The object was to show liberal arts students how deeper knowledge is achieved through fluency in, and integration of, multiple disciplines.

"So we arranged to teach this course, which spanned two terms," said Ray, ". . . and the idea was to try to get students to think seriously and carefully about how humans had tried to make sense of the larger universe both from a philosophical view and from also a scientific point of view or even a theological point of view. At the time the earliest sort of a prehistoric record we have of people having had astronomical knowledge [was] Stonehenge."

The class would work best if the chemistry between them worked. Bob was quieter by nature, but he relished the art of conversation even if his tendency was to respectfully listen. He drew out the opinions of others and often made his points with questions rather than assertions. He had the quiet authority of a patient school master, too slim to have physicality on his side. He modeled humility in the style of Socrates who told us, "The only true wisdom is knowing you know nothing." In my conversations with Bob, on multiple occasions, he had an interesting way of exhibiting intellectual self-confidence by expressing self-doubt and openness to contradiction. Conversation was an invitation to a dialogue, not a lecture.

His students remembered his gentle touch. When one student's essay made no logical sense whatever, Bob penned in the margin, "I understand you as if through a cloud."

"Bob was a pedagogical genius," said Marilyn Gaye Piety, a student who now teaches philosophy at Drexel University. "I remember very little about what he said in class because he was so subtle. His objective, clearly, was to get his students talking, and that he did." To keep the conversations from becoming free-for-alls, "Bob would ever so gently direct the discussion in productive directions. He was never dogmatic, though, never told us how we should interpret anything. He was a genius at getting his students thinking, at getting the best out of all of his students."[6]

⊕

Could this softer-spoken philosopher's tendency to look inward and self-analyze mesh with a more animated and outgoing scientist whose focus is the widest-imaginable physical world? Was this Plato meets Buzz Lightyear?

6. Marilyn Gaye Piety, email to the author, May 16, 2024.

Ray's style was less ponderous, more mission-driven and methodically scientific: make a hypothesis, find the data and reasoning to support it, or toss it out. Ray believed in intellectual humility too, but his demeanor did not always model it. If Bob asserted something, he was quick to express self-doubt. Ray was more boldly declarative. They both welcomed counterargument, but in differing ways. Bob liked their counterbalance in style, but he also saw that—style notwithstanding—they had in common an appreciation of healthy skepticism and challenges to their own assumptions.

"When Ray said one day early in our conversations something like 'we seldom think about how really hard it is to know anything,' I knew I wanted to work with him."

Ray wasn't one to show deference to a senior faculty member, and Bob enjoyed Ray's irreverence. Bob compared Ray to the physicist and Nobel laureate Richard Feynman who called philosophy "low level baloney."[7] Bob told a story of Feynman meeting with his faculty advisor, a man of so little patience he would place an expensive watch on his desk to keep visitors mindful of his demanding schedule. Feynman responded by placing his own Micky Mouse watch on the desk next to it. Ray shared Feynman's irreverence, Bob said. He loved that about Ray.

As Bob recalled about their dean, "He saw an opportunity to put a philosopher who he saw was interested in cosmological questions, and a physicist whose field was cosmology, together in a course that would bring the students in the sciences and humanities together." They would be the embodiment of what C. P. Snow called "two cultures," the literary or philosophical intellectuals on one side, the scientists on the other.

"There seems to be no place where the cultures meet," Snow complained. "I am not going to waste time saying this is a pity. It is much worse than that. . . . But at the heart of thought and creation we are letting some of our best chances go by default. The clashing point of two subjects, two disciplines, two cultures—of two galaxies, so far as that goes—ought to produce creative chances. In the history of mental activity that has been where some of the breakthroughs came."[8]

⊕

7. Horn and others attribute this quote to Feynman, but the closest to an original source I could find was Feynman, *Surely You're Joking, Mr. Feynman!*, 232.

8. Snow, *Two Cultures*, 17.

Their dean believed it could work in part because Bob was fully immersed in the topics of Stonehenge and archaeology long before Ray's arrival. Stonehenge was all the rage in the 1960s. Gerald Hawkins's bestselling book *Stonehenge Decoded*, published in 1965, described the author's use of new-fangled computers to develop the then-startling theory that prehistoric people arranged the landmark's enormous stones to align with astronomical events, particularly the summer solstice. Many thought this was quackery. Archaeologist Richard Atkinson said Hawkins's book was "tendentious, arrogant, slipshod, and unconvincing." The builders of Stonehenge, said Atkinson, were "howling barbarians."

But the mysteries of Stonehenge resonated in the hippie culture of the time, and it was a popular topic with students. Back when Bob was preparing for his own first term at Earlham in 1966, well before Ray's arrival, he received a letter from his new dean asking him if he would be interested in leading a freshman seminar program. Based on a Harvard model, "the idea was to engage a faculty member in teaching a group of freshman students in a field that was not his own, a field that you wanted to explore . . . with a group of students who were doing the same thing." Teacher and students would learn a new subject together.

"He gave me a list of possible topics, none of which I particularly liked, so I wrote back and said I am interested in doing that [kind of class], but I'd like to take the theme of Stonehenge." Thus, Bob could pursue the passion for archaeology that dated to his boyhood.

"Hawkins had written a book in which he was arguing that Stonehenge was a celestial computer," recalled Bob. "I was quite skeptical about that, but I was also interested in the claim he was making."

The class was to be limited to fifteen students and Bob called it "Megalithic Cultures of Western Europe," omitting "Stonehenge" from the course title because he didn't want to "attract a crowd that's not really willing to work hard at it." He interviewed students who applied and selected the best.

In October of 1967, Bob caught a lucky break, a coup for a new teacher at a small, lesser-known Midwestern college. He convinced Gerald Hawkins himself to visit campus and be the star attraction of a three-day Earlham seminar on Stonehenge. Students were given rigorous research assignments to prepare for Hawkins's visit so they could hone their critical-thinking skills and challenge Hawkins's theories about ancient astronomy. More than fifty years later, Bob still spoke with pride about the seminar. "The students studied Hawkins's book literally inside and out and back toward the ground. Hawkins said it was the best critique of his work that he had anywhere. So that created a seedbed for interest in Stonehenge and similar questions. And that survived."

Years later, after Ray arrived at Earlham in 1972, public interest in Stonehenge was accompanied by even wilder conjectures about ancient monumental archeological sites. Could their construction have been aided by extraterrestrial visitors? Erich von Daniken's book, *Chariots of the Gods*, published in 1968, eventually sold in the tens of millions. A 1972 documentary, *In Search of Ancient Astronauts*, featured Rod Serling, Carl Sagan, and Werner von Braun. How, they asked, could "primitive" people move Stonehenge's massive stones and align them so perfectly with solstices? How could Peru's ancient Nazca lines be drawn without airborne vehicles? The 1968 movie *2001: A Space Odyssey* built a fictional narrative around alien-installed black monoliths of rectilinear perfection.

While these extraterrestrial questions were not taken so seriously by academia, Ray and Bob's dean saw that Stonehenge could bait students to pursue bigger, harder topics. For Ray's part, he, like Bob, was highly skeptical about claims that Stonehenge marked astronomical events at all and looked forward to showing students how to apply science and critical thinking skills to Hawkins's work. Bob would introduce philosophy, history, and the study of how humans perceive the world—and worlds—around them. The humanist and the astronomer would themselves model how a mixing of perspectives and challenging criticisms can point to larger truths. So in 1974 their joint venture began.

⊕

If archaeological sites such as Stonehenge were to frame their students' coursework, it was fortuitous that Earlham enjoyed proximity to an abundance of archaeological curiosities. Native American earthworks like the ones in Newark are scattered across Ohio, into Indiana, Illinois, Wisconsin, Michigan, Kentucky, Tennessee, Pennsylvania, and far beyond. Many were simple conical mounds, others dome- or loaf-shaped burial places of various sizes. Others were geometric, without any evidence of burials. Like Stonehenge or the Nazca lines, their construction required purposeful and thoughtful planning, and orchestration of large workforces. Ohio's giant circles, squares, and octagons seemed to be sophisticated representations of something, but no one knew what. Though Stonehenge was older by more than 1,500 years, the mounds of Ohio were likewise a product of "prehistoric" cultures. The words "prehistoric" and "mounds" are out of favor today because they can be pejorative, suggesting lack of intellectual or artistic sophistication. "Earthworks" is now preferred. The word "prehistoric" is generally associated with written records as Westerners think of them. Is it really useful to describe an event that happened on the Scioto River in, say, 400 CE, by using a word that also time-stamps dinosaurs? One scholar of Potawatomi ethnic heritage told me that "'prehistoric' isn't in my vocabulary."[9]

Sixty miles southeast of Earlham College's home in Richmond, Indiana, was a historic site called Fort Ancient. "Fort" was a misnomer adopted by early explorers. The site consists of earthen walls lined with "moats" that traced the contours of hilltop ridges. It was later found there was no evidence of walls or timbers built atop the earthworks, and the "moats" were *inside* the enclosures, making the combined structure fairly useless for defense purposes. It's now believed the walls defined an interior ceremonial gathering space and the moats were lined with clay to help them retain water, making them more like decorative or sacramental pools than barriers. In all, the structures at Fort Ancient enclosed a full one hundred acres.

On a pleasant day in the 1974–1975 school year, Ray and Bob took their students there. As fascinating as the enclosures were, there was another curiosity at Fort Ancient they wanted them to see: the "foursquare." Within the northern enclosures stand four small mounds arrayed to form the corners of a square, rather like a baseball diamond except this one has sides 512 feet long, large enough in area to hold more than twenty-five baseball diamonds. Each corner mound was just a few feet across and no more than waist high. Originally the corner mounds were covered by slabs of limestone that were blackened and scarred, suggesting bonfires.[10] The mounds had been surveyed originally in the nineteenth century, but Ray and Bob weren't aware of anyone doing a closer examination of their geometry.

Ray and Bob aimed to change that, and they would use the site to combine a lesson in archaeology with another in the basics of land surveying. Here they unpacked a plane table, a simple but accurate way to map a site's three-dimensional characteristics. The device consisted of a horizontal drawing

9. Dr. John Low, interview with the author.
10. Ancient Ohio Trail.

surface mounted on a tripod equipped with bubble levels. Atop the leveled table they placed an alidade, a telescopic sight that they aligned to whatever distant objects they were mapping. Distances, compass angles, elevations and triangulations were recorded on paper on the plane table. In this way the students measured distances between mounds and angles relative to one another and to cardinal points on a map. They couldn't establish good sight lines for all four mounds because somebody made the unfortunate choice of positioning the site's small museum right inside the square. But they could site the alignments of three mounds and what they found was stunning. Imaginary lines connecting three points of the square formed a near-perfect 90-degree right angle. How was it that such a "primitive" people could get their math so right, two thousand years ago, over such extended distances without surveying tools, at least like ones we know? Bob recalls they discovered the "intimations" of a near-perfect square.

Surveyors later proved them right. The foursquare's corners are indeed geometrically precise. Archaeologists say the builders lived otherwise simple lives: hunting, gathering, cultivating fruits, nuts and vegetables, using flint arrowheads, spears and tools of stone or bone. They lived in small hamlets not big enough to be called villages. Nonetheless, the students' survey revealed an ancient knowledge of basic geometry that seemed more sophisticated than anyone seemed to be talking about at the time.

"Of course, they were very excited about that and so they began to talk about the precise geometry of the site," recalled Bob. The students wanted to share their research findings. But the professors knew their data was "flimsy." Much more would need to be studied. For example, were the mounds still in their precise position as constructed, or had earlier excavators slightly changed their positions? Their measurements needed extensive confirmation.

As the professors and students continued to discuss their findings, the subject of Stonehenge and astronomical alignments inevitably came up.

"I was always very skeptical frankly," said Ray. "I understand very well the cynicism and skepticism that many people have for archaeoastronomy because I was exactly one of them in the beginning. I thought it was all nonsense and it was very easy to go to any prehistoric structure and just start drawing lines between distant things and points. They'd always point to some place on the horizon. If you just stick enough lines you can always find solar alignments or lunar alignments or anything you want. And so the whole thing seemed like pseudoscience and nonsense to me.

"I remember saying to Bob, when we were talking about it, that if he could just give me some ramshackle prehistoric sites somewhere I could go

FIGURE 2.1. From left: Ray Hively, Bob Horn, archaeologist Brad Lepper and University of Cincinnati architecture scholar John Hancock, at a symposium on the Newark Earthworks held in 2011 in Granville, Ohio. Photo by Timothy E. Black / Newark Earthworks Center.

out and I guaranteed him I could find evidence for it being aligned as much as at Stonehenge and it wouldn't matter what the site was or what it was extracted from."

Bob remembers Ray betting the students he could draw random lines and find landmarks aligned to the summer solstice at any archaeological site.

"The whole thing was so silly," Ray said. "I could always find the alignments and he [Bob] said, well, he knew a site. We can put that to test at a site called the Newark Earthworks. At that point, even though I considered myself educated I'd never heard of them. Like most people, I never knew they existed."[11]

Bob recalled, "I knew enough about Newark to know that it looked as if it was precise geometrically." You could see that on nineteenth century maps. "It would be a much more challenging problem. So I said, 'let's go to Newark.'"

11. McAlister, "Mounds' Lunar Alignment," 6.

Ray put it this way, "If you had a prehistoric site that was not aligned to anything, what number of alignments would you expect to find by chance? The theory was that we could find as many alignments at Newark as there were at Stonehenge."[12]

"And so we drove down there," Ray said. It was all sort of tongue-in-cheek, an academic exercise to show that archaeoastronomy was a bunch of hooey.

12. McAlister, "Mounds' Lunar Alignment," 6.

CHAPTER 3

Invention and Deception

> I wish that the persons who go thither would make very exact descriptions of what they see of that kind, without forming any theories. The moment a person forms a theory, his imagination sees, in every object, only the traits which favor that theory. But it is too early to form theories on those antiquities. We must wait with patience till more facts are collected.
>
> —Thomas Jefferson, letter to Charles Thomson, concerning Indigenous "monuments"

More than one thousand years before Christopher Columbus landed on a Bahama island and named it for Christ the Savior, or San Salvador, Indigenous earthworks decorated the entire North American landscape from the Great Plains eastward. When white explorers found that Indigenous people had no consistent explanation for the earthworks,[1] they began inventing their own narratives. People continue doing so to this day.

Hively and Horn followed a long succession of early European explorers curiously seeking explanations, forming theories. Which brings us to the story of David Wyrick, a sorry victim of inventive theorizing and misinformation, if ever there was one. Born in Pennsylvania in 1804, he moved to Newark, Ohio, in the 1840s,[2] eventually becoming the Licking County Surveyor and an avid "antiquarian." Before archaeology became the true scientific discipline it is today, amateurs like Wyrick liked to unearth ancient graves and other Indigenous sites in search of artifacts. Little consideration was given to the expelled people who regarded their ancestors' remains as sacred and inviolable.

1. Lepper, "Early Historic American Indian," 8.
2. Find a Grave. "David Wyrick."

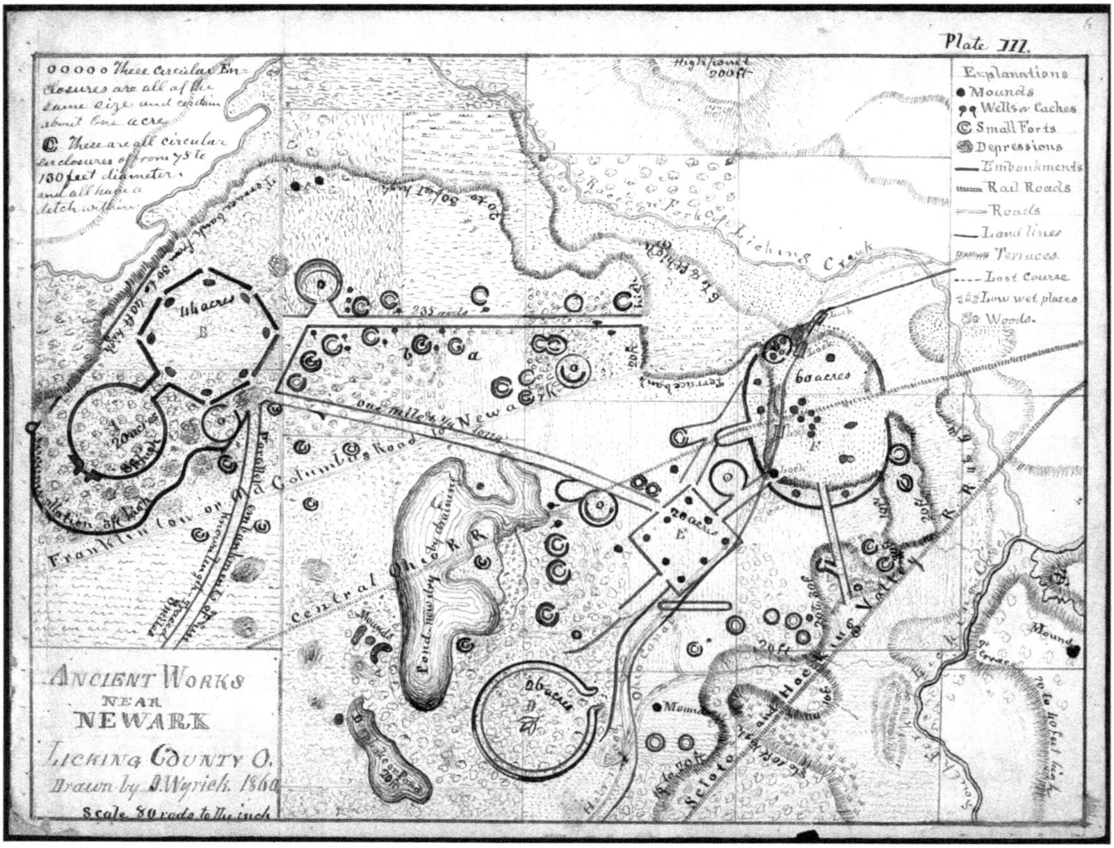

FIGURE 3.1. David Wyrick's 1860 map of the "ancient works" of Newark, Ohio. David Wyrick Collection, William L. Clements Library, The University of Michigan.

By 1859 Wyrick was suffering from rheumatoid arthritis. His friend, the respected archaeologist Charles Whittlesey, said Wyrick's "fingers were swollen and distorted, and his feet so much enlarged as to render them almost useless . . . and that his appendages were so disfigured as scarcely to retain their human aspect, he was everywhere regarded with commiseration." Wyrick used a drug called laudanum, a bitter-tasting mixture of opium and alcohol that was then growing in popularity as a pain killer. Civil War soldiers who used opium products soon popularized them further and by the end of the nineteenth century about one in two hundred Americans were addicted to opium and morphine powders, most of them middle- and upper-class women. They were the OxyContin of their day.[3]

3. Trickey, "Inside the Story."

Wyrick's ailments drove him to retire as a surveyor, but he was strong enough to create excellent maps of the Newark earthworks, in addition to collecting artifacts. Many earthworks were sprawling constructions, overgrown by centuries of trees and brush, and surveyors like Wyrick were uniquely able to measure and document them. Like so many, he sought clues to their origin.

For the most part, Wyrick shared the colonizers' view that Native people could not have built the earthworks. Western thinkers were blind to Indigenous intellect. Many theorized the mounds were created by ancient visitors to North America from Europe or the Middle East. Columbus was not the first to cross the seas, they reasoned. They speculated about the ancestral line from Adam and Eve that begat the Indigenous American. What blessed children of God could build something so monumental? Surely not Indians! They came to a theory that to modern ears may sound bizarre. The builders must have been the descendants of the Lost Tribes of Israel!

Within a few short years of Columbus' last voyage, beginning in the early 1500s, the idea of Israeli Indians, or, alternatively, Hebrews later displaced by Indians, started gaining traction. The idea faded from public consciousness for a time, then returned to serious consideration between the late eighteenth and early nineteenth centuries, with innumerable books, newspaper articles, pamphlets, sermons, and speeches making the case.[4]

Who were these Lost Tribes of Israel? What did Indigenous Americans have to do with them?

The first thing to know about the Lost Tribes is that if they're ever found and reunited in Israel, you're looking at the second coming of Christ and the complete triumph of good over evil. The Old Testament spells this out in language that Christians believe foretold the coming of Jesus, including a passage in which the prophet Ezekiel described ten of twelve tribes who, 2,700 years ago, were exiled by the Assyrians from the Kingdom of Israel. According to Ezekiel's prophecy, once these Lost Tribes are found, returned to the Holy Land, and reunited with the other tribes, a new Messianic Age will ensue. Folks in those days took this stuff seriously, and some do today. If the Bible said the Israeli tribes are wandering somewhere in the world, why not America? They must be somewhere.

Over the centuries, theorists placed the Lost Tribes variously in Kenya, Ethiopia, West Africa, Nigeria, Crimea, Siberia, Australia, China, and Ireland.

4. Dougherty, "Land of the Jewish Indians," 1.

Some have claimed to have found them in Peru or elsewhere in South America. Much effort was made to examine foreign languages for hints of Hebrew words and phrases, or local customs that seemed to echo Jewish traditions. One fellow generated a long list of Japanese words that in his mind bore suspicious resemblance to Hebrew ("Goi," for example, the word for a non-Hebrew, was said to be related to "Gai' Jeen," a prefix used to describe a non-Japanese person).[5]

Knowing what I've learned about the centuries-long preoccupation with the Lost Tribes of Israel, it was an oddly disorienting experience when I drove my car through Chillicothe, Ohio—a major center of Hopewell culture earthworks—and found my eye distracted from the road by a sign on a tired-looking storefront. It was the headquarters of the "Lost Tribe Motorcycle Club." A collection of Harleys was lined up in front. The tradition of the Lost Tribes is not only old, but continuously evolving.

The earliest proponent of the theory of Lost Tribes in the Americas was probably Bartholeme de Las Casas, whose intentions seemed good on the surface. As early as 1515 he became an advocate for ending the mistreatment of Indigenous people by the Spanish. A Catholic priest, Las Casas first defended the rights of aboriginal people in the Americas, then advocated their conversion to Christianity. "These Indians can bring near the redemption," he wrote. "If we treat them humanely in this world and convert them to Christianity, we are preparing for the redemption of the Western world in the messianic era. Their conversion is apt indeed, as I am convinced the Indians originate in Ancient Israel. Indeed, I can bring proofs from the Bible that they are of the Lost Tribes."[6]

This may all sound tangential to our story of the Newark Earthworks, but it's not. Stay with me.

In the late 1700s, James Adair spent some forty years living among Native Americans and exploring territory between the Appalachians and the Mississippi before publishing his "History of the American Indians" in 1775. He described what he mistakenly thought were earthen fortresses: "Through the whole continent, and in the remotest woods . . . We frequently met with great mounds of earth, either of a circular or oblong form."[7] For almost two hundred pages he offers evidence "on the descent of the American Indians from the Jews." He writes, "From the most exact observations I could make

5. PBS, "Lost Tribes of Israel."
6. PBS, "Lost Tribes of Israel."
7. Adair, *History of the American Indians*, 377.

in the long time I traded among the Indian Americans, I was forced to believe them lineally descended from the Israelites, either while they were a maritime power, or soon after the general captivity; the latter however is the most probable."[8]

A few years later, Yale College President Ezra Stiles addressed the Connecticut General Assembly and described in detail his theories about Indians being "Canaanites of the expulsion of Joshua."[9]

It all sounds quaint, but consider that people of European origin had never before witnessed the skin pigmentations and cultural expression they discovered in America. In her 2020 book *Caste: The Origins of Our Discontents,* Isabel Wilkerson wrote, "Before Europeans expanded to the New World and collided with people who looked different from themselves, the concept of racism as we know it did not exist in Western culture." She quotes historian Dante Puzzo, who wrote, "Racism is a modern conception, for prior to the sixteenth century there was virtually nothing in the life and thought of the West that can be described as racist."[10]

As they dispersed across the American continent, many European colonialists would of course make the enslavement of Black people and the expulsion of Indigenous people central to their idea of progress. Look in the Bible hard enough, add a heaping dose of creative interpretation, and you'll find any self-serving rationalization you wish for viewing people of color as inferior or hostile. Proponents of slavery and Indian removal believed scripture offered divine endorsement of their views.

The myth of the Lost Tribes of Israel and the mystery of the earthworks became deeply entangled with one another and with debates about race. As we will see, to this very day, in some corners of American subculture, that tangled pseudo-history of the Indigenous mounds still sticks to the rhetorical fingers of many people who embrace perverse racial and religious agendas.

⊕

Back to Ohio. The Reverend Charles McIlvaine, an Episcopalian Bishop in Cincinnati, wrote the preface for an 1839 book called *Antiquities of America,* and predicted then that artifacts in ancient Indigenous burial places would

8. Adair, *History of the American Indians,* 13–14.
9. Silverberg, Mound Builders, 26.
10. Wilkerson, *Caste,* 68.

one day confirm an origin described in the Bible.[11] An abolitionist, McIlvaine said somewhere buried in the mounds was proof that, "all races of men have descended from one common stock."[12] This proof would also show the barbarism of slavery by proving us all to be kin in the family of man.

Enter David Wyrick in the year 1860. Like many scholars, Wyrick was on the side of those who believed in the Lost Tribes theory of mound builders. Bringing that frame of reference, he used his surveying skills to create detailed maps of the four-square-mile Newark earthworks complex, from the Octagon to the west to the Great Circle to the south to a massive now-lost ellipse to the northeast. He looked for artifacts too. On June 29, with his son of eight or nine at his side, Wyrick strode onto the grounds of the earthworks at Newark looking for a good place to dig. He chose a spot about two thousand feet east of the edge of Newark's Octagon. Today the spot is along a street called Camp Alley, just southwest of a funeral home. Earlier, Wyrick's friend, another important surveyor of Native sites and foremost authority on mounds, Ephraim Squier (whom we will meet later), suggested he "examine the 'dug holes,' conceiving they might be caches or hiding places—cemeteries or bone pits."[13]

The specific spot selected may have been chosen by Wyrick alone, or perhaps it was suggested to him. It is likely that others knew where he was digging. But into one spot he leaned with his tools, sifting lumps of clay, stone, and other objects through his fingers. At a depth of only about twelve inches or so he said he found a large clump of clay and began scraping it apart. Slowly revealed was something elongated and triangular. It was fewer than six inches long and two and a half inches across at its widest. Brownish in color, he spit on it to wipe it clean, finding a surface surprisingly smooth and polished. Its shape was compared to a plumb bob, the pointed weight bricklayers suspend on a string to define vertical lines. Clearly it was carved by a human hand. Strangest of all were the inscriptions, figures like letters of an unfamiliar language, covering all its surfaces. Indigenous people were not believed to have a written language.

He knew it must be an exceptional discovery; nothing quite like it had been found in Native earthworks. "Almost frantic with delight," as one report later put it,[14] Wyrick rushed straight back to Israel Dille, a friend who shared

11. Lepper and Gill, "The Newark Holy Stones," 22.
12. Lepper, "Archaeology: Newark 'Holy Stones.'"
13. "Remarkable Archaeological Discovery," 2.
14. "Remarkable Archaeological Discovery," 2.

his interest in antiquities. Fortuitously, Dille was entertaining a visitor who would become Wyrick's friend, Charles Whittlesey, an early and respected leader in the infant science of archaeology. His articles about the Ohio earthworks had been published by the Smithsonian Institution. Together, they made an extraordinary observation. The writing on the stone—found in a place where other artifacts predated Columbus by hundreds of years—was *Hebrew.* Could this be what it seemed? Evidence of the Lost Tribes, living in America, among Indians, hundreds of years ago?

Unable to read the inscriptions they hastened to the local man most fluent in Hebrew, the Reverend John Winspeare McCarty of the local Episcopal church. The inscriptions, said McCarty, were indeed Hebrew and consisted of four phrases:

Law of the Lord
Word of the Lord
Holy of Holies
King of the Earth

For those who interpret their Bible literally, this news was jaw-drop-slap-your-forehead big. The first newspaper to report the discovery was *The Cincinnati Commercial,* an outlet believed to have been selected by Reverend McCarty to impress his superior in the Episcopal Church, the Cincinnati bishop, Reverend McIlvaine, the very person who predicted such a discovery would someday be made.[15]

Within days, Wyrick became front-page news across the country. *The Daily Exchange* in Baltimore was one of many asking, "Can it be possible that these works are of Hebrew origin? If so, what has become of the lost race?"[16] The news appeared in *The Chicago Tribune, The Brooklyn Evening Star* and on page two of *The New York Times,* under the headline "Remarkable Archaeological Discovery in Ohio."[17]

Skepticism was just as immediate. The shape of Wyrick's wedge-shaped find reminded some of a Masonic "keystone," and Whittlesey soon came to believe, as did others, that this must have been left there in more recent years

15. Much of this account is drawn from the work of Lepper and Gill who have extensively researched and written about the chronology of the Newark Holy Stones. See in particular Lepper and Gill, "The Newark Holy Stones."

16. *The Daily Exchange,* 1.

17. "Remarkable Archaeological Discovery, " 2.

by a Freemason. For one thing, the shallowness of its location in the ground was not deep enough to place it in the strata of Native artifacts.

As images of the find began to circulate, Hebrew-language scholars examined the carved lettering and spotted incongruities. Some Hebrew characters appeared modern, while other characters matched those found in ancient texts. This hinted at forgery. Then there was the smooth polish and pristinely preserved carved lettering. Where were the signs of wear one would expect on a many-centuries-old buried relic?

A *Chicago Tribune* headline called it "A Curious Discovery or a Great Hoax." Quoting the Cincinnati newspaper that first reported the news, it said, "There have been so many egregious hoaxes of a literary, theological and scientific character that we confess a very considerable degree of skepticism in relation to the integrity of the Holy Keystone."[18]

Writing in *The Cincinnati Daily Commercial,* William D. Bickham said on July 10, 1860, "(It was) quite possible and even probable that the stone may have been expressly prepared, inscribed and deposited by some facetious fellow to furnish sport for him at public expense."[19]

In a letter to *The New York Times,* published just weeks after the discovery, Henry H. Schoolcraft wrote of Wyrick's stone, "It lacks nearly all the evidences of scientific accuracy."[20]

Particularly harsh was *Harpers Weekly* which, in its September 1 edition, published a page one article by D. Francis Bacon who claimed that images of the Keystone were being circulated "with no little pecuniary gain to its contrivers and promoters." Though Bacon quoted various Newark-area residents as vouching for Wyrick's integrity, the author nonetheless quoted an unnamed source as saying Wyrick was "poor, and to have taken the antiquarian trade, hoping to realize something from it to support himself and his family." If Wyrick wasn't trying to profit from the object's display or its tracings or castings, Bacon offered an alternative explanation. Citing Wyrick's reputation for honesty, he wondered whether Wyrick himself might be the victim of a hoax. "We are bound to believe that in this matter he has been and is a victim, and not a 'victimizer.'"[21]

As crushing as this must have been, it did not slow Wyrick down. His acquaintances encouraged him to dig for more. Four months after the Keystone discovery, Wyrick traveled eight miles south of Newark to Jacksontown

18. *Chicago Tribune,* 1.
19. Johnson-Humrickhouse Museum, "Newark Holy Stones."
20. Schoolcraft, "The 'Hebrew Stone' in Ohio."
21. Bacon, "The Ohio 'Holy Stone,'" 1–2.

Stone Mound, better known today as Reservoir Stone Mound. It was originally more than forty feet high, 180 feet wide and covered in stone, making it the largest pre-Columbian stone structure north of Mexico. Radiocarbon dating later placed its construction in the first or second century CE.[22] Like so many monumental Indigenous works, it was decimated by colonizers In the 1820s builders of a reservoir used thousands of wagonloads of its stones for erosion control. Despite the damage, archaeological finds remained to be discovered below the hill's surface.

Here on November 1, 1860, Wyrick went to work. This time he brought more witnesses, including a local dentist named John Nicol, who encouraged him to dig deeper at one spot where a wooden burial platform had previously been found.[23] Out came a new discovery, even more remarkable than the Keystone. This time the object was encased in a carved-stone box, preserving a richly engraved and shaped stone within. An elongated oval about seven inches in length, the stone was inscribed on almost every surface. On its front was an image of a bearded, robed figure.

As before, Wyrick and his companions sought Reverend McCarty. The text, the reverend said, consisted of the Ten Commandments. Letters above the bearded figure's head identified him as Moses. The object became known as the Decalogue Stone.

"Mr. David Wyrick has gone and done it again," declared *The Cincinnati Daily Press.* "Somebody tells of strokes of lightning running in a family. Finding holy-stones seems to be inherent in Mr. Wyrick . . . in order to have witnesses of his discovery, to put scoffers at holy-stones to shame, he discovered it and dug it up in the presence of several gentlemen."

The response of most was: if it sounds too good to be true, it probably is. As with Wyrick's previous find, comparisons were made to previous hoaxes and to Joseph Smith, the founder of Mormonism, who claimed to have been guided by an angel to a collection of inscribed golden plates containing the Book of Mormon, with its own version of American history before Columbus. Most Americans thought Smith was a fraud too.

Brad Lepper, senior archaeologist for the World Heritage Program of the Ohio History Collection, and his collaborator, Jeff Gill, a Newark pastor and "avocational historian and archaeologist," have done as much as anyone to piece together the puzzling story of David Wyrick and the Newark Holy Stones. Because of renewed interest in the stone, Lepper and Gill felt it necessary to scrutinize evidence of the stones' authenticity as a relic of

22. Lepper, "A Radiocarbon Date for a Wooden Burial Platform," 8.

23. Bush, Kocher, and Lepper, "The Newark Holy Stones," 83.

FIGURE 3.2. The Newark Holy Stones, unearthed by David Wyrick in the 1860s, still draw tourists today. Johnson-Humrickhouse Museum, Coshocton, Ohio.

ancient Hebrew origin. Much of the preceding account came from the exceptional work of Lepper and Gill, including a 2000 article called "The Newark Holy Stones," that appeared in *Timeline,* a publication of the Ohio Historical Society.

Lepper points out that it is simply too convenient that the Decalogue Stone directly answers every one of the criticisms leveled against the Keystone. It was buried much deeper in the ground than the Keystone's twelve inches, resting amidst Native archaeological remains. The Decalogue stone showed no resemblance to Masonic heraldry, setting that issue aside too. The pristine preservation of this stone and its carvings was explained by its placement in a protective stone container. The effort to mimic ancient Hebrew was better than on the Keystone, perhaps, but Gill could spot flaws with his own less-trained eye. Lepper and Gill sought the assessment of a preeminent Harvard University scholar of Hebrew language, who called the Decalogue stone a "grotesque . . . forgery."[24]

While they can't prove it, Lepper and Gill tend to agree with those who early on suspected Wyrick was hoaxee, not hoaxer. Moreover, they believe they have a motive for the crime. They even have suspects.

What, you might ask, could possibly motivate somebody in 1860 to create fake evidence of Lost Tribes of Israel wandering their way into what today is the vicinity of Columbus, Ohio? The key, say Lepper and Gill, is to understand the times in which this unfolded. During the summer and fall of 1860, while Wyrick was making his startling claims, the nation's eyes were all on another Midwesterner named Abraham Lincoln, then running for president. Lincoln's abolitionist supporters were amassing all the evidence they could unearth to show that slavery was a moral abomination. Slavery's proponents in the South were doing likewise to defend their position, even inventing "scientific" anatomical evidence in support of their bogus claims of the inferiority of non-white races. The pseudo-science of polygenesis emerged, which, among other things, held that only the white race descended from Adam and Eve. "The White, Red and Black Races are not descended from one pair,"[25] wrote one of the architects of this line of thinking, Josiah Clark Nott. He argued that races of humans arose independent of one another in different geographic "provinces."

Not only did Nott argue that Native American and Black races arose separately, he said they existed before Moses, even before Adam and Eve. Nott wrote of "the countless aborigines found on this [American] continent, which we have reason to believe were building mounds before the time of Abraham."[26] If abolitionists could show that in fact the Hebrews and aboriginal people coexisted, then a cornerstone of white-supremacist polygenism would crumble. It would prove the "unity of the human species" and the sinfulness of slavery.

Thus, finding Hebrew inscriptions among Native artifacts was of greater than academic interest. It supported the abolitionist cause. Finding the

24. Lepper, "Conclusive Proof."
25. Nott, *An Essay on the Natural History of Mankind*, 5.
26. Nott, *Types of Mankind*, 58.

Decalogue stone just five days before an election with Lincoln on the ballot would be exceptional timing.

As for the question of whodunit, the most likely culprits include the ambitious Reverend McCarty, the sole person in Newark with enough knowledge of Hebrew letters to guide a carver's hand. McCarty's bishop, as we noted earlier, hoped for precisely such a find in the archaeological sites of Ohio. The local stonecutter, Elijah Sutton, was the one person with the skills necessary to do the carving. It was noticed that Sutton's tombstones happened to be about equal in thickness to the keystone. As for the person most likely to have planted the stones in the dig sites? That was the dentist, John Nicol, not only on location to witness the Decalogue find, but later involved in similar hoaxes involving "Holy Stones."[27]

As news reports shed doubt on Wyrick's claims, and as some said he might have been scammed, Wyrick himself began to have doubts. No doubt he had culprits in mind. And, like many victims of a scam, he felt stupid. Looking back, he recognized the possibility that people he trusted—people who knew where he was digging—might have planted the Holy Stones for him to find. Now he was a national embarrassment. In 1863, Wyrick wrote a letter to Joseph Henry, secretary of the Smithsonian Institution, stating "The Hebrew Stones I fear has [*sic*] done the evil. I wish to God someone else had found them than myself." He said he had "a fear in my mind that someone has been trying to hoax me. Especially as my opinions have been strong and firmly held."[28]

The following year, in 1864, Wyrick opened a bottle of his laudanum, drank it down, and died. The stonecutter Elijah Sutton—the very man suspected of carving the fake Hebrew stones—is believed to be the craftsman who carved the tombstone for Wyrick's grave. Wyrick's original gravestone is still at Newark's Cedar Hill Cemetery three miles from the Newark Earthworks. Unlike the Holy Stones of Newark, his own stone is now weather worn, broken and barely readable.[29]

The story of David Wyrick is more than the tale of one poor naïve victimized soul, assuming he was unaware, of course. His is the story of the white man's struggle to grasp and make sense of the rich but very foreign-to-him cultural phenomena of Indigenous America. Hard as white people tried to see them as a lesser race, reality got in the way. David Wyrick was awed by the great earthworks at Newark. He used his skills as a surveyor to painstakingly

27. Bush, Kocher, and Lepper, "The Newark Holy Stones," 78–93.
28. McCulloch, "Newark Hebrew Stones," 5–10.
29. Find a Grave, "David Wyrick."

record their size and geometry and dig for clues to their meaning. Where others saw unremarkable mounds of dirt, Wyrick and those like him beheld exceptional human achievement, even as they invented bizarre narratives to explain them. We are still trying to arrive at a better understanding of the earthworks of Ohio, and, as we will see, we are still getting diverted from that understanding by modern charlatans, people still motivated by religion or racial grudge. Fortunately, in unsteady steps, some forward and others back, we have inched our way onto a better path to understanding.

What became of the Holy Stones themselves? Wyrick sold them shortly before he died and they were eventually donated to a small museum in Coshocton, Ohio. For decades, that is where the Holy Stones sat, relics of a great hoax, stashed in a desk drawer, all but forgotten. Until 1980, that is, when they created a whole new stir, and for many are forgotten no more.

⊕

Wyrick, dead in 1864, wasn't the only surveyor in the county interested in the mounds. In 1862, while Wyrick was mired in the scandal he had unearthed, two brothers, James and Charles Salisbury, took up some of the work Wyrick was beginning to put behind him. Residents of Newark, the Salisbury brothers had wide-ranging interests. In the 1840s James was a physician ahead of his time, advancing theories about germs as causes of illness. With the onset of the Civil War he saw Union soldiers crippled by severe gastric illness, often fatal. For the troops he invented a chopped, beef-based, easily digestible source of protein better known today from the frozen dinners harried parents guiltily put in front of their kids. He invented the Salisbury Steak.

At home in Newark, the brothers developed an interest in the ancients. They took up surveying tools and mapped Native earthworks in exacting detail. Much of the actual manmade topography of Newark, now lost, was recorded with precision by the Salisburys in 1862. But not long after they were created, the Salisbury maps were filed away and forgotten too, like the Holy Stones, as erased from memory as most mounds themselves would soon be. All but lost for more than a century, the chance rediscovery of the Salisbury documents in 1989 would prove invaluable to Hopewell scholars.

CHAPTER 4

Newark, Ohio, 1975

> That the knowledge at which geometry aims is knowledge of the eternal, and not of aught perishing and transient.
> —Plato, *The Republic*

Bob Horn brought Ray Hively on his first tour of the Newark Earthworks in the summer of 1975. Ray was naturally curious about it as an archaeological site, but his larger purpose was to show that claims of astronomy in places like Stonehenge were mostly claptrap. The term "archaeoastronomy" was just coming into wider use at that time, having been proposed in a 1973 academic journal article as the name for a new field of research that combined anthropology, archaeology, astronomy, engineering, geometry, and more.[1] The way Ray talked about it, as far as science is concerned, archaeoastronomy might as well be astrology.

Bob was skeptical of archaeoastronomy too, but he was willing to take Ray up on his bet that he could find random unintended celestial alignments anywhere. He didn't expect Ray to pull that off. And Bob was drawn to Newark at any opportunity because of his interest in Native mounds. That interest did not immediately rub off on Ray.

"Initially like most people, I wasn't particularly impressed," said Ray. "Initially when I saw the site, it didn't dawn on me what was going on there because when you stand there all you see are the relatively modest walls . . . five feet high, they sort of trended off into infinity . . . You can't even see what the structure is. And so I thought well okay, so they built these long walls. So what?"[2]

Like the Nazca Lines in Peru, the Newark Earthworks are best seen from the air. Nazca's wonderful spiders, monkeys, and bird shapes, covering hundreds of square feet, come to life only in an airplane.

1. Baity, "Archaeoastronomy and Ethnoastronomy," 390.
2. Squier and Davis, *Ancient Monuments of the Mississippi Valley*, 68.

FIGURE 4.1. A groundskeeper at the Moundbuilders Country Club in 2024. Photo by James W. Graham.

So they set about surveying the property, studying the compass bearings of the lines formed by the walls or by various alignments between mounds or gaps in the walls. They gathered and charted their data with a plan to later compare them to movement of the sun or other objects in the sky. "The idea was to survey the site and then be able to pick out random alignments that would show that anybody can do this and it's meaningless," Ray said. The idea was to "debunk archaeoastronomy at Stonehenge."

Viewed from inside, the long walls of the Newark Octagon and its adjacent circle make steady, straight, horizontal lines and arcs, equal in height, in any direction you look. From outside, where the land slopes in spots, you can see how the original builders intentionally built the walls higher. By leveling the ground inside and raising the sides outside, the visual effect within surrounds you with an eye-level straight horizontal borderline of enclosure far off into the distance.

The Great Circle—not to be confused with the circle immediately adjacent to the Octagon—is a mile to the southeast. Its diameter is about one-fifth bigger than the one mated to the Octagon, and has walls as high as 14 feet in

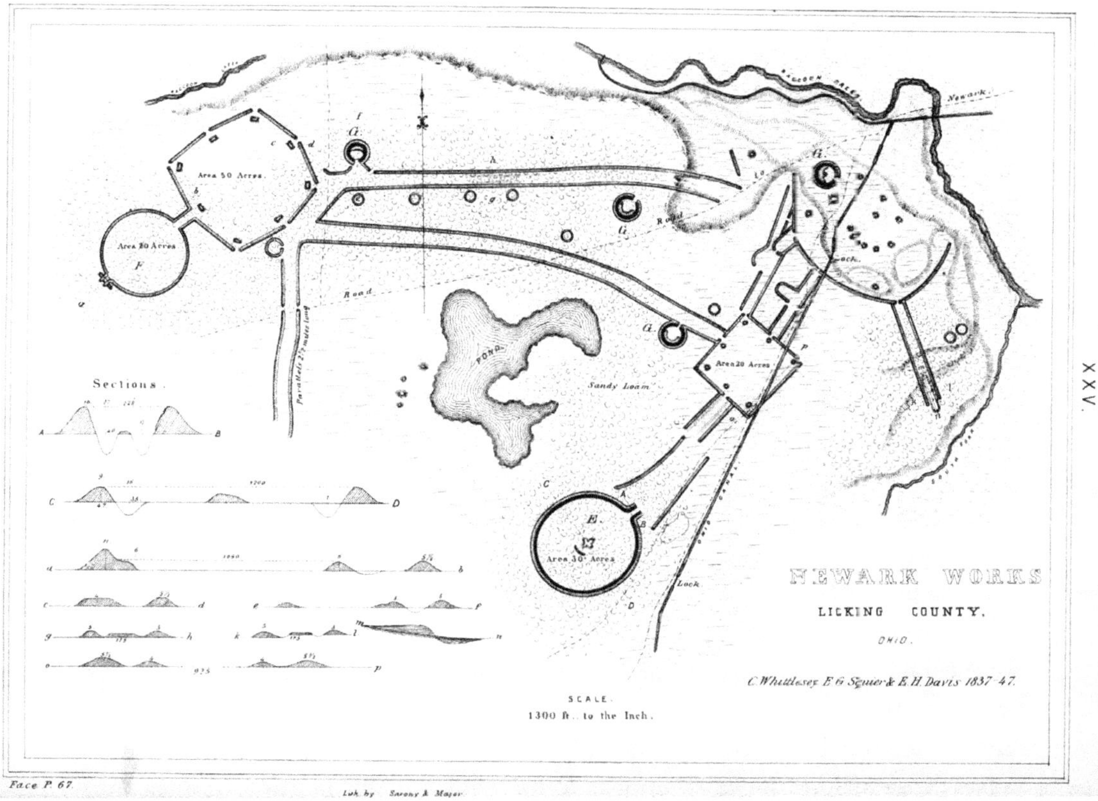

FIGURE 4.2. Ephraim Squier and Edwin Davis's 1847 map of the four-square-mile Newark complex of earthworks. The Newark Octagon is at left and the Great Circle at bottom. These two survive today and are among the best-preserved Hopewell earthworks, but only a few small fragments of the other walls remain. Today, a tour guide and Hopewell expert, Jeff Gill, can help you find them. From Squier and Davis, *Ancient Monuments of the Mississippi Valley*, World Digital Library, Library of Congress.

places, including at the entrance, giving visitors a grander, more humbling, welcome. All the major earthworks in Newark are National Historic Landmarks, but the Great Circle is treated as such, with a small museum outside and modern additions removed from inside. Unlike the Newark Octagon, the Great Circle is lined on the inside with a moat-like ditch. It's believed the moat contained water in its original conception, making it a decorative, probably sacred, feature to further impress a visitor. Better preserved and unobstructed by golf, Ray and Bob could experience the Great Circle more like ancient people did. There are no known human constructions up until that era, east of the Rockies, that are so dauntingly impressive. No wonder evidence shows ancient people traveled many hundreds of miles to step into, and be encircled by, its walls.

⊕

Bob's curiosity was particularly drawn to the geometry. Absent any written record as we normally think of it, here was a writing of a different kind, the universal language of mathematics. Given the evidence of Indigenous geometry at the Fort Ancient "foursquare," what strange arithmetic might they find at Newark on an even grander scale? What does the geometry reveal about the mind of its builders? As far as they knew, nobody had really delved into that aspect of the construction. They saw nineteenth-century drawings, surveys, and narrative descriptions that expressed admiration for the sophistication of the designs, but those surveyors were generally cataloging sites rather than thinking harder about their meaning or purpose.

"The hunch that I had when I suggested to Ray that we go to Newark was that the site might very well be geometrically regular. Squier and Davis in their early surveys talked about geometric regularity of a number of the sites."

Between 1845 and 1847, Ephraim Squier and Edwin Davis initiated one of the earliest scientific examinations of ancient Native mound sites, creating a voluminous record of surveys, drawings and written descriptions of the more than one hundred sites they personally inspected. Of the mounds they saw, those around Newark appear to have impressed them more than any. Upon visiting the Great Circle, they wrote, "At the entrance, which is towards the east, the ends of the walls curve outwards, for the distance of a hundred feet, leaving a passageway eighty feet wide, between the deep ditches on either hand. Here . . . the work presents a truly grand and impressive appearance; and, in entering the ancient avenue for the first time, the visitor does not fail to experience a sensation of awe, such as he might feel in passing the portals of an Egyptian temple, or in gazing upon the silent ruins of Petra of the desert."[3]

As Squier and Davis collected data at Newark and other sites, they discovered something surprising and inexplicable. "Several extraordinary coincidences are exhibited between the details of these works," they wrote. Examining the Newark circle-octagon, they noted that the circle's area of twenty acres was "nearly identical in size" with another circular earthwork known as Hopeton, about fifty-five miles to the southwest, near Chillicothe, Ohio. These two circles were, in turn, both equal in size to a third known as

---

3. Squier and Davis, *Ancient Monuments of the Mississippi Valley*, 68.

High Bank, a few miles south of Hopeton. "The square has also the same area with the rectangle belonging to the Hopeton, and with the octagon attached to the High Bank Works. It is not to be supposed that these numerous coincidences are the result of accident," they wrote.[4]

The work of Squier and Davis was compiled into an 1848 book, *Ancient Monuments of the Mississippi Valley*, the very first publication of the Smithsonian Institution, at that time just two years old. Many of the earthworks Squier and Davis documented have since been destroyed by plows and earthmovers, so their work is to this day an invaluable record of lost archaeological wonders.

Bob had studied Squier and Davis, but he and Ray could not be sure of the accuracy of their measurements, including the "coincidences" they identified. As Ray and Bob compared the Squier and Davis surveys to their own measurements, occasional inaccuracies appeared. Nonetheless, the evidence they found themselves, combined with that of earlier surveys, suggested mathematical precision that was astonishing, even by modern standards.

Bob said, "What confirmed that early on was Ray and I set up an appointment with Martha Otto who was then the curator of archaeology of what was then the Ohio Historical Society."

Added Ray, "We wanted to find out what the archaeologists had found out about the earthworks, and she was the leading archaeologist in the state."

"We went in for our appointment with Otto and on the wall outside her office was a photograph," said Bob. "It looked as if someone who imagined a perfect circle connected to an octagon had drawn their fantasy. But it was aerial photography."

Ray remembered that photo well: "That octagon looked like it had been laid out by an engineer on a drawing table." It was obviously the earthworks at Newark in an oversized enlargement, but it was black and white and decades old, when the area was largely rural without suburban sprawl that now surrounds it.

"As soon as we got into Martha's office we asked her, 'wherever did you get that?'" Bob remembered. "She said, well that's a photograph that was taken by Dache Reeves."

"Who's Dache Reeves?" they asked.

Great question. With a name only a Hollywood agent would dream up, Dache Reeves was a pilot who flew with the American Expeditionary

4. Squier and Davis, *Ancient Monuments of the Mississippi Valley*, 71.

FIGURE 4.3. Ray and Bob vividly remember the day they discovered a poster-size enlargement of this Dache Reeves's photo on the wall at Martha Otto's office. National Museum of the American Indian, Smithsonian Institution (P13208).

Force in France during the First World War. In 1918 he was executing aerial reconnaissance in a balloon when enemy aircraft, armed with machine guns, attacked. His balloon burst into flames and Reeves leapt from his gondola, parachuting to safety. Another balloon was promptly inflated and Reeves went right back up. Two weeks later Reeves was once again balloon-borne when a "circus of fifteen enemy airplanes" attacked. Again he leapt to safety. Incredibly, just two hours after this second feat of derring-do, he did it yet again, falling from another burst of flames to one more safe landing.[5]

5. "Dache Reeves," Military Times.

He's best remembered now not for those balloon feats and the Distinguished Service Cross he earned, but for his work in the cockpit of airplanes. In the 1920s he became a pioneer in aerial photography, even writing what is said to be the first book on the topic.[6] It was an extraordinary turn of luck, then, that he somehow landed in Ohio in the 1930s, a time when countless Indigenous earthworks were not yet completely destroyed, but soon would be. As Bob Horn heard the story, "When he returned [from the war] he was itching to be able to fly and they put him in a desk job at Wright[-Patterson] Air Force Base in Dayton."

Reeves knew about the earthworks and was interested in archaeology. A British flying acquaintance of Reeves's had made a name for himself by completing aerial surveys of Roman archaeological sites in Europe. That gave Reeves his idea. "He could schedule flights over the earthworks as a part of cartographic training for people that he was in charge of," Bob explained. "He did some of the flights himself. So he started the program of photographing earthworks. There are nine hundred photographs he took, most of them of the earthworks in Ohio, but some of them from areas further west."[7]

If you think archaeology means lots of digging on hands and knees, the words "aerial archaeology" might sound oxymoronic. Reeves pioneered that too, and today it has graduated to satellite imagery, garnering magnificent results. The value of Reeves's work was soon recognized and in 1936 *Scientific American* published his article about Ohio's Great Serpent Mound, one of the most sculpturally beautiful of all the Native earthworks in the Americas, especially if you see it by air. He flew over the Newark Octagon, too, and discovered a previously unknown pair of parallel earthen walls approaching it from the south. The walls were shown in century-old Squier-and-Davis drawings too, extending for more than two miles, but those were thought to have been erased by farmers and others. Reeves found previously unknown remnants, as did another 1930s aviator, Warren Weiant Jr., who found faint traces of parallel walls extending a full ten miles south. Reeves wrote that, "This Newark avenue is the longest straight line of parallel embankments constructed by prehistoric builders and demonstrates a considerable knowledge of elementary surveying."[8] Not much was made of Reeve's discovery until Brad Lepper took a harder look at those 1930s photos six decades later.

6. Reeves, *Aerial Photographs*.

7. Interview with Bob Horn, Jane Horn, Ray Hively, and Susan Hively, July 21, 2021, Richmond, Indiana.

8. Reeves, "A Newly Discovered Extension," 189–93.

Like Hively and Horn, Lepper found them revelatory and would offer an extraordinary new hypothesis about Reeves's "Newark avenue."

⊕

The more Ray and Bob studied documents and images from libraries and archives, including Reeves's images, the more evidence they uncovered about geometric earthworks spread all throughout southwest Ohio, but now mostly destroyed. Luckily their precise locations and dimensions had in many cases been carefully recorded. They made full use of Earlham College's librarian, who pulled resources together from distant collections, including the Reeves archives at the Smithsonian.

In 2022, when I visited Ray and his wife Susan at their home in Atlanta, he invited me to sit on a bar stool at their kitchen island where, spread out before us, was a huge enlargement of a vintage 1930s aerial photograph of the Newark circle and octagon, taken in winter when the leaves on trees did not obstruct the view. Ray had a straight edge and pointed out small circular earthworks that existed in Reeves's time but were long since obliterated by developers who had scraped the land clean of its Indigenous past. Ray pointed to one of the now-vanished circles and wondered aloud whether there was an alignment with one side of the octagon that he hadn't noticed before. His questioning never ceases.

Back in the summer of 1975, Ray and Bob were making journeys to Newark to conduct land surveys and using them to check the accuracy of nineteenth century surveys. They also wanted to know if subsequent occupants of the existing earthworks made any alterations during the twentieth century. Could the country club have changed anything over the decades? Before the arrival of golfers, the Newark site had been used by the Ohio militia which, at one point, "restored" some mounds. Who knew what they changed? Ray and Bob wanted to determine what was truly Indigenous and what was altered. The surveying gear available to them in the 1970s had none of the electronic conveniences we take for granted now. Bob or Ray would peer through the lens of a tripod-mounted theodolite while the other walked the ranging pole some distance away, dragging a tape and pulling it taught to measure distance. The theodolite gave them the vertical elevations and the horizontal compass bearings.

How Indigenous builders drew the Octagon was a particular mystery. The giant circles could be laid out simply enough using a rope tied to a stake in the center. But the Octagon? Just try drawing one with a pencil on a piece of paper. The easiest way is to start with a square, then overlay another identical square turned 45 degrees to form an eight-pointed star. Connect the points and you have an octagon. Ray and Bob charted their data on paper and reverse-engineered the Newark Octagon, drawing squares on paper where the builders might have drawn them on the ground to create their shapes. Overlayed on their survey data of the Octagon, the resulting squares were precise in a way one just wouldn't expect of a people who were still hunting with spears and atlatls. The opposing sides of the Octagon were, for the most part, as perfectly parallel as the nearby circle was perfectly round, even though the Octagon's sides were about a quarter of a mile apart. Odd patterns emerged. Comparing the adjacent circle, known as the "Observatory Circle," they found its diameter precisely matched the lengths of the sides of one of the imaginary squares they drew to connect the vertices of the Octagon. Not all of these patterns were immediately apparent in those early months, but there were hints, trails of evidence to follow. When there's a bit of gold dust in your pan, you look for nuggets, hope for a vein.

The more they found the more they were mystified. The need to make sense of it grew overpowering. That both Ray and Bob found this esoteric stuff so interesting was a sign they had both found not just a potential unexplored path into America's distant past, but a kindred pathfinder too. Despite their differing ages and backgrounds, despite the fact that the pursuit of archaeology did nothing to advance their respective careers in astronomy or philosophy, they were on this strange road together and sticking to it.

The fall semester of 1975 began and the weather turned colder, so the two re-immersed themselves in full-time teaching, leaving less time for the earthworks. As much as they loved teaching, they were eager for the following summer's opportunity to return to Newark. As for Bob, the life path that brought him to teach at Earlham was never straight. He had moments of awful misfortune and tragic turns before, and he would find more soon.

CHAPTER 5

Armed with Good Intentions

Nature does not proceed in a straight line, it is rather a sprawling development.
—Robert Smithson, land artist[1]

Though he would graduate from and later teach at Earlham College, Bob Horn's youthful interest in the French horn made him first enroll as a freshman at Oberlin College, renowned for its music program. That experience was cut short when one day, inexplicably, he became so ill that his vision blurred and then doubled. He could barely read. A diagnosis was slow in coming and at one point his doctors feared leukemia. It turned out to be mononucleosis, a disease Bob said was not well understood in the 1940s. Then he developed hepatitis on top of that. His symptoms were severe and his recovery slow, forcing him to drop out for the semester. When he recovered he had time to kill before he could return to Oberlin, so he filled it by taking a job as a reporter for a Richmond newspaper, *The Palladium-Item*.

It was during that time that a high school classmate invited Bob to join him on a blind date with a young woman named Phyllis. Soon, she and Bob were inseparable. So inseparable, he abandoned plans to return to Oberlin. He now had a powerful new reason to keep his newspaper job and enroll instead at Earlham College.

They married in 1952 and were an exceptional match. At Earlham, as Bob discovered philosophy and the world of Kierkegaard, he dived so deep into his studies of the Danish philosopher that he grew suspicious of the reliability of translations then available. He told Phyllis he had found an apartment for them that was ideal primarily because its landlord was Danish and could teach him the language. She not only agreed, she took up the language herself. In 1953 she traveled with him to Denmark to further pursue his new

1. Smithson, "Cultural Confinement," 155.

academic interest. The following year they moved to New York City so Bob could work on his graduate studies at Union Theological Seminary. These were good times on a promising path.

By 1958, Bob and Phyllis had been married six years. She followed him to Haverford College, which had offered him both a teaching position and a few months of freedom to work on his dissertation before the start of classes in the spring. As it happened, that was the second year of one of the century's worst global influenza pandemics, one that took the lives of 100,000 Americans. A month after arriving in Haverford, on September 23, 1958, Phyllis became one of its victims. Bob was a widower at age 29.

The awesome grief would be crippling enough, but at Haverford Bob had no shoulder to lean on. "I was very much alone. I was new at Haverford. . . . I really hadn't gotten acquainted with many people." His apartment could not feel emptier, nor the distance to his small town in Indiana greater. His trauma made it impossible to focus on his dissertation, so he let that slide. When the spring term eventually came, he forced himself to begin the teaching assignment that was his reason for being there.

He did slowly make acquaintances. Haverford did not admit women until several years later, but it had a sister college, Bryn Mawr, and there were occasional joint academic conferences and social events. Bob was at one of them when an attractive young student named Jane glanced his way, spotted his nametag, and said, "Your name is Horn. I play the horn."

This was serendipity. Bob Horn also played the horn and Jane was studying philosophy. Jane recalled he was "a very fine horn player. . . . I was a very mediocre horn player, but I love to play the fourth horn," the least demanding part of an ensemble. The two colleges had joint musical performances, "so I insisted he come to the orchestra."

"So I went to the orchestra," said Bob, adding cheekily, "and it wasn't very long before we exchanged mouthpieces.

"Jane was one of the first people I got acquainted with and she was also the first person I could talk to about my grief over losing Phyllis. I found she was a superb listener. That and the French horn. We both loved playing the French horn. We thoroughly enjoyed each other and that grew and grew and two years later we got married.[2]

Bob said it would not be accurate to say they spent their honeymoon touring Native American earthworks, however it is nearly so. During their travel

2. Robert and Jane Horn, both interviewed by the author, 2021–2022.

as newlyweds he took her to see his family in Indiana and, along the way, toured many of the Ohio archaeological sites that had so interested him since childhood, including one called Mound City near Chillicothe.

Before long, Bob's connections at Union Theological Seminary paid off anew and he was given an offer to return there to teach. So he and Jane became New Yorkers and began thinking about raising a family. That's when the couple's common interest in Native culture took a momentous and exceptionally personal turn. Jane happened to pick up a copy of *Ladies Home Journal* and saw an article that told of the hard lives of Indigenous people living on America's tribal reservations, and of the plight of Native children in need of adoptive parents and good homes. Jane was moved and told Bob about it. Why not us?

They reached out to the Child Welfare League in New York City, which had entered into an agreement with the federal Bureau of Indian Affairs to find parents for children deemed to be in need. Under their Indian Adoption Project, the authorities were experimenting with placements in non-Native homes, theorizing that an upbringing in a more economically advantaged (i.e., white) setting would yield better outcomes for the child. The operating premise was that such children would be better off relocating away from the reservation. The full story was much more complicated, or so Bob and Jane would learn. But with the best of intentions they applied and waited.

In the meantime, Bob was offered yet another teaching opportunity, this one at his alma mater, Earlham College. Like the fortuitous undergrad scholarship that united him with his first wife, here came Earlham once again with a new opportunity. Jane, who had grown up in New York City, did not want a big city upbringing for her own children. She wanted someplace smaller, more family friendly. Bob's hometown of Richmond would do just fine.

In 1967, the Child Welfare League brought Jane and Bob the news for which they had long waited. They adopted a two-year-old girl, Mary, whose birth family had been members of the Menominee Nation near Green Bay, Wisconsin. A son, Jonathan, joined the family soon afterward. Just eleven months old, he was from the same tribal community.

At Earlham, Bob's earnest interest in Native people showed in the topics he chose to teach during their years of starting a multiracial family. He taught a class based largely on a book by Roy Harvey Pearce titled *Savagism and Civilization,* first published in 1953. He was strongly interested in the deeply harmful racism that lay behind the so-called "civilizing" of Indigenous people.

More than fifty years later, when I first asked Bob to tell me more about his and Jane's adoption of two Native American children, his response surprised me. In an email he mentioned the Child Welfare League and said, "Their policy has turned out to be unwise, but we were idealistic and naïve." Separately, Jane too described the decision as "naïve." At the time I thought it was an odd thing to say about the program that made their family possible. I learned later why it made sense.

⊕

Fast forward to the fall of 1975. Having set their work at Newark temporarily aside so they could resume teaching, Ray and Bob were midway through the academic year when Bob felt a strange weakness in his legs. It worsened by the day. He tried to ignore it, hoped it would go away. It was December, and he was standing in line at a toy store waiting to buy Christmas presents. "I suddenly felt very weak and disoriented. The shock was severe."

This feeling in his head and limbs was something he could no longer ignore. "At once I thought 'I could die right here.' It revived vivid memories of the first time Phyllis told me the same thing a few weeks before she died." The fear was real, but then the symptoms passed. He stayed in hopeful denial long enough to attend a Christmas Eve church service and "play a very challenging composition for the French horn and organ" by the Danish composer Carl Nielsen.

Jane recalled, "I was planning thyroid surgery in December, so Bob did not tell me as he was feeling worse and worse. His legs stopped working in early January and he was hospitalized with grave neurological symptoms. He was devastated as his students visited him in the hospital and he could not recall enough in philosophical terms to discuss their papers. He tried to read philosophy and found it completely opaque. He was very acutely ill for the next several months."[3]

When a diagnosis was finally made it was Guillain-Barré Syndrome (GBS), sometimes called French Polio. "It was a paralytic disease. Not a lot was known about it then," said Bob. His physicians chose not to tell Bob that just a year earlier an Earlham student sought treatment for the same symptoms and died of GBS within two days. Bob's long-term prognosis was guesswork

3. Jane Horn, email to author, Dec. 12, 2022.

at that point; all the doctors could say was if Bob didn't see improvement in the months immediately ahead he might never get better.

The symptoms resembled those of a severe stroke. His memory of previously familiar words in non-English languages, like Danish or Greek, eluded him. "He suffered from terrible insomnia," Jane said. He "was desperate for distraction." After six months he still could not walk twenty feet.

"I despaired of returning to teaching as I still could not talk without exhaustion," said Bob.

"I worked hard at the bibliotherapy," Jane said, "with the help of a wonderful librarian at our public library who was experienced in stocking the bookmobile for shut-in men. His ability to read returned slowly and he spent months with books about World War II, science fiction by Isaac Asimov, and everything he could find about the Manhattan Project. After months of that he eased into other languages, trying, for example, some Hans Christian Andersen stories in Danish. There was endless physical therapy too."[4]

There was slow improvement and it appeared Bob would eventually walk again with a cane. As for their work at Newark, Bob told Ray, "You go ahead and do the survey. God knows when I'm going to be able to do anything. The odds are against my going on with it, so you go ahead."

Ray refused. "I won't touch it. I'm not going to do a bit more on Newark until you can go."

Bob insisted: "I won't be any good to you."

"Look," said Ray, "if you can hobble around with a cane you can hobble around with a ranging pole."

For now, Earlham College was willing to wait too. But Bob and Jane and their children wondered how long it would take.

⊕

Not everything about Newark came to a complete stop. Ray secured the aid of an able assistant in the form of a talented sophomore named Jane Dorney. As a freshman, Dorney had taken Ray and Bob's course on cosmology, which she described as a "big commitment to make for students and faculty alike," requiring a two-class block of time in each of two trimesters.

She remembers learning how different early cultures saw their place in the universe and how belief systems, science, and philosophy evolved

4. Emails from Jane Horn to the author, Dec. 13, 2022, and from Robert Horn to the author, Dec. 17, 2022.

through time. "Bob was the expert on ancient cultures and did more of the lecturing at the beginning of the course." He made the students learn the Greek alphabet so they could transliterate from the original texts. "We ended with modern physics and the scientific viewpoint of the cosmos, so Ray did most of the lecturing for that segment. But they also worked together very well and the movement through time and cultures seemed seamless to me. Bob was the philosopher, with a very rational, analytical approach, who understood the world views of the ancient cultures. And Ray was the scientist with a data-driven, logical approach. Both were good at pulling out and seeing even bigger concepts and patterns from the things in front of them."[5]

This was the class that took excursions to see the Fort Ancient earthworks where Bob and Ray first experienced the precision of ancient Native geometry. With her classmates, guided by an art instructor, Dorney also helped assemble an exceptionally good scale model of Stonehenge, which the school displayed in a lobby for decades afterwards.

Dorney's high school in Green Bay, Wisconsin, had been equipped with an observatory of its own, so she knew her way around a telescope. She became Ray's teaching assistant and was enlisted to temporarily fill Bob's shoes on Ray's journeys to Newark, a drive of more than two hours each way.

"The surveying we did was with standard surveying equipment of the era," Dorney recalled, "which required two people to do—one to sight through the transit and the other to hold the measuring stick. He taught me how to use the instrument and we took alignments along each straight edge of each mound in the mound system. . . . It took several day trips to be able to complete it all and it was hot. I remember driving back to Earlham with the car windows rolled down to try to cool off. And yes, the golfers were playing the course as we were working."[6]

Dorney said Ray's plan was to document the lines made by all the mounds and then match them to the sun's rise and set points on the horizon.

"We would take our lunch and we'd meet in the morning and drive over there, and then we would survey the mounds. He figured out the whole plan of what he wanted to do, I just followed him. . . . The precision and the accuracy were extremely important. . . . We'd stand on those long mounds of geometric shapes and we'd sight down those mounds, get those sightings, get those bearings, get the numbers.

5. Jane Dorney, email to the author, Aug. 17, 2021.
6. Jane Dorney, email to the author, Aug. 17, 2021.

"We were mostly measuring the angles, so where on the compass basically was it pointing? . . . It's not as much about the length of the mound but about the angle it's pointing at. Or if you had an avenue, if you had a parallel avenue, you wanted to sight right down the avenue. That kind of stuff. So the focus was really on the angles on the compass."

Dorney could do more than hold a ranging pole, of course. She was herself a budding astronomer and had a knack for the necessary arithmetic. Back at Earlham, Ray put her to work running the numbers. Handheld electronic calculators were in their infancy, and electronic spreadsheets were decades away, so much of the work was by hand.

"I can remember some hot days sitting in my apartment, with no air conditioning, crunching numbers. I had pages and pages and pages of numbers and filling out tables," Dorney recalled.

Ray was unable to take time off from teaching to do the research, so it all transpired over an extended period of time, said Dorney. And the alignments Ray thought would be so easy to find were becoming frustratingly illusive.

"I remember him talking about the solar alignments. They did not line up with the solar alignments at all. . . . Randomly there would have been some, and that really piqued his interest, that none of the alignments matched any of the solar alignments at all. It was very unusual that that would happen."[7]

Remembering his frustration, Ray joked at the time that perhaps he was discovering an ancient "culture of solar avoidance." Maybe the solstice and equinox lines weren't so randomly found after all. Maybe the astronomy of Stonehenge wasn't so accidental. Ray started to think differently about archaeoastronomy. And what to make of Newark's extraordinary geometry? How could people who hunted with flint-knapped arrowheads also have a common unit of measurement, employed over long distances, and a grasp of plane geometry they expressed on such ambitious scale? There was clear intent behind those designs of sculpted soil and clay, but what intent, exactly? No archaeologist or anthropologist had figured it out, so what made them think they could?

7. Jane Dorney, telephone interview with author, Aug. 24, 2021.

CHAPTER 6

Native Americans of Richmond, Indiana

> Life must be understood backwards. But . . . it must be lived forwards.
>
> —Søren Kierkegaard, *Journals IV.A. 164*

Bob's recovery was agonizingly slow and the separation from his work torturous. Jane helped him down the endless slog of rehabilitating mind and body to do what once was second nature. His rehab regimen was like that of stroke victims. This befell them in the years they were raising two children who had challenges of their own. Mary was about eleven years old and Jonathan about eight. The children grew healthier after years of challenging respiratory illnesses, though they continued to suffer from allergies. With their maturity came new cultural and social adjustments.

Compared to today, Child Welfare League policy of the 1960s placed minimal value on a Native child's own tribal heritage, and maximum value on economic opportunity and assimilation with the dominant American culture. Removal to distant white families was considered progressive. Bob and Jane nonetheless understood that Mary and Jonathan lost something precious when they were made to trade their culture for white social advantage. They wanted to reconnect their children to their Wisconsin Menominee heritage, but that would take time, in part because of the struggles the Menominee people faced stemming from the US Congress's termination of its federal recognition as a tribe in 1954, something not restored until almost twenty years later.

The tribal termination movement that took hold in the 1940s through the 1960s had a complicated history, growing in a soil of mixed intentions, some good, but some born of white resentment. Cloaked as an effort to liberate Native people from federal government "wardship," termination sought to end the sovereignty and federal support of reservations and transition their occupants toward assimilation and self-sufficiency. The reality was something else, of course, and robbed tribes of the kinds of government support that the rest of America took for granted—things like policing and health care. Sometimes lifelines are chains. The Menominee had grown a successful lumber industry and were thus deemed by Washington authorities to be among those most ready for "liberation" from federal backing. The Menominee were also forced to accept termination in exchange for an $8.5 million legal settlement they earned after federal agencies were found to have mismanaged their forests. Justice came at a price. The Menominee lost their status as a tribe and their economic fortunes headed into rapid decline.

In the 1960s, when Mary and Jonathan were born, there were no Menominee community schools for Native children to attend. Had they stayed, they would have been bussed to a local public school where, Jane believed, they would have been treated as "second-class citizens" by a local white majority population with whom there had been racial frictions. In Richmond, Indigenous children were a novelty and Bob and Jane hoped that racial animus toward them was less ingrained.

Bob and Jane aspired to give them the best of both worlds, raising their adopted children in a loving home while also gradually reacquainting them with their Menominee culture. In the earliest years the challenges of parenting Mary and Jonathan would be familiar to any parent. They were filled with so much energy that keeping up was challenging. When Mary was just three, they took her and Jonathan to visit the Navajo Nation reservation, followed by a visit to the Grand Canyon. At the gorge where the Little Colorado flows into the Colorado River, there was no fence or railing, and as soon as the car door opened, Mary "literally flew out the car door and headed, of course, to the rim, as fast as she could go," recalled Bob. "I went off after her and got to the rim and she stopped and turned around and commented in a perfectly rational and laconic way, 'I could fall.'" That was "life with Mary."

When Mary started first grade in Richmond she discovered a boy from India in her class. "I think the first-grade teacher handled that quite well," said Jane. "The two children could have been taken for brother and sister. The teacher said 'we have two Indian children in our class, one from India and one American.'" Both children later endured teasing that made them unhappy, Jane recalled. "Most teachers were not prepared to help children deal with racial differences."

They wanted the children to be fully exposed to Western culture too. Jane remembered one spring when both children performed in an interfaith, church-sponsored performance of Benjamin Britten's family opera *Noye's*

Fludde. Jonathan, six, played a squirrel, and dance-loving Mary, ten, was a wave. Jane recalled how well the opera was constructed to engage children throughout the performance, and how it harnessed Mary and Jonathan's abundant energy. In Jane's recollection, "That performance did a great deal to help our kids feel a part of the Richmond community," in addition to other activities they enjoyed: playing the cello, learning ballet, and doing gymnastics at the YMCA.

In 1976, Mary and Jonathan's school asked children to wear Halloween costumes to honor the nation's bicentennial, so Mary was Sacagawea and Jonathan was the Cherokee humorist Will Rogers. Within Indigenous culture there is distinct tribal diversity, a fact perhaps not top-of-mind in Richmond at the time.

Although there are tribal presences in cities throughout the Midwest, Richmond, Indiana, is a long way from the nearest reservation or Indigenous population center. There were powwows in Indiana and Ohio, so the family started visiting those, particularly the Boy Scout–affiliated Tecumseh Lodge in Indianapolis which brought powwows to county fairgrounds in the region. These were great family activities, with good barbecue and potluck food, new friends, and opportunities to meet Indigenous people.

"For Bob and me, having grown up with ominous Indian drums in the movies, the drums became friendly." They were grateful, too, for the warm welcome Mary and Jonathan received.

But Mary looks back at them as inauthentic, dominated by white "hobbyists" and "wannabes." White people were allowed too much influence over the conduct of Native powwows; they inappropriately participated in dancing and wearing of regalia. Over the years Mary saw that the powwows she attended as a youngster lacked what she recognizes today as ritual necessities. There was no "smudging" with smoke from sage, sweetgrass, or tobacco, which Mary explained was a way of ridding a place of negative energy, or "bad mojo." Later, after her Menominee community proudly bestowed on Mary the hard-earned right to carry eagle feathers, she was confronted at a powwow by a non-Native authority who challenged her right to carry the feathers of an endangered species. That was an affront she would not forget.

Bob and Jane came to befriend another couple who had also adopted two Native American children. They lived in Green Bay, not far from their children's native Menominee homeland. On one visit to Green Bay, their Wisconsin friends suggested they visit the Menominee Fair, where they would see "Indian dancing," an "Indian pageant," horse racing, and boxing matches featuring the Menominee Indian Boxing Club. The children loved it. While there, Jane expressed an interest in buying a pair of moccasins. She was told to visit the St. Anthony's gift shop the following Monday.

While browsing the gift shop, an older woman of Native appearance was there, watching Mary carefully for a time, showing a look of recognition. Remarkably, the woman turned out to be Mary's biological grandmother. The reunion was tearful and filled with hugs. The grandmother, was, in fact, the family member who had decided to give Mary a new life with an adoptive family. "We have always told our children they were given up out of love," Jane said. Years later, as Mary grew older, she made visits to the Menominee community a frequent part of her life. The brush with her grandmother turned out to be a fleeting one, and she did not reconnect with her birth family, but she gained new friends and discovered a place that welcomed her in a way that was missing from her Richmond community. Richmond was where Mary remembered the teacher telling the class that there were no Indians left in America. She raised her hand and begged to differ, returning the next day with a long list of federally recognized tribes. To this day, Indigenous students still wince at such classroom indignities and worse, and not just in primary schools. As for Jonathan, the teasing from classmates was bad enough that it sometimes led to occasional schoolyard fistfights.

"It's either people don't think I speak English because of the way I look, or they want to stay and hear my whole life history. But then they want to challenge it, they want to challenge me," Mary told me. In Wisconsin, by contrast, "I don't have to justify my existence, I don't have to justify who I am or where I'm going."

Mary pointed to local Walmart stores to illustrate. At the Walmart in Richmond, a store employee with a suspicious look might walk up to her and say "Can I help you" in a tone more investigative then assistive. She recalled a store employee who saw her tribal ID card. "Oh yeah, that's the one where you get free stuff!"

Another employee noticed her "Native Pride" ballcap and asked Mary about it.

"I got it at a powwow."

"Oh, you're one of those Natives."

"Yes, ma'am, I'm Native American."

"Oh! My great, great grandmother is Cherokee."

"Oh Lord," Mary would think to herself on this occasion and other similar ones, smiling and listening patiently.

Others have called this the "Cherokee Syndrome." In his classic book, *Custer Died for Your Sins,* Vine Deloria Jr. wrote, "During my three years as Executive Director of the National Congress of American Indians it was a rare day when some white didn't visit my office and proudly proclaim that he or she was of Indian descent. Cherokee was the most popular tribe of their choice. . . . All but one person I met who claimed Indian blood claimed it on their grandmother's side. I once did a projection backward and discovered that evidently most tribes were entirely female for the first three hundred years of white occupation. No one, it seemed, wanted to claim a male Indian as a forebear."[1]

By contrast, Mary could shop at Walmart near her tribal home in Wisconsin and bask in the warmth of unremarkable anonymity, or better still, bump into new Native friends.

What Bob and Jane came to appreciate was that the challenges and, in fact, the morality of such adoptions were profoundly more complicated than they realized. The institutions facilitating such adoptions were driven by misguided good intentions and blind to the richness of the Native culture and communities they were all but erasing. Indigenous parents faced loss of custody over spurious grounds. "Poverty, poor housing, lack of modern plumbing, and overcrowding are often cited by social workers as proof of parental neglect," wrote William Byler, executive director of the Association of American Indian Affairs (AAIA), in a devastating and influential 1977 critique of such adoptions. Alcohol abuse was often cited as cause for separation, but Byler noted that "in areas where rates of problem drinking among Indians and non-Indians are the same, it is rarely applied against non-Indian parents. . . . Ironically, tribes that were forced onto reservations at gunpoint and prohibited from leaving without a permit, are now being told that they live in a place unfit for raising their children."

As human rights advocates have shown, one brutal way to destroy a culture is to rob it of its children. The sheer scale of Indian adoption programs of the 1960s was in that sense stunningly destructive. AAIA surveys in 1969 and 1974 showed that fully 25 to 35 percent of all Native children were "separated from their families and placed in foster homes, adoptive homes, or institutions." In Wisconsin, the birthplace of Mary and Jonathan, Native children had a 1,600 percent higher risk of separation from parents, compared to

1. Deloria, "Custer," 3.

non-Native children. Minnesota data showed that among children adopted by nonrelated couples, 90 percent of those couples were non-Native.[2]

Critics had long despised boarding schools and by the 1970s they redirected their ire at the forced assimilation of adoption programs. Just eleven years after Bob and Jane lovingly welcomed their first child, Mary, into their lives, Congress passed the Indian Child Welfare Act, putting a stop to such adoptions. Some years after that, in 2001, the Child Welfare League's new director, Shay Bilchik, issued a public apology for the very program that had made Bob and Jane's family possible. "No matter how well intentioned and how squarely in the mainstream this was at the time, it was wrong; it was hurtful; and it reflected a kind of bias that surfaces feelings of shame, as we look aback with the 20/20 vision of hindsight." It was "a hurtful, biased, and disgraceful course of action . . . we see (these events) as both catastrophic and unforgivable."[3]

Ben Barnes, chief of the Shawnee Tribe that was the dominant Native presence in Southwest Ohio at the time of European contact, is also a national leader on the topic of truth and reconciliation for Native American victims of the nation's old boarding school system. I asked him about the family adoption programs of the 1960s. He said, "That's the callousness of liberalism, you know? It happens oftentimes with Native peoples that people who are of progressive minds want folks to do better, but they haven't talked to them about what the definition of 'do better' is." He doesn't blame the parents who welcomed Native children into their families. "These families are part of a structural racist system in these specific geographies. It doesn't have anything to do with them as a people."[4]

Bob and Jane's intentions were noble, to be sure. How could such parents anticipate the changing moral and political landscape, or know the harmful motivations behind adoption programs? Bob and Jane deeply understood their children's need to find a bridge to their cultural birth heritage. As they entered the decade of the 1970s, the failings of such adoption programs were barely entering public consciousness outside of tribes. Meanwhile, Bob and Jane had children to raise. Many of the challenges they would face were still ahead. They wanted and needed to figure out how to help their two children straddle two worlds. Bob and Jane had a lifelong interest in Native culture, but when it came to Native life in modern America, they knew they had more to learn.

---

2. Byler, "Destruction," 1–4.
3. Tribal Law Updates, "Apology."
4. Barnes, interview.

⊕

FIGURE 6.1. Mary (in Native regalia), Jane, and Bob Horn (front row) join former Earlham students who were among a group that made trips together for more than fifty years, shown here in 2019. Two students shown here were in Bob's 1969 seminar class the year that he brought Gerald Hawkins, coauthor of a landmark 1965 bestseller on Stonehenge archeoastronomy, to Earlham. Hawkins told the students their critique of his work was the best he had heard by scholars at any level. Photographer unknown.

The path that brought Mary and Jonathan from the Menominee tribal community in the Northwoods of Wisconsin to the mostly white, Quaker-influenced Richmond in East-Central Indiana, was similar in ways to the path many Native American children took in the decades when the goals of Native adoption and schooling programs were primarily "assimilation." There was one other Native girl of particular note who also traveled that strange path from reservation to Richmond, some seventy-five years before Mary and Jonathan. The year was 1895 and the young woman was known then as Gertrude Simmons. Her journey to Richmond and beyond is a truly epic tale that was almost lost to history until it was rediscovered and popularized in the 1990s. Like almost everyone else, Mary, Jonathan, and their adopted parents knew nothing about Gertrude in the 1970s and 1980s, which is sad because they might have found inspiration in her story.

Gertrude was a nineteen-year-old Yankton Dakota graduate of Indian boarding schools when she arrived in Richmond. Thin, with long straight black hair, she was beautiful, though not in a delicate way. Elegantly statuesque, she would not want for male suitors. Her arrival was made possible by an invitation to attend Earlham College, and she was surely as nervous as any freshman confronted by its high brick facades, towering trees and the manicured lawn of its campus quad. What made it much harder for Gertrude was the tortured trail that took her there. Her mother's name was Taté I

FIGURE 6.2. Zitkala-Ša, also known as Gertrude Simmons Bonnin. Photo by Joseph Turner Keiley. National Portrait Gallery, Smithsonian Institution.

Yóhin Win, "Reaches for the Wind" in their native language. Gertrude, born in 1876, the year of the Battle of Little Bighorn, spent her earliest years in what she described as "a wigwam of weather-stained canvas" on a reservation in South Dakota. Three times daily she and her mother carried water from a muddy stream.

Of her childhood on the reservation, Gertrude wrote, "I was as free as the wind that blew my hair, and no less spirited than a bounding deer."[5] At age eight she was lured away from her happy birthplace by missionaries who promised not just education but the adventure of a journey by train and the

5. Zitkala-Ša, "American Indian Stories," 68.

sweet taste of red apples you could pick right off Indiana's trees. She first attended White's Manual Labor Institute, a Quaker boarding school north of Indianapolis. Arriving in moccasins and wrapped in a blanket, she objected to wearing the tight-fitting lacey clothes she and her classmates were given. She found them immodest. Everything about the place was foreign.

"The annoying clatter of shoes on bare floors gave us no peace," she later wrote. "The constant clash of harsh noises, with the undercurrent of many voices murmuring an unknown tongue."[6]

On her first day a classmate warned they would cut her long black hair and said there was no use fighting it.

"No, I will not submit! I will struggle first," she replied. "Our mothers had taught us that only unskilled warriors who were captured had their hair shingled by the enemy."

She snuck away and hid under a bed. "I remember being dragged out, though I resisted by kicking and scratching wildly. In spite of myself, I was carried downstairs and tied fast in a chair. Not a soul reasoned quietly with me, as my own mother used to do; for now, I was only one of many little animals driven by a herder."[7]

⊕

She adjusted nonetheless, even excelled. In a few years' time, her Quaker teachers secured an invitation for her to attend a Quaker college downstate, bringing her to Earlham.

"As I hid myself in my little room in the college dormitory, away from the scornful and yet curious eyes of the students, I pined for sympathy. Often I wept in secret, wishing I had gone West, to be nourished by my mother's love, instead of remaining among a cold race whose hearts were frozen hard with prejudice."[8]

Gertrude showed a talent for language and oratory, earning her the respect of her Earlham peers. She was picked to represent the college in a statewide oratorical contest where a competing team displayed a taunting white-sheet banner with a crude caricature of what she described as "a most forlorn Indian girl," labeled with a racist slur for a Native female.

6. Zitkala-Ša, "American Indian Stories," 89.
7. Zitkala-Ša, "American Indian Stories," 91.
8. Zitkala-Ša, "American Indian Stories," 101.

"Such worse than barbarian rudeness embittered me." Nonetheless, she took one of two top prizes and was celebrated by her classmates.

"The evil spirit laughed within me when the white flag dropped out of sight, and the hands which furled it hung limp in defeat."[9]

Her academic success took her to Pennsylvania where she was given a teaching position at one of the most infamous of Indian boarding schools, the Carlisle School. Its founder was Colonel Richard Henry Pratt, who believed himself well-meaning but whose ignominy was secured when he declared that to advance the interests of the Indigenous it was necessary to "kill the Indian in him, and save the man."[10] Many of his school's Native students nevertheless held him in esteem for his efforts on their behalf, and Carlisle School helped create a class of "educated" elites among Indigenous students. Although the education was Western in orientation, they informally broadened their Native knowledge by forming lasting relationships with members of other tribes whom they might not otherwise have met. Thus was established a leadership core of a budding pan-Indian civil rights movement. The larger legacy of the Carlisle School, the source of its infamy, was its role as a model for countless other boarding schools that devolved into a system that did soul-crushing harm to the culture and well-being of thousands of Indigenous children removed from tribes, scrubbed of their language and traditions, and often brutally mistreated.

Aside from her work teaching at Carlisle, Gertrude continued to stand apart. She was a violinist so gifted she played at the White House for President William McKinley. She crafted beautifully written depictions of her childhood, critical of boarding schools, gaining a wide audience when they were published in *The Atlantic Monthly* and *Harper's Magazine.*

She worked to give women an equal role in efforts to form an organization of Native Americans dedicated to ridding themselves of white people's patronizing control, reform the bitterly maligned Bureau of Indian Affairs, promote educational advancement and advocate for people living on reservations. Gertrude likened reservations to prisoner-of-war camps. When one close male friend described the proposed leadership of the new organization as being led exclusively by men, with women given a separate auxiliary organization, she was having none of it.

"Your organization seems a plausible project," she wrote. "Why do you think the men are able alone to do it—and in a queer after thought suggest

9. Zitkala-Ša, "Old Indian Legends," 32.

10. Pratt, "Mingling Indians with Whites," 46.

the Indian women should have theirs too. . . . Am I not an Indian woman as capable to think in serious matters and as thoroughly interested in the race as any one or two of you men put together?"[11]

She felt increasing bitterness toward government efforts to assimilate Indigenous people into white society by smothering Native culture. "I hate this eternal war between being wild and being civilized."[12] She responded by translating Native American stories into modern English for all readers and she cowrote the first Indigenous American opera, *The Sun Dance*, about a Native American ceremony that at that time was banned by federal law. A deeply meaningful religious ritual for many Native people, the Sun Dance as practiced by some tribes involved physically grueling aspects that white Americans found shocking and "primitive."

The dream she shared of an organization by and for Native people became a reality. The first meeting of the Society of American Indians was held—with intentional irony—in the city of Columbus, Ohio, on October 12, 1911, Columbus Day. Fifty leaders of numerous tribes came together from all parts of the United States to discuss education, employment, conditions on reservations, and much more. Gertrude did not attend that meeting but took leadership roles in later years.

At the close of that historic first pan-Indian meeting in Columbus, a group of Native leaders traveled together to see Ohio's distinctive monuments to its Indigenous past, its ancient mounds. They visited one such site and, according to a local news account, "Before leaving the Indians gathered on top of the mound and sang 'America,' and following that the younger Indians gave an impromptu war dance on the same elevation."[13] It is likely the white reporter covering the event lacked awareness of the difference between a "war dance" or any other Native ritual.

A century later, in an effort to commemorate that momentous 1911 meeting of Native Americans, came another curious illustration of how, even among the most enlightened and well-intentioned people, the puzzling Newark earthworks can play tricks on historical memory. On Columbus Day weekend, 2011, Ohio State University hosted a "Society of American Indians [SAI] Centennial Symposium." Leading Native American intellectuals, scholars, and writers attended. A Native American keynote speaker at the event later wrote, "Attendees of the first [1911] SAI meeting traveled from Columbus to

11. Zitkala-Ša, "Letters, Speeches," 39–40.
12. Zitkala-Ša, "Letters, Speeches," 23.
13. Ohio State Journal, "Columbus Red Men," page number obscured.

the Newark Earthworks, a side trip that those of us who attended the anniversary gathering replicated."[14] Another conference attendee wrote a similar account for the same publication: "The SAI delegation had learned of ancient earth enclosures built by their ancestors in nearby Newark. It is said that they visited the Octagon Earthworks and sang 'America.'"[15] The 2011 attendees organized a reenactment, visiting the Octagon and singing the same song. A third writer, a noted poet and professor of English and American Indian studies, described the poignant irony of the songs at Newark, that day and a century earlier.[16]

I wanted to know more about that 1911 gathering at Newark. Curiously, I struggled to find contemporary or original sources from that year. Then I discovered a funny thing. Although the dancing and the singing of "America" did happen in 1911, the trip to Newark almost certainly did not. That detail seems to have been made up somewhere along way. I eventually found a local newspaper account reporting that the 1911 SAI delegation traveled not to Newark but to "the Pope farm on the Dublin Pike, where there is an Indian mound of considerable size."[17] It appears that the OSU trip to Newark in 2011 replicated an event that never actually happened at that site.

Sadly, the mound at Pope Farm is long gone. The 2,400-year-old, thirty-foot-high mound, built by people of the Adena culture, was leveled in 1954 to make room for a truck repair business.[18] There, in suburban Columbus at the corner of Adena Drive and Dublin Road, a nondescript trucking business remains in operation to this day.

⊕

When Gertrude married, she took her husband's name and became Gertrude Bonnin. Later she embraced another new name for herself: Zitkala-Ša, meaning Red Bird, the name for which she is best known today. Some years afterwards, a successor organization to SAI, the National Council of American Indians, elected Zitkala-Ša to serve as its president. After American women won the right to vote in 1920, she traveled the country speaking to women's

14. Warrior, SAI, 224.

15. Chaatsmith, "Singing," 182.

16. Noodin, "Bundling," 237–40.

17. *Ohio State Journal*, "Columbus Red Men," page number obscured. The author thanks the Franklin County Genealogical and Historical Society for locating this account.

18. Carlson, "Grandview Heights Moment."

suffrage groups about the plight of Native Americans. Her female audiences were impressed to see a woman in a position of leadership, representing a culture where matriarchal authority had deep roots. Her message to women was simple enough: those who worked so hard for voting rights for American women should be first to recognize the injustice done to the first Americans, who still had not been granted citizenship, let alone suffrage. By 1924, the Indian Citizenship Act was passed.

Zitkala-Ša was a fierce critic of the Indian boarding school system, but she was nonetheless aware of the educational advantages she had received. Speaking to a largely white audience in 1928, she began by saying, "At the outset, permit me to explain that I did not learn English in the Government Indian Schools. I attended Earlham College, Richmond, Indiana."

Then she noted, perhaps somewhat patronizingly, "I want to give all the credit if I have accomplished anything in trying to learn, to the Friends (Quakers) who have helped me. They have succeeded somewhat perhaps in subduing the wild impetuosity of a Sioux Indian woman. Someone has asked me when I was addressing an audience, after this fashion: 'Are you a civilized Indian?'" Here her audience laughed. "I told them I did not know, because civilization is a word that is very hard to define and to understand. I don't know what you mean by civilization. We send out little Indian boys and girls to school and when they come back talking English, they come back swearing. There is no swear word in the Indian languages and I haven't yet learned to swear."[19]

Zitkala-Ša died in 1938, when Bob Horn was a seven-year-old boy in Richmond with a growing curiosity about Native American mounds. Her story slipped from public memory until the 1970s when a Duke University English professor, searching for something unrelated in old copies of *The Atlantic Monthly*, happened upon Zitkala-Ša's essays from 1899–1902. By the 2000s, those and other of her writings were published in new collections, and biographies appeared. Mary and Jonathan were adults by then. Today the journey of the Yankton Dakota writer, musician, and activist is widely celebrated.

19. Zitkala-Ša, "Letters, Speeches," 257.

CHAPTER 7

Return to Newark

The question is not what you look at, but what you see.
—Henry David Thoreau

In the year 1975, Bob and Jane faced dual challenges. Bob's rehabilitation remained slow even as the needs of their growing children grew. Ray Hively was, by contrast, living the more carefree life of a bachelor—for the moment at least. Before long, he received an invitation to dine at the home of Earlham's president, Franklin Wallin, which would prove consequential to Ray's marital status. The guest of honor, a friend of Wallin's, was Anthony Aveni, an astronomer on his way to becoming a founding father in the nascent study of archaeoastronomy, then barely accepted as serious science. Aveni's 1977 *Native American Astronomy* was among the first of more than forty books he would write on that and related topics, many of them concerning Mayan and Aztec archaeological sites. Aveni came to dinner, and knowing of Ray and Bob's work at Ohio's earthworks, President Wallin invited Ray so they could meet.

Wallin's secondary motivation for the dinner was hinted at in his seating arrangement, which placed Ray next to Aveni on one side and to Wallin's daughter, Susan, on the other. At one point in the evening, Susan left the room to put her young daughter to bed, and as she returned she overheard her father talking to Aveni about her: "You know that marriage you attended a few years ago? It didn't take." Ray overheard the remark too but pretended not to. Susan returned to the table and Ray, feigning ignorance, asked, "So, is your husband traveling?"

Susan remembers that as an effort by Ray to "make sure everybody was on the same page," regarding Susan's availability. They were indeed. So much so, that before long Susan and Ray were engaged to be married. One measure of how comfortable Susan's family was with Ray as her fiancé was an incident that occurred on a trip to Michigan where they visited her grandparents in their cottage. As Ray and her father engaged in a conversation about Hopewell mounds, her grandfather's ears perked up, and he then spoke excitedly about Hopewell mounds in nearby Grand Rapids. Susan's grandmother interrupted her husband, also named Franklin, urging him to get ready to go to lunch. So, in an effort to simultaneously converse about Native mounds and tuck in his shirt, "he dropped his trousers to his knees and got everything tucked in, just engrossed in the conversation, and then he belts it back up. It didn't even faze him, and my grandmother was absolutely horrified."

"Franklin!" she exclaimed.

As the June 1976 date of their wedding approached, Ray and Susan needed a minister and did not have to look far. As a young man, Bob Horn had been ordained in the Disciples of Christ Church. Compared to other faiths, that was a denomination with relaxed standards for ordination, and accepting the ministry fulfilled a wish of Bob's father even if Bob's long-term goal was teaching, not preaching. For the wedding, though wobbly on his feet and reliant on walkers and canes, Bob gracefully officiated.

Bob's influence extended to Ray and Susan's choice of newlywed destinations too. They spent the night of their wedding at the Holiday Inn in Newark. The late June date was close to the summer solstice, so they rose before dawn and headed to the Moundbuilders Country Club in search of alignments. There were no golfers at that early hour, and no pointers to the rising sun either, at least none Ray could find.

"I was never certain that Susan was as interested in spending her wedding night at Newark, Ohio, as I was," wrote Ray. "But I improved my standing by subsequently taking her on a somewhat more romantic honeymoon: a week-long sailing trip in the Caribbean."

Ray still likes to kid Bob about the questionable validity of his marriage license, but this was a marriage that took. More than forty years later, Ray and Susan were still very much together.[1]

⊕

By the summer of 1980 Bob finally "exchanged his cane for a stadia rod," as Jane put it, and returned to surveying earthworks with Ray, focusing on Newark's Octagon.

1. Interviews with Horn Sept. 08, 2021, and Hively, Horn, and Susan Hively and Jane Horn, July 21, 2021.

"We undertook a survey of the site utilizing a transit and steel tape," they later wrote, leaving out of their published accounts the obstacles encountered. Far from fully recovered, walking was still a challenge for Bob.

"We just went out there and dodged the golf balls, but nobody ever bothered us," said Ray. "I think there was only one time when somebody came and said, 'what the hell are you doing.' But then he backed off. He was a big burly guy. But mostly they just played around us and we had to patiently stay out of their way."

They remembered one groundskeeper "was expressing frustration with the historical society because he thought they were so small minded. These mounds have really kept them from getting the kinds of tournaments they wanted. All he wanted to do was improve them. He wanted to put in new landscaping that would make the mounds better than they were! He couldn't understand why all these people were upset about these old Indian mounds when all he wanted to do was make them more attractive."

Many golfers and area residents "had no conception," said Ray. "You have people who live in Newark who are like people who live in Paris and have never been to the Eiffel Tower. There are people in Newark who don't know anything about the mounds."[2]

The fieldwork was essential to understanding the exact location of every earthen wall and mound, not just as it was situated that summer, but how they might have been altered by all the previous occupants of the property. Beginning in the 1890s it was a campground used by the Ohio National Guard, which described it then as "the Octagon and Circle Forts of ancient earth-works, constructed by an unknown race of people, who inhabited this section of our country prior to the Indian."[3] Guardsmen camped, drilled, bathed in the neighboring Racoon Creek, dug trenches and built a firing range and stables on land outside the earth enclosures. In 1893, the Guard went to work "restoring the grounds to their early condition." Even after the "restoration" they continued camping there, 6,149 strong on one August week in 1903.[4] Forty years after the army's work, a Depression-era restoration was made to the Octagon's neighboring Observatory Circle.[5] How reliably true to the original could either of these "restorations" be, and what of

2. Hively interview, accompanied by Horn and Susan Hively and Jane Horn, July 21, 2021.

3. "Annual Report of the Adjutant General," 378.

4. Murphy, "Ohio National Guard Activities," 4.

5. Hively and Horn, "Geometry and Astronomy," S5.

the other unknown disturbances over the years? These questions mattered, for how could you prove an alignment to the heavens if mounds had been relocated?

Ray and Bob labored over these questions and over the nineteenth century maps that held important clues. Not always accurate, sometimes not agreeing with one another, the old surveys nevertheless gave useful evidence and confirmation. Later aerial photography by Dache Reeves luckily predated 1936 restoration work and gave further confirmation of the original Indigenous construction.

Another complication was the local topography. If you were going to test whether something on the ground aligns to a winter solstice, you have to know more than just the compass heading of that day's sunrise. The compass points to a spot on the horizon. What if there is a hill in the way? In that case they had to calculate where the sun would first send its rays over a hilltop visible from the earthworks. Any alignment pointing to sunrise over the hill would be a couple of degrees south of the horizon-level sunrise, depending on the height of the hill.

Combining their own measurements with those recorded by surveyors as far back as 1820, they slowly recreated on paper what they believed was an accurate depiction of the original earthwork as it was built sometime between sixteen hundred and two thousand years ago. The geometry of Hopewell earthen design had intrigued Ray and Bob from the beginning. As interested as they were in supposed alignments to the heavens, it was the geometry that drew them in too. Studying the plane geometry carved out of the flat surface of the earth, the new information Ray and Bob gathered was startling. Fascinating patterns emerged. "The first point to be noted regarding the geometry of the earthworks is their remarkable regularity," they later wrote. The octagon was exceptionally accurate, with walls precisely parallel and vertexes symmetrical, although it had a curious anomaly that they would later struggle to explain. But, if you draw an "X" using the vertices opposite one another, their intersections create near-perfect right angles. Modern surveyors would be hard pressed to achieve that.

At the Newark Octagon, the adjacent Observatory Circle measures 1,054 feet across. Readings made at various points around the perimeter showed that 1,054-foot diameter never deviates by more than four feet—a circle 99.6 percent true. They had earlier noticed that the length of the diameter precisely matched the length of the sides of a square drawn by connecting alternate vertices inside the octagon. It seemed coincidental until they

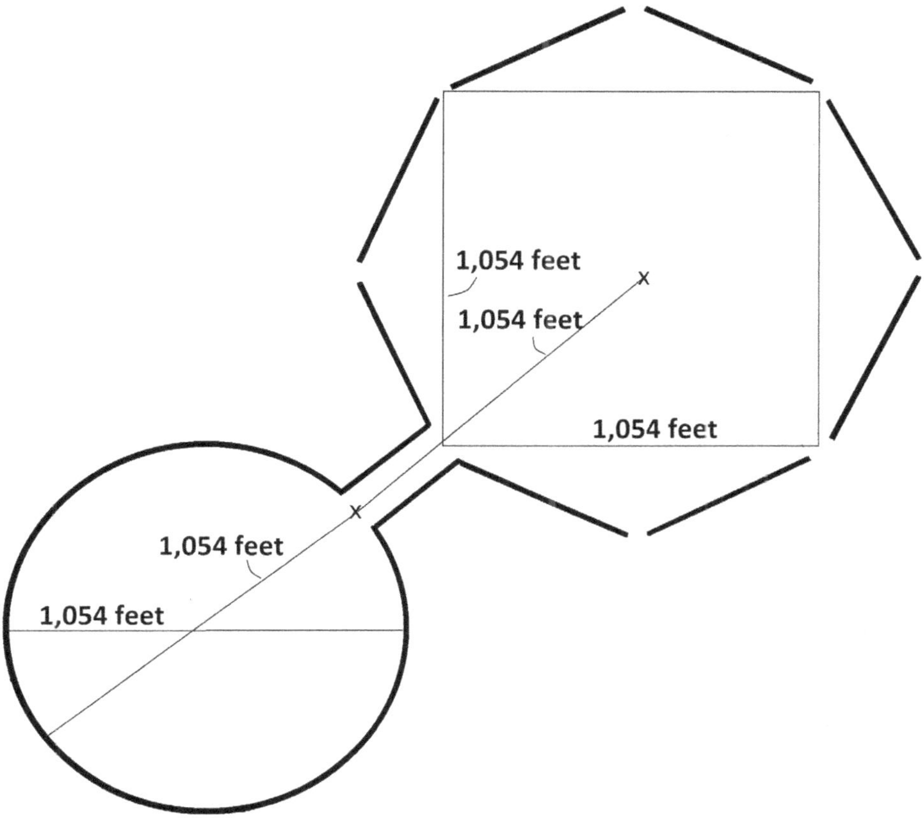

FIGURE 7.1. Ray and Bob called the 1,054-foot observatory circle diameter one "OCD," a common unit of measurement that, in time, was discovered at earthworks throughout southwest Ohio. Courtesy of the Ohio History Connection, with modifications.

discovered that same number—1,054—repeating itself again and again like Easter Eggs waiting to be found. Ray and Bob called that unit of measurement one "OCD," for Observatory Circle Diameter. They compared the Newark Octagon to the only other Hopewell earthwork that combines a circle and octagon. Known as High Bank, it is sixty miles south near Chillicothe. Now mostly flattened by farm equipment, its outline had been precisely revealed using a magnetometer that located disturbances in the soil. The High Bank circle's diameter? One thousand fifty-four feet, or one OCD, almost exactly.

The Newark Octagon sits within a four-square-mile area that until the nineteenth century featured a much larger arrangement of geometric earthworks. The Great Circle, about a mile away, was thankfully saved from bulldozers, but not so fortunate were other nearby mounds eastward, one forming a vast ellipse and another a great square, known as the Wright Square. We do know their former locations however, thanks to nineteenth-century surveys and modern detective work. Armed with that information, Ray and Bob measured from the center of the Observatory Circle to the center of the Great Circle. That 1.2-mile distance, 6,313 feet to be precise, equals 5.99 OCDs. The distance between the centers of the Octagon and the Square? 6.02 OCDs. Those reasons alone strongly suggested at least two things: first, a common unit of measure much more sophisticated than the "arm's length" that most people think of as a measure used by ancient people. And, second, a great ancient masterplan connecting all these monumental works to one another. And Ray and Bob were just getting started.

These discoveries of feats of geometry were not entirely new. Nineteenth-century surveyors found other extraordinary patterns. For example, the Squier and Davis book published by the Smithsonian shows a curious feature of the Hopeton Earthwork, sixty miles south of Newark. Here, where a great circle adjoins a square, they showed that the area of the circle *equals* the area of the connected square—both twenty acres. Likewise, the Squier and Davis map of the four-square mile collection at Newark showed that the Observatory Circle at the Octagon is also twenty acres in area. The Wright Square, six "OCDs" from the Octagon? An equal twenty acres square. Squier and Davis found Easter Eggs too.

The geometric challenge of "circling the square" dates back to the ancient Greeks. How, they asked, can a square be drawn that is equal in area to a given circle, using only a compass and straightedge? For millennia, no one could find an answer, and as a puzzle for the academically inclined, many tried. Lewis Carroll of *Alice in Wonderland* fame tried. The philosopher Thomas Hobbes tried it. Dante mentions it. A then-little-known former surveyor who was a contemporary of Squier and Davis, working in Illinois, once tried his hand at the problem. Named Abraham Lincoln, his law partner remembered finding his friend in an exasperated state over the problem. William Herndon wrote, "He was sitting at the table and spread out before him lay a quantity of blank paper, large heavy sheets, a compass, a rule, numerous pencils, several bottles of ink of various colors, and a profusion of stationery and writing appliances generally. He had evidently been struggling with a calculation of some magnitude, for scattered about were sheet after sheet of paper covered with an unusual array of figures. He was so deeply absorbed in study he scarcely looked up when I entered."

Herndon claimed he worked at it for two days "almost to the point of exhaustion . . . having ended in failure, we, in the office, suspected that he was more or less sensitive about it and were therefore discreet enough to avoid referring to it."[6] It wasn't until 1882 that Ferdinand von Lindeman proved to the satisfaction of most experts that "squaring the circle" couldn't be done.

Somehow the people of the Hopewell culture managed to square-the-circle in location after location. No, it wasn't the same as finding the formula to do it on paper with a compass and straight edge. But the presence of that quirky mathematical feat, etched all over the ancient Ohio landscape, was greatly puzzling to nineteenth century surveyors, and it remains so today. Those Indigenous builders were wicked smart, to say the least.

⊕

So Ray and Bob had identified the original locations and compass bearings of the earthworks. They accounted for alterations by country clubs and army brigades. They accounted for topographical elevations. It was time now to consider what connections, if any, existed to objects in the sky.

An octagon, by definition, is formed by eight lines, and the Newark Octagon's lines are defined by walls that average about 550 feet in length, vertex to vertex, each side almost as long as the Washington Monument is tall. That makes for very long, straight and precise pointers. There are also openings at each vertex, with small mounds the builders placed just inside of each opening, creating gaps for other possible reference points to the horizon. Solstice alignments were alleged to be at Stonehenge, and they could have practical uses such as tracking seasons, so Ray continued looking for those. But try as he could, Ray continued to find nothing about the Octagon that tracked the sun. He had until then sworn that solar alignments could be found anywhere. It seemed to defy the odds that absolutely none of the linear shapes or vertex openings pointed to any solar event, even accidentally.

It was during this period of frustration that he was on an airplane "passing the time reading a book on statistics and how things can be proven to be probable or improbable. I remember thinking of all the linear features of Newark and none of them pointed anywhere close to a solstice. That seemed

6. Ellenberg, *Shape,* 10.

FIGURE 7.2. The southeast wall of the Newark Octagon. Photo by James W. Graham.

very improbable. How do you explain this? The only way I could think of was they must be pointing at something else. Saying they were a cult of solar avoidance wouldn't get you very far. They had to be pointing to something."

Ray and Bob understood that these builders knew exactly what they were doing, at least as far as geometry was concerned. The question was: what exactly *were* they trying to do? The deliberate laying down of these giant shapes must have had a purpose. Ray liked to say that the casual observer walking amidst these earthen structures would be unaware of any geometric patterns. You wouldn't build this to impress your girlfriend, he said, because the patterns are invisible at ground-level. So what was the point?

If the Newark Earthworks did not point to the sun, there were other options. There were stars and constellations—the North Star, Orion's Belt, the Big Dipper. All of these figure into Indigenous cultural traditions, as they do other cultures. The constellation Pleiades was known to Native Americans variously as the seven sisters, boys, or children. The Ojibwe refer to it as "the hole in the sky," and the Navajo, or Diné, say it signals planting and harvesting times.

But the most obvious and prominent alternative to the sun is the moon, of course. The moon plays a big role in Native cultural traditions across many tribes, so it's a logical alternative. The problem with the moon is that, unlike the sun or constellations, its location in the sky is a much more complicated thing to forecast and mark. The sun rises and sets in predictable fashion with the seasons, appearing at horizon points that move slowly, steadily north on the horizon each day until reaching its northern limit—the summer solstice—where it appears to "stand still," rising and setting at the same point on the horizon for several days before moving south again, day by day, inching to its farthest southern point at winter solstice and another stand still. The sun repeats that pattern over and over, six months northward, pause, six months southward, pause, reversing course on nearly the same days each year at the same points on the horizon. A relatively easy pattern to understand.

The moon, however, has a personality all its own. In our electric-lit world, people barely notice it, let alone understand it. For starters, the moon's rise and set points head north and south and back again, like the sun, but instead of a year, it does it in less than a month—27.3 days to be more precise.[7] That's not so complicated, but one astronomical curve ball is a thing called the "precession of the lunar nodes." Sounds like 1950s sci-fi, sure, and you'll thank me when I say a deep understanding of this is not necessary for our purposes, but a couple of concepts are helpful. First, imagine a circular disk, or plane, formed by the earth's orbit around the sun. That is known as the ecliptic plane (related to the word "eclipse"). The earth's axis is tilted 23.5 degrees relative to that ecliptic plane. That's the tilt that gives us seasons. The moon's orbit around the earth is close to the ecliptic plane, not the equatorial plane, except that it is off by about five degrees from the ecliptic. In addition to those two "tilts" in orbits, a third dynamic comes into play. This is the gravitational pull of the sun on the moon. The sun pulls the plane of the moon's orbit into a slow circle, so the place above earth where the moon crosses the ecliptic plane moves westward 19.4 degrees each year. Multiply 19.4 degrees times 18.6 years and you get 360 degrees, a full circle around the earth (remember that number, 18.6). It's a bit like a spinning top that's wobbling a bit, one side leaning just a little bit further around its wobbling path with every rotation. As the moon travels around the earth, those three factors work together: the tilt of earth's axis (23.5 degrees), the tilt of the moon's

7. The 27.32-day north-south movement of the moon is known as the sidereal month. This is different from the moon phases, which happen over a 29.53-day period known as the synodic month.

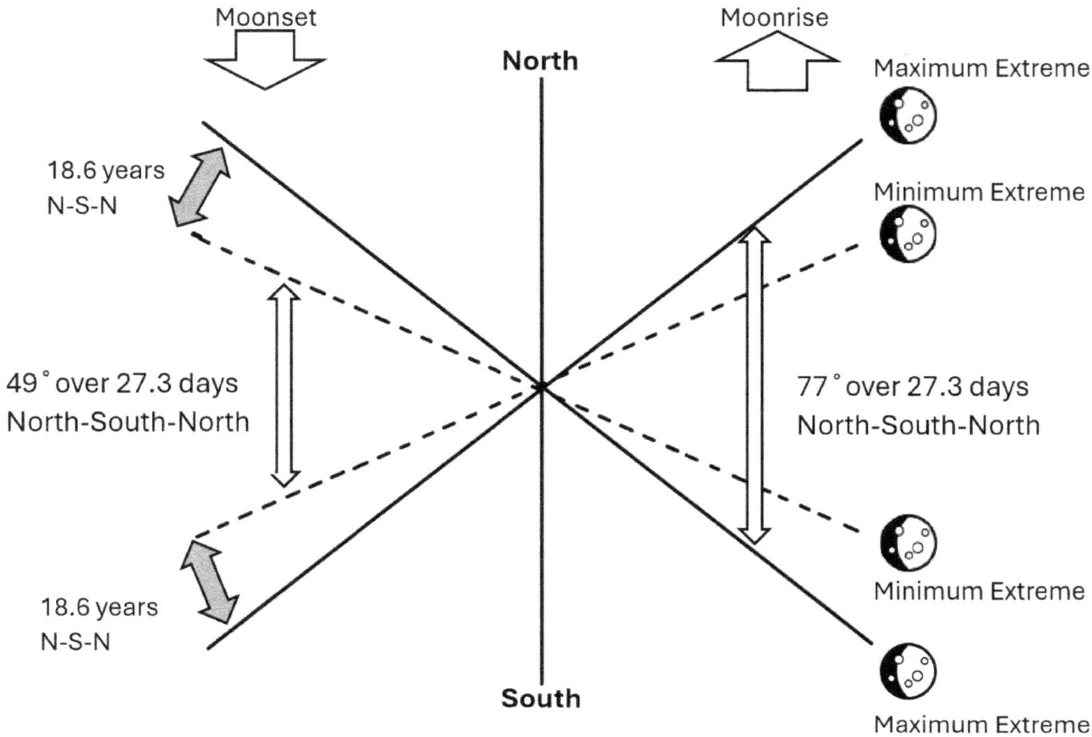

FIGURE 7.3. The 18.6-year cycle of moonrises and moonsets. Diagram by James W. Graham.

orbit (five degrees), and the pull of the sun on the moon. If you could stick a pen in the moon like a toy spirograph you would get a lovely, lacey 3D pattern that takes 18.61 years to repeat. And like a spirograph, the line rejoins and retraces its path after that time.

If you find this complicated, you're not alone. Isaac Newton told a colleague that completing a theory of the moon "made his head ache and kept him awake so often that he would think of it no more."[8] Ray and Bob were already skeptical that the builders of Stonehenge were pointing to summer or winter solstices, so it seemed truly ludicrous to think Indigenous peoples would build massive earthen monuments to track an 18.6 year lunar cycle, one that's so complicated few of us understand it even today. What would be the point? Unlike the sun, the moon's path has no effect on weather or seasons. Tides, yes, but tides aren't a thing in Ohio.

Nonetheless, Ray and Bob decided to humor themselves and see how a moon-tracking Ohio "Stonehenge," half a mile in length, might work. For this

8. Brewster, *Memoirs*, p. 157.

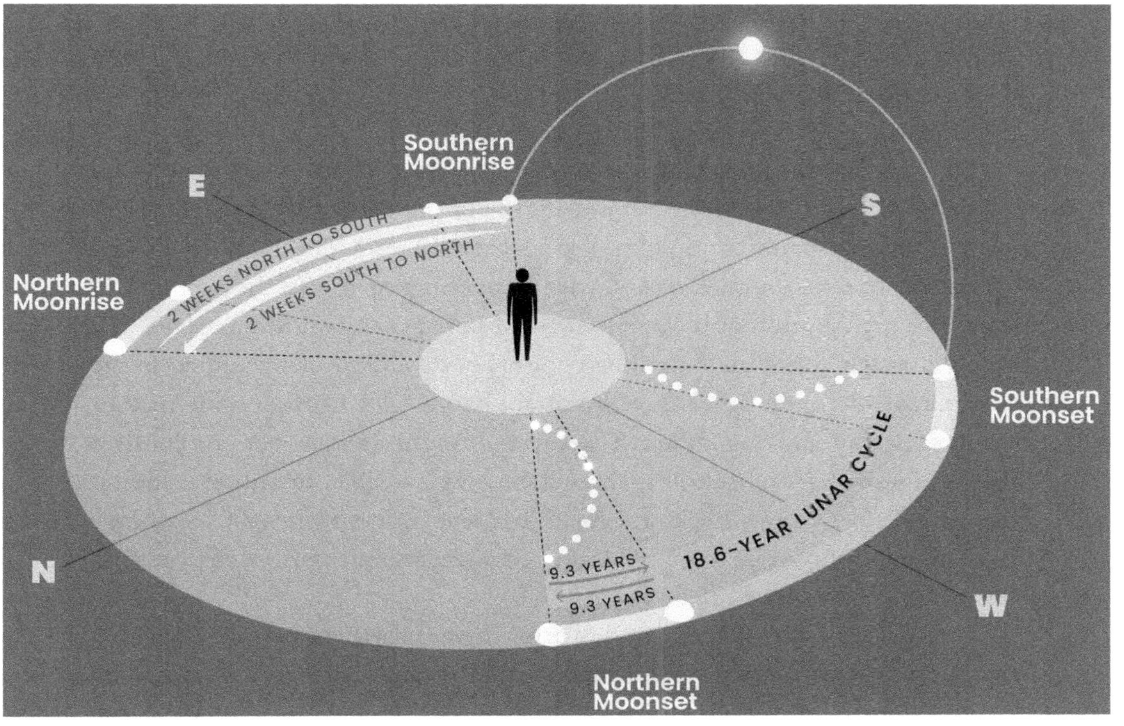

FIGURE 7.4. Every 18.6 years, moonrises and moonsets occur at their northernmost points on the horizon. Then, for about two weeks, moonrises and moonsets occur a few degrees further south each day until they reach their southernmost extreme and return northward again. The pattern repeats for months, defining a "standstill." After the extreme standstills, for nine years, the distance between northern and southern moonrises slowly narrows until it reaches the extreme minimum, or "minor standstill." Then the angle widens for nine years more. Courtesy of Ohio History Connection.

they had to consider how the moon's long orbital cycle would be observed from the ground. The lunar counterpart to a solstice—a "lunistice"—is referred to by astronomers as a lunar "standstill." Lunar standstills bear some resemblance to a pendulum's swing. Imagine you're on a very big swing set, going as fast and high as you can. You speed through the bottom of your downward arc, then rise and slow to a moment of weightlessness, a pause, before you speed backward toward another pause on the opposite end. For a kid, the pause is the magic, holding you there for a breath of a moment.

A lunar standstill is a swing set's pause expressed in the grandest of scales. The moon "stands still" in two ways. First, the moon's rise and set points move northward for about two weeks, then they appear to pause, and for as much as three days the rises and sets occur over nearly the same spots without seeming to change. If that stopping point is, say, a mountain, it might make a memorable impression on the viewer. Then it reverses direction and each day the moon's rise marches south for about two weeks, along the horizon, pausing again before returning north. So roughly every month there are two standstills, one north, one south.

The second way in which the moon "stands still" is referred to as its "maximum" and "minimum" standstill. Over the course of that long 18.6-year cycle, maximum standstills repeat themselves monthly for a period of several months, with the moonrise happening at the farthest points to the north and south that it ever reaches. Moreover, at its north extreme, the moon is visible for more than fifteen hours per day and transits higher in the sky than at any other time. Then, for about two weeks, its rise occurs further south each day, moving as much as seven or eight degrees per day, until it reaches its southernmost point. There the moon is visible for only nine hours per day. That extreme back-and-forth, highest transit to lowest, northern-most to southern-most, continues for a several-month period of time that repeats only once every 18.6 years.

Facing east, if you point your two arms toward the two rise and set points that are two weeks apart and at their farthest points north and south, your arms will form an angle of about 77 degrees. For the next nine years, as the moonrises swing north and south each month, the distance narrows between north and south, your arms go closer together, and at the end of nine years your arms are forming a much narrower angle of just 49 degrees. When your arms are widest apart, that's the major standstill. When they are closest together, that's a minor standstill. Counting moonrises and moonsets, north and south, that makes four minor and four major standstills, or eight noteworthy, time-marking occurrences in all.

What's going on, if viewed from space, is the changing relationship, or declination, between the moon's orbital plane and the equatorial plane. Remember that the moon's orbit is wobbling five degrees off the ecliptic plane aligned to the sun. That means that sometimes the orbit is farthest from the equator, at maximum standstill, and then nine years later it is closest to the equator, for the minimum standstill.

In ancient times, in a valley where there are low hills making a jagged horizon of reference points, that pattern could be easier to spot. Let's say your daughter is born near the day you see the moon rise at its northern-most point over a specific distant hill you have named Mount Luna. Each month's northern-most turning point makes a slow march southward over nine years, then turns northward for nine more, never again making it as far north as Mount Luna. Finally, for the first time in more than 18 years, it returns for its long magical pause over distant Mount Luna to the north, as if saying, "Behold, I have returned for my epochal moment. It has taken 18 years. Your daughter has grown from child to child-bearing."

Astronomers don't normally pay much attention to where the moon rises and falls on a horizon because it isn't relevant to understanding the workings of solar systems or the wider universe. If you work on voyages to the moon, as Ray had, you pay attention to the path of the moon around the earth so you can intercept it accurately enough to stick a landing on the Sea of Tranquility. But Ray and Bob understood that a standstill might make an impression on ancient people in North America, living in the nighttime embrace of a river valley in Ohio, so they calculated the points on the horizon where those eight major standstills would occur. They compared that data to the lines formed by various features of the Newark Octagon.

⊕

Observatory Circle, the western half of the Newark Octagon configuration, has gone by that name for decades, and nobody quite knows why. Its name predates anyone having a serious idea that it might actually be an astronomical observatory. At the southwestern edge of that circle stands "Observatory Mound." It is positioned directly opposite an earthen causeway connecting the circle to the octagon.

Using astronomical data, combined with topographical maps for elevations at the horizon, Ray calculated that the moon rose at its 18.6-year northernmost point at 51.6 degrees, or just east of northeast. He calculated similar compass bearings for the other three major lunar standstills and the four minor ones. Then he compared them to the directions of the walls of the octagon and to other lines formed by looking through gaps at vertices or along other points along the paths of the circle, causeway and octagon.

This was the same exercise they used to find pointers to the solstices, yielding nothing. Now he looked for pointers to the moon. They were opening a drawer they thought was empty, and found a box of gems, each a luminescent lunistice, a stunning standstill.

"It all fell into place," said Ray.

⊕

The Octagon's south-southwest wall draws a ruler-straight 550-foot line pointing to a place on the horizon that corresponds to 130.3 degrees on a

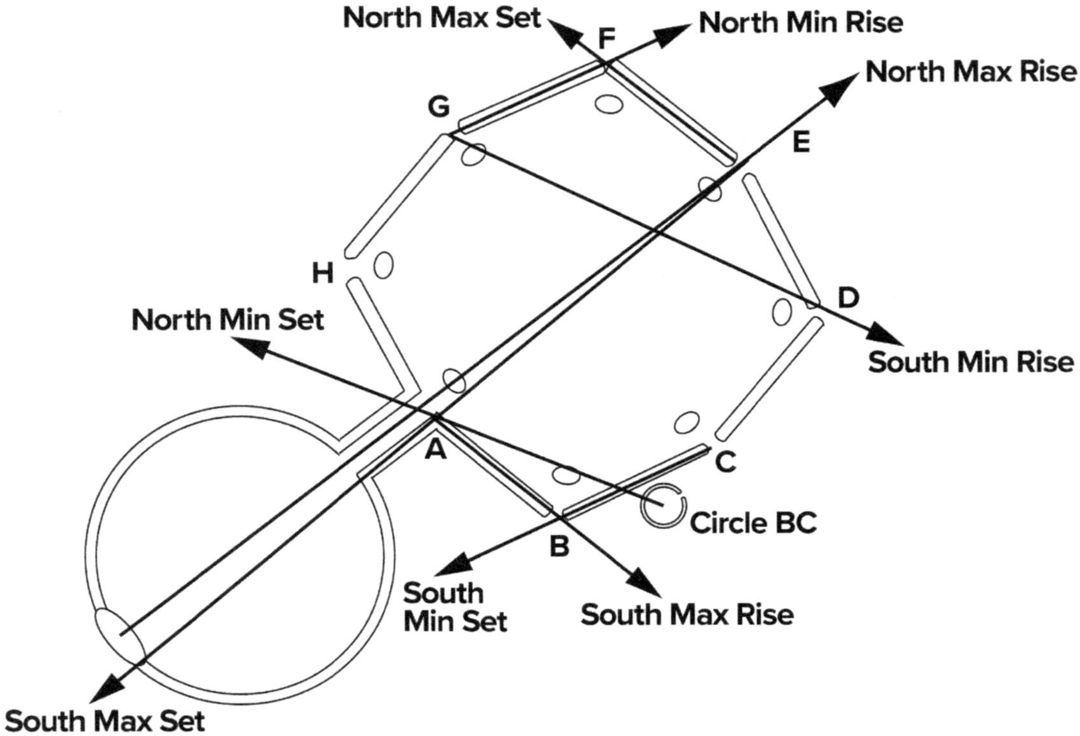

FIGURE 7.5. Newark Octagon alignments identified by Ray Hively and Bob Horn. Illustration by Ray Hively.

compass. By their calculations, that turned out to be the place on the horizon where the moon rises at its southernmost point, within three-tenths of a degree of accuracy. The Octagon's north-northwest wall points to the moonrise at north-minimum standstill, within two-fifths of a degree. There were others too, but the crowning alignment was the one viewed by standing atop the observatory mound, the highest point in the earthwork, at the circle's west end. From there, look straight through the center axis of the circle, through the center of the causeway, straight down the axis of the octagon, a straight line traversing the center of the entire half-mile length of the combined earthworks. That axis points to 51.6 degrees, northeast, at the precise point, within one-fifth of a degree, where moonlight peeks out over the horizon at its northern-most point. For a period of about two years, every 18.6 years, the moon returns to that point about once a month and "stands still," rising there again and again for up to three days, before moonrises start to swing far southward, a little each day. On that day of northern standstill, the period of visible moonlight is the longest in a generation. If these

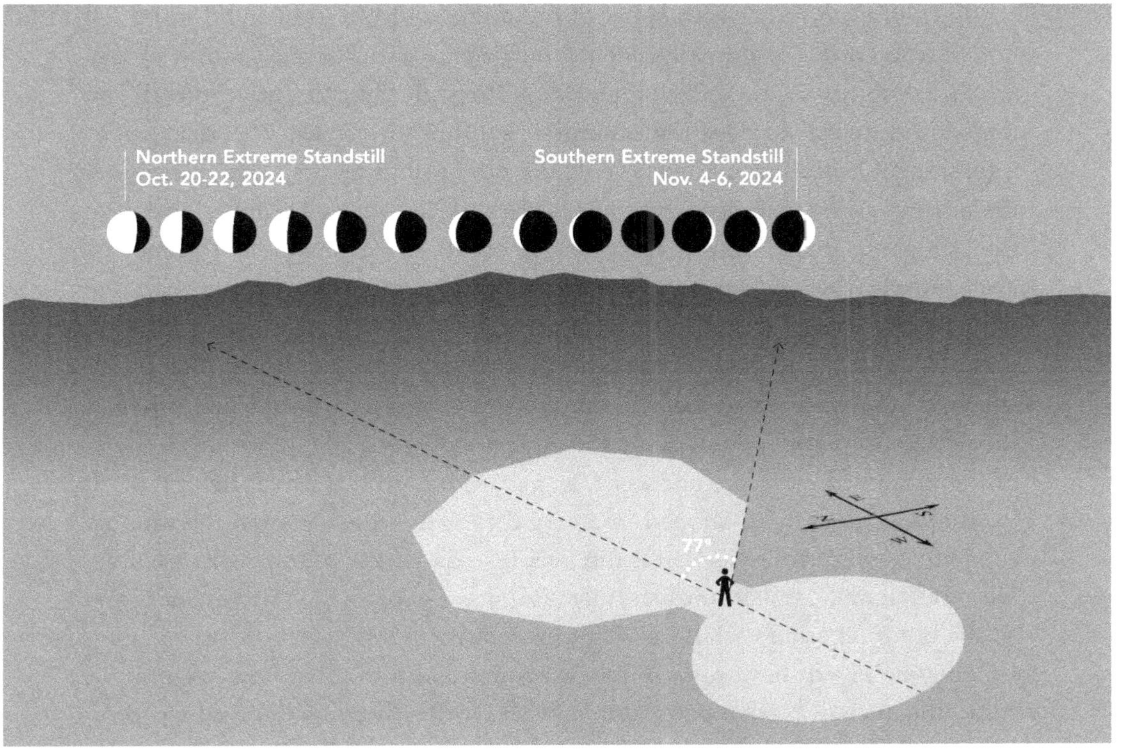

FIGURE 7.6. When moonrises reach their northern and southern extremes every 18.6 years, an observer can see the northern-most moonrise align and "stand still" with the central axis of the Newark Octagon, as it did for a group of observers on October 21, 2024. For about two weeks afterward, the moon rose each day at a slightly more southerly point on the horizon until reaching its southern extreme standstill. It then reversed course. Illustration by Kevin Stone and James W. Graham.

great earthen enclosures were meant to serve as gathering places for a mass of people, imagine that moonrise as everyone stood facing where the earthworks told them to look. It could be an awe-inspiring show rivaling the great medieval cathedrals.

In all, Ray and Bob found evidence that the Octagon pointed to all eight of the lunar standstills that occur in the moon's generation-long orbital journey across the heavens.

"It seemed that the more convincing the evidence appeared to be, the more we came to suspect our own ingenuity," said Bob. "Were we somehow projecting our own view into the material we had accumulated? It took a long time before the two of us were ready to go beyond saying, 'Well, it's possible,' to state really that the Hopewell intended what was there."[9]

9. Holden, "Moon Maze," 6.

By their own admission, some of the alignment points seemed more ad hoc than others. For one alignment you had to stand at the mound at the southeast vertex of the Octagon and look through the gap between walls at the southern vertex to see the minimum southern moonset. Was that really intentional? But what made some of the odder alignments convincing was the quirky ways the original builders added small asymmetrical variations to the Octagon's shape, despite their proven ability to create perfect symmetry. For example, the west-southwestern wall is some thirty feet shorter than the other walls, and a mound in front of the gap on its north end is set slightly to one side, creating a wider gap and thus a neat sight line to the maximum southern moonset. Elsewhere a small circular mound placed just outside the octagon creates a viewpoint through a west-facing gap, giving a view of the minimum northern moonset. In fact, although it is a parallelogram, it is otherwise slightly ill-shaped in a way that "gives the Octagon the unique capacity to align four sides and the avenue axis with the lunar standstill(s). No other shape can accomplish this," Ray later explained. Why make these subtle but deliberate variations if not for a purpose?

They believed they were on to something that redefined how we understand the ancient Native people of Eastern North America. Certainly, it profoundly changed their own perspective on these people. There was, however, one anomaly in the earthwork construction they found so troubling it made them doubt themselves. Most of the alignments they found were accurate to within less than half a degree (a compass, of course, has 360 degrees). However, by comparison, one wall was way off. To fit the pattern it should point to where the moon touched a hilltop. Instead it pointed to a spot on the horizon where it set if the hill was not there, a spot not visible from the Octagon.

"All the alignments on the octagon made sense. But there was one which was an alignment to the north-most moonset. Instead of being off by a few tenths of a degree, it was off by one degree and nine-tenths.[10] The reason for that was because it ran directly into a hill that was north of that wall. Ray and I used to say if we could just strip down that hill we'd have a virtually perfect set of alignments. It was genuinely anomalous." And it made no sense.

These people were brilliant, sure, but they would need an airplane to align that wall to a spot on the horizon hidden by a hill. They couldn't fly for heaven's sake.

10. Their 1982 paper described the error as 1.7 degrees.

CHAPTER 8

Will Anyone Take Us Seriously?

It were not best that we should all think alike; it is difference of opinion that makes horse races.
—Mark Twain, *Pudd'nhead Wilson*

Anomaly notwithstanding, Ray and Bob now had reason to believe the Newark Octagon was a kind of giant ancient moon-dial, ticking off not hours of the day like a sundial, but months and years over a generation's time. They were confident their discovery was important, but they also knew many scholars would be just as skeptical of such ancient astronomy as they themselves had been.

"Once Ray and I thought we had a case for geometry and astronomy, I felt we needed the severest critic we could find," said Bob. "And that man was Olaf Prufer."

Severe to say the least. A Harvard trained anthropologist, Prufer taught for four decades at Ohio's Kent State and no student forgot him. "He hated intro classes and freshman, as a principle. He delighted in scaring them," recalled a former student who claims to have taken twelve classes with him. "He was a little mean, a lot scary and simply brilliant."[1] His short profile was counterbalanced by wideness of girth, a broad, bushy beard, and a belligerently confrontational manner. F-bombs so pleased him he named his cat F***knuckles, sans asterisks. He emigrated from Germany, where his father had been a Nazi and Hitler's ambassador to Brazil before emigrating to Switzerland in 1943.[2] Olaf retained a German accent and Bavarian-like reputation for fondness of drink. But the older students could tell he enjoyed teaching them, so they remember him with affection.

As a young archaeologist, Prufer upturned theories of how ancient Ohioans lived. Until the early 1960s, most scholars believed Ohio's large

1. Kohl, "Olaf Prufer."
2. Prufer, Curt, *Rewriting History*, dust jacket text.

earthworks were remnants of large human settlements, but no one had been able to find solid evidence of population centers, such as foundations of dwellings. Like suspicious parents looking for beer cans, archaeologists searched for evidence of habitation, mundane artifacts of daily living, things like cooking tools or butchered deer bones. They found none. Then, in the early 1960s, a farmer named Alva McGraw told friends he was finding random artifacts of various kinds on his property south of Chillicothe, where Paint Creek meets the Scioto River. McGraw pleaded with Olaf Prufer to have a look. Prufer, who had been coming up mostly empty-handed at a dig site just a few miles south, reluctantly agreed. The result would be a great step toward modern understanding of the Hopewell lifestyle, and it cemented Prufer's reputation as the foremost authority on Hopewell culture at that time.[3]

The model Prufer described became variously known as the "vacant center-disbursed hamlet" theory. The earthworks were not for living in, he argued, they were for ceremonial gatherings and other purposes. Prufer theorized that people lived in small hamlets scattered all throughout the surrounding area and came together for rituals and other purposes. Ever since Prufer, archaeologists modified, but did not significantly change, his description of Hopewell life.

Over the years, he built on that success and his dominating presence in the classroom was no smaller when he joined peers at academic conferences. One young graduate student remembers attending a conference on Hopewell research. "I was a little bit shocked and maybe afraid because I was about to come to grad school in Ohio. And here's this guy that would stand up and yell at the presenter and yell at other people in the audience. Essentially, everybody was dumber than him. Which may be true, but he didn't have to share it."[4]

Like invasive but necessary surgery, an interrogation by Prufer was obligatory for all scholars interested in Hopewell postulating. Bob had a sense of what he was in for because years earlier, after bringing Stonehenge scholar Gerald Hawkins to Earlham, he asked Prufer for his views on the British megalith.

"Prufer was entirely disgusted with Stonehenge," said Bob. "He thought Hawkins was crazy. He thought there wasn't any reason the people who

3. Carr, "Scioto Hopewell," 463.
4. Jarrod Burks, interview with author, May 20, 2024.

were supposed to have built Stonehenge could ever have done anything of the kind."

When Bob and Ray asked for a meeting, Prufer, true to his reputation, suggested they meet in a pub, not quite the setting they had in mind for a professional evaluation of their work. There, Prufer's reaction was not entirely surprising.

"You guys are crazy," Prufer said, as Bob recalls it. "There's no way, no way whatsoever, the people who lived there at the time could have built this. They had next to no social structure. We never found a Hopewell village. We don't know how they lived together. As far as we can tell they lived together on family farms. And what about the kind of organization that would have been required to build this kind of thing! You need a chieftainship! Without a chieftainship it's next to impossible!"[5]

Bob chuckles when he looks back at the Prufer meeting, but Ray sees the episode differently. Ray was quite adamant that I not turn Prufer into a caricature of the stubbornly closed-minded. Prufer was opinionated, sure, but in Ray's view his reputation as an authority was well deserved and he welcomed Prufer's critical analysis. Skepticism is healthy; it's how science is done. In talking to me about Prufer, Ray wanted no part in criticizing him just because they did not once see eye-to-eye. But Prufer's reaction was a gloomy outcome for Ray and Bob.

The archaeologist might not have taken the philosopher-astronomer pair as seriously as they hoped, but he didn't dismiss them entirely. "Before you go any further you've got to talk to Alva McGraw," Prufer told them. So they did, and as soon as McGraw heard them mention astronomy, he in turn said the person they had to meet is named N'omi Greber. "N'omi's working on my site and she's doing excavating here and she's interested in astronomy, so you gotta talk to her."

Greber was herself an emerging figure in Ohio archaeology, and she would be a leader of the generation stepping out from Prufer's shadow. Some archaeologists dabbled in multiple historical eras, but Greber remained focused on the culture of the Hopewell. Students remember her as a rigorous tutor and exceptionally disciplined at dig sites in the field. She made scrupulous use of checklists and insisted others do the same. Gather the data, she taught one of them, "and make sure you have two points of reference for

5. Bob Horn, interview with the author, May 12, 2021.

everything. Don't take everything at face value that somebody tells you, do the research yourself if you want to corroborate it."

But that discipline in the field seemed to soften once she shook the dirt off her boots and got behind the wheel of her car. More than one person I interviewed let their story swerve onto the topic of her driving habits.

She would drive down the center lane of interstate highways, doing fifty-five while others were "blowing her doors off" at eighty, recalls student Jamison Kilby Brizendine. Merging from one freeway onto another she would come to a complete stop and wait for the traffic. "What are you doing!" her student pleaded. "When you're going to merge with traffic you can't stop!"

"Are you sure you don't want me to drive?" he would ask Greber.

"Oh it's fine," Greber would say.[6]

Jarrod Burks, another acolyte and future leader in the field, remembers that when she drove with him across the Ohio countryside, she made aggressive use of the brake. A maternal reflex would send her right arm over his chest to keep him from flying toward the windshield.

But Greber survived her own driving and enjoyed a long career, producing more than sixty papers, articles, chapters, and presentations, mostly about Hopewell culture. In many ways, Greber was the perfect archaeologist for Ray and Bob. She had previously studied astronomy and mathematics, and her husband's career as an aeronautical engineer included work for NASA. She recognized the potential behind Ray and Bob's meticulously collected data. So from her they had the encouragement they needed to pursue publication of their work.

For a publisher, Ray and Bob had their eye on *Science* magazine, a respected journal that was celebrating its centennial year. Its founders included Thomas Edison, and it was a publisher of articles similar to one Ray and Bob were drafting. One from 1980, for example, described ancient Mayan canals.

For help in refining their draft article they turned to Anthony Aveni, the pioneer in archeoastronomy whom Ray knew through the dinner party hosted by Earlham's president, and to Martha Potter Otto, the archaeologist whose display of Dache Reeves's aerial photo jump-started Ray and Bob's enthusiasm. Both read their paper and offered helpful suggestions.

---

6. Jamison Kilby Brizendine, interview with the author, Sept. 7, 2024.

A third reviewer who agreed to analyze their work was John Eddy, a respected astronomer who, like Ray, had strayed out of his academic bubble to investigate how humans had observed the heavens in the past, and what their observations and methods might tell us today. Eddy held a position at the High Altitude Observatory in Boulder, Colorado. Around 1970 he came across an article in the Sunday magazine of *The Denver Post* that described the Bighorn Medicine Wheel, located about five hundred miles north of Boulder in Lovell, Wyoming. Compared to the earthworks of Ohio, the Medicine Wheel is just a fraction of the size, closer to the diameter of Stonehenge, but of a much simpler construction. Its age is harder to guess. Many believe it predates European contact because Native people appear to have been visiting it for thousands of years. The Medicine Wheel consists of arrangements of stones, each small enough for a single human to pick up and move, and so remotely located that it seems plausible it was undisturbed for hundreds of years. Eighty feet in diameter with twenty-eight spokes, it resembles a wagon wheel, and outside it are six smaller stone cairns roughly sized to fit a seated human. In 1972 Eddy arrived there with a surveyor's transit and steel tape and looked for Stonehenge-like alignments. He was not disappointed. He found pointers to the summer solstice sunrise and sunset, and additional alignments to the horizon where three of the brightest stars rise at key times of the year: Aldebaran, Rigel, and Sirius.

When Eddy published his findings, they tantalized a public still fascinated by Stonehenge. Not so fascinated were his peers at the High Altitude Observatory, who found his interest in the discipline of archaeoastronomy undisciplined and unwelcome. Serious people did not take that stuff seriously. Eddy's forays were seen as outside the institution's mission, and they told him so in as threatening a way as they could: his performance evaluations. In 1973, when the observatory's funding was cut, he was let go.

Despite the temporary loss of academic backing, his article about the Medicine Wheel was accepted by *Science* in 1974. Perhaps even more scientifically momentous was another paper Eddy wrote of a different kind. This time, Eddy turned to astronomers from another era—nineteenth-century England and Germany—who had described earlier observations that sunspots and other storm-like behavior on the sun's surface had calmed between the years 1645 and 1715. This contradicted conventional wisdom, which held that solar activity was relatively constant. Eddy dug deeper into solar observations from around the world going back to Galileo. Then he turned to yet another scientific discipline, examining carbon-14 in tree rings, another indicator of solar activity. He even correlated historical shifts in solar activity to weather patterns on earth. He called the calmer solar period the Maunder Minimum because he liked the alliteration that a nineteenth-century astronomer's name gave his theory. This paper was published in *Science* in 1976, and it helped make his reputation, despite the astronomy establishment's disapproval of his methods and chagrin over his popularity.

As a follow up to his work on the Medicine Wheel, Eddy looked elsewhere for Native American sites that might have astronomical connections, including the nineteenth-century maps of Ohio's earthworks by Squier and Davis. Remarkably, in roughly the same time period before 1977, when Ray and Bob were gathering data on the ground starting in 1975, Eddy noticed something extraordinary simply by looking at an old map of Newark. Using compass-bearings indicated on the map, he made an extraordinary guess: "I have found by simple map examination that a line through the axis of symmetry of the octagon, the center line of the causeway, and the center of the connected circle coincides very nearly with the direction of northernmost rise of the moon at the latitude of Newark . . . reached in cycles of 18.61 years." He summarized his Newark idea in a single paragraph of a 1977 book edited by astronomer E. C. Krupp called *In Search of Ancient Astronomies*. He hadn't done the hard work of collecting data that Ray and Bob were doing, so publishing that single paragraph was not something to be taken seriously until more was known. The following year, however, in 1978, Eddy visited Newark for two days and surveyed it himself. Ray and Bob never knew of Eddy's visit, and although Eddy shared his findings with colleagues, he never published them.

Ray and Bob did eventually learn of Eddy's work at Newark and at the Medicine Wheel, so they included Eddy's observations in their own paper, giving him proper credit for being first to notice the possibility of a lunar alignment. Eddy had been published twice in *Science*, so Ray and Bob sought his endorsement of their work and hoped it would help convince the editors of *Science* to publish them too. They sent Eddy their paper and crossed their fingers.

Eddy was impressed and said so to the editors at *Science*: "Personally I find it very hard to write a judgment on it, because it is a momentous case. I almost wish the authors hadn't written the paper so well or so carefully. It is beautifully done. Hively and Horn have been careful to look carefully into past work, and to put the site into its proper archaeological context, and to do the fieldwork of archeoastronomy scrupulously and well. I feel particularly qualified to say this for in 1978 I also spent two days at the Newark site and surveyed it with a transit and our measurements agree. I have also taken pains to check the calculations of moonrise and moonset that Hively and Horn invoke, using the same reference and my own computer printout for the site. The result of all of this is to confirm all parts of their paper that deal with measurements and number."[7]

Now it was time for *Science* to render its judgement. According to Ray, the magazine had three reviewers responsible for deciding whether their paper would be published. Two said yes, but the third was a no, and that was sufficient to kill it. An upset Ray called the editor, Philip H. Abelson, but Abelson declined to talk to him and instead had an assistant explain that Abelson considered it "too early" to publish their piece. In hindsight, Ray thinks that the claims they made about Newark were too sensational, too controversial to gain easy acceptance. Abelson wanted other experts in the field to take their work seriously before he would be willing to do so.

Next they approached a more specialized publication: *The Cambridge Archaeological Journal*. Their reviewers were initially positive, but the editor eventually told them it wasn't the sort of thing they publish. Ray interpreted that to be a commentary on their methodologies. No archaeologist turned a shovel for their findings. Their focus on astronomic measures wasn't really archaeology.

In the end, they found a publisher. A quarterly called *The Journal for the History of Astronomy* featured Hively and Horn's paper in its Archaeoastronomy supplement in 1982. This was a bit like aiming for Carnegie Hall and getting a night club gig instead. An organization that ranks the influence and impact of academic journals gave *Science* a 7.63 and *The Journal for the History of Astronomy* a 0.34.[8]

⊕

Even in the town of Newark the now-published work was barely noticed. Local news outlets ignored it, as did all of the media in Ohio and beyond. The small community of people who were interested in Ohio archaeology did give them an audience, however, when N'omi Greber invited Ray and Bob to speak to the Midwest Archaeological Conference in Cleveland. This was a place where one competed for attention with a rapid-fire series of

7. John Eddy, private correspondence, Dec. 17, 1980.
8. Clarivate, Web of Science.

presentations on topics such as "Native American Gunflints of Hixton Silicified Sandstone: Verification by Experiment." One of Greber's students gave a presentation at a similar conference and remembered Greber coaching her in advance with a stopwatch to make sure she was no more than thirty seconds over or under her allotted five minutes.

Ray and Bob were given a bigger role than that, and it was the first time they showed their findings to a large audience of archaeologists. Ray fell ill with laryngitis, so Bob had to present the paper without him—a professor of philosophy, a Kierkegaard scholar, speaking to a room full of archaeologists. There are few who remember that conference now, but one person in the audience who listened intently was Patricia Essenpreis, a thirty-three-year-old Harvard-trained archaeologist who would later take oversight responsibility for archaeological work at Fort Ancient, including the "foursquare" that Ray and Bob first visited with students years earlier, sparking their interest in Hopewell geometry. Essenpreis would remember what she learned that day, and use it to inform her own research, with impressive consequences to come.

So their paper was published and the local archaeological community was now fully informed. It was up to others to prove the worth of the Hively-Horn field work. Ray and Bob weren't finished though. There was another earthwork potentially just as interesting as Newark's located sixty miles south, near Chillicothe, on a terrace of land by the Scioto River less than two miles south of Alva McGraw's farm. This was High Bank Works, the only other earthwork featuring a circle-octagon shape like Newark's. Walking around it today, it is barely discernable, flattened by farmers. But its precise dimensions were well documented in nineteenth-century surveys, twentieth-century aerial photography, and more recent magnetic imagery. There was little worry that walls were moved because unlike the Newark Octagon and Great Circle, High Bank had never been put to uses other than farming. No golfers or troop encampments. No fairground or roller coasters like those once at the Great Circle. Surely if the ancient builders at Newark intentionally created alignments, wouldn't those show up at its geometric twin to the south? And if there were similar lunar alignments at High Bank, it would be much harder to call them all coincidental.

⊕

Three features at High Bank quickly stood out. First was the fact that the entire structure was turned clockwise, almost exactly ninety degrees southeastward

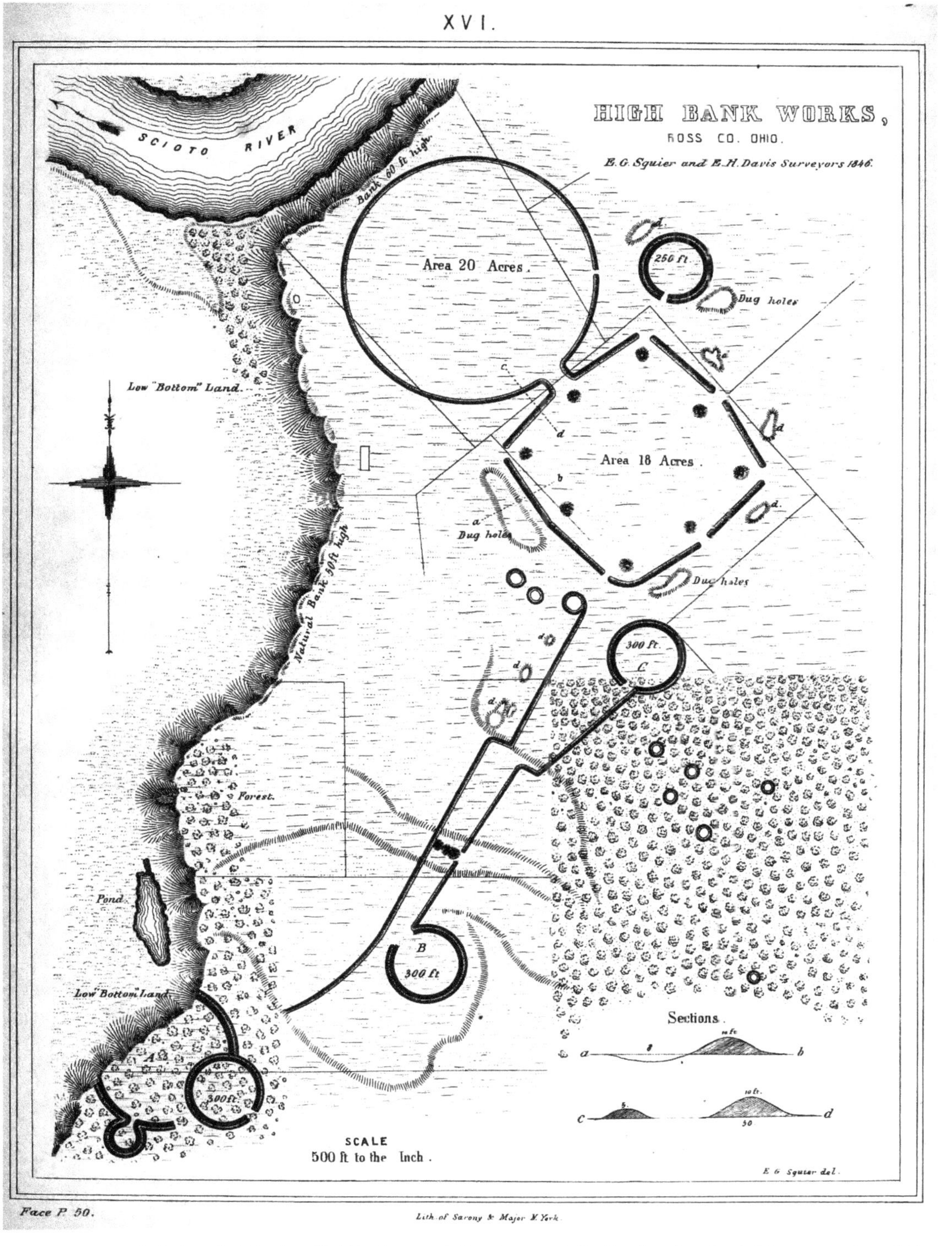

FIGURE 8.1. High Bank Works, 1846. From E. Squier and E. Davis, *Ancient Monuments of the Mississippi Valley,* World Digital Library, Library of Congress.

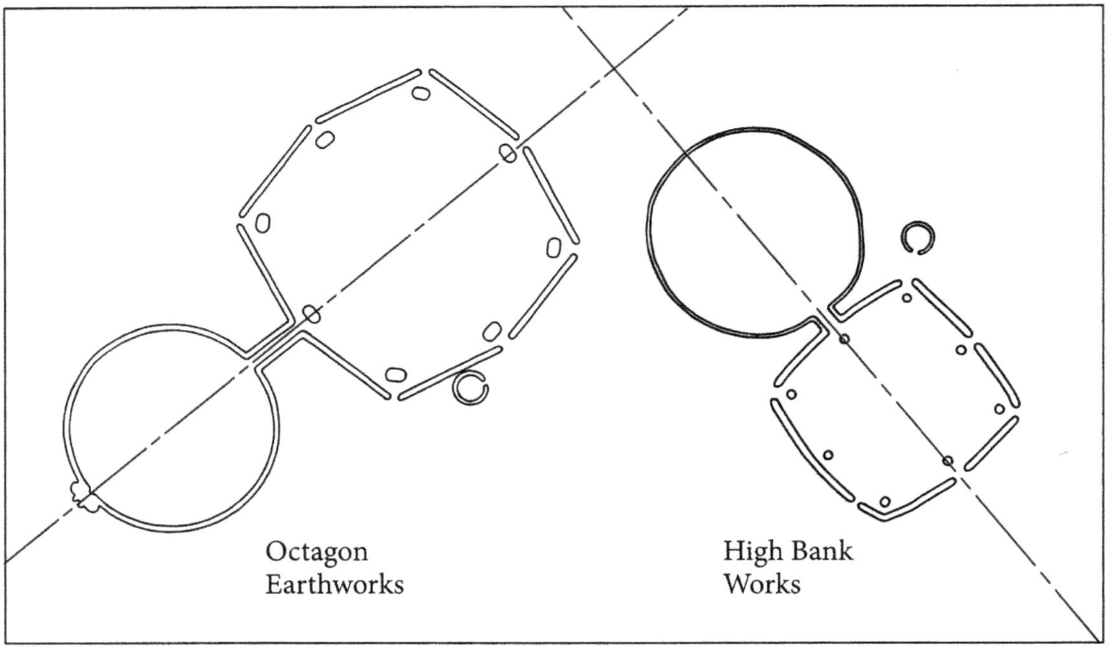

FIGURE 8.2. Though sixty miles apart, the directional orientation of the Octagon Earthworks and High Banks Works appears related. The axis of High Bank Works has a compass bearing that differs from Newark's by precisely 90 degrees. Illustration by John Hancock, after Hively and Horn, courtesy of the Ohio History Connection.

when compared to Newark. If you could lay one atop the other, their central axes would be at right angles to one another, to within one degree of accuracy. Second was the geometric symmetry with Newark, including an identical 1,054-foot-diameter circle—one OCD as they called the common unit of measure discovered at Newark. Its connected octagon was smaller, but measuring the octagon from the middle of one wall to the middle of its opposite parallel wall yields that same magic OCD, 1,054 feet, in all directions.

The other standout feature was the presence of inexplicable imperfections that strayed from the perfect symmetry the builders were otherwise perfectly capable of achieving. They knew how to create neatly equidistant vertices, for example, but the southernmost vertex of the octagon was weirdly misshaped, cut off by short linear walls instead of the sharp corner seen at the seven other vertices. Each vertex had a gap between adjoining walls, but that odd southern corner shifted the gap to the northwest by 170 feet. The wall on the octagon's west-northwest side was several feet longer than it would be if it were proportional to other walls. And what about that weird little gap in the eastern side of the circle? Based on similar anomalies at Newark, they knew these were clues to something.

They repeated the process of identifying key moon- and sunrise and set points on the horizon, accounting for the altitude of surrounding hills that might move the first and last peaks of light southward by a degree or so. Then they laid it all out and looked for the kinds of alignments evident at Newark. Some things did not make sense at first, but soon it all came together.

Strangely, the axis that bisects the whole circle and octagon did not create a line that pointed to anything at all, or so they thought. At Newark it made that glorious line to the northernmost lunar standstill. At High Bank, by turning the whole structure 90 degrees, they found a pointer to the northernmost moonrise marked by a line straight across the octagon, rather than lengthwise into the circle. As for the short wall that cuts off the south vertex, an old map puts its original length at 144 feet long and Ray and Bob found it pointed straight at the northernmost standstill. What of the oddly placed gap on the southern corner of the octagon? It turned out that if you stand at the easternmost vertex and look across the octagon through that gap, you'll see the moon set at its minimum south standstill. And Ray was particularly surprised to find at High Bank a major feature missing at Newark. After Ray spent all those months looking for solstice alignments in Newark, here at High Bank he found four—sunrises and sunsets at the winter and summer solstices, all marked! When they studied the wall on the octagon's north-northwest side, for example, they saw it pointed straight to sunrise at the summer solstice.

In total, High Bank pointed to all twelve standstills of the moon and sun. It turned out the central axis pointed to something as well. It tells you where to stand on the northwest side of the circle in order to see sunrise on the winter solstice, shining through that one small gap in the circle wall that until then seemed to serve no purpose. As at Newark, some of the alignments seemed conjectural, while others seemed clearly intentional because of the anomalies of the construction.

The fact that such alignments were now evident at two separate Ohio earthworks made their discovery doubly hard to refute. In 1984 the partners Hively and Horn published their second academic paper, again in another archeoastronomy supplement to *The Journal for the History of Astronomy*. If accepted by the larger archaeological world, it would be a major discovery, now twice found. Nowhere else in the world were there monumental structures of this size that demonstrated so much sophistication on so many

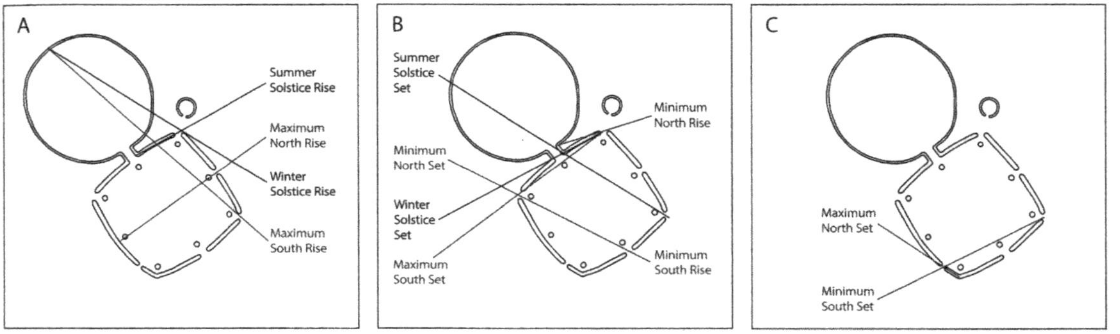

FIGURE 8.3. The twelve celestial alignments at High Bank Works, pointing to every northern- and southernmost rise and set point of the sun and moon. Illustration by John Hancock, after Hively and Horn, courtesy of the Ohio History Connection.

levels—geometry, astronomy, landscape engineering—all by a people known until then for hunting, gathering, small-scale gardening, and living in tiny hamlets scattered across the countryside.

It was a breathtaking find. But outside the tiny world of Ohio archaeology, hardly anyone seemed to care. Who were these two making these claims? A philosopher? An astronomer? From tiny Earlham College?

⊕

Archaeologists literally spend time in trenches. Ray and Bob rarely got their fingers dirty. If archaeologists were to ever warm up to their hypothesis, it would be an awkward embrace. Tyler Swinney, a tribal liaison and authority on Native American archaeology at the Cincinnati Museum Center, said to me, "A geology professor I had my freshman year told me there are two types of people in the world. There are people who look up and there are people who look down and archaeologists tend to be downward looking people as a whole. And I think that obviously, astronomers and any number of mathematicians, they are people who tend to look upward."

Later in his career, the astronomer John Eddy, whose forays outside his field into archaeology attracted criticism, told an interviewer, "I truly believe the sayings that there is no hope for the satisfied man and that without fear there is no learning. Entering a new field with a degree in another is not unlike Lewis and Clark walking into the camp of the Mandans. You are not one of them. They distrust you. Your degree means nothing and your name is not recognized. You have to learn it all from scratch, earn their respect, and learn a lot on your own. But I also think that many of the most significant discoveries in science will be found not in but between the rigid boundaries of the disciplines: the terra incognita where much remains to be learned. It's not a place that's hidebound by practice and ritual."[9]

⊕

In 1977, back when Hively and Horn were just beginning their study of Ohio earthworks, astronomer Jerry Ehman was working just forty miles away at a much more modern observatory established at Ohio State University. He was studying computer printouts of signals captured on the "Big Ear," a massive radio telescope laid flat across almost an acre of land and aimed skyward at a site north of Columbus. It was part of the SETI project, the Search for Extraterrestrial Intelligence, the brainchild of Philip Morrison, an astrophysicist who coincidentally had been a member of the thesis committee overseeing a younger astronomy student named Ray Hively. As Ehman scanned a few days' worth of signals, he came across one that lasted seventy-two seconds, the most powerful one he'd ever seen. He took a pen and wrote the word "WOW" next to the alphanumeric record of the signal. Now known as the "WOW! Signal," it was just the kind of narrow-band signal they were looking for, and its origin has never been fully explained.

By 1998, funding ran out and the radio telescope was demolished so investors could redevelop the property and expand a neighboring golf course from nine holes to eighteen.[10]

9. Eddy, "Interview."
10. Betz, "Wow! Signal."

CHAPTER 9

Who Were These Ancient Builders?

Here, the earth is sanctified, sacrament caressed.
—Allison Adelle Hedge Coke, *The Mounds*

Who were these ancient people who seem to have decoded the mysterious movement of the moon? Bob had taught a class on the tragic consequences of Euro-American efforts to "civilize" Indigenous Americans by erasing their rich intellectual and cultural traditions. But Bob also taught about the philosophy, mathematics, science, and art of the ancient Greeks. Even he and Ray did not expect to unmask ancient Indigenous knowledge that Western cultures normally associate with "advanced" civilizations.

The Native people of two thousand years ago who populated the eastern half of North America from the Great Lakes southward, though culturally diverse, have been categorized collectively by modern scholars as "Eastern Woodland." In the 1980s it was simply not understood that Eastern Woodland Indigenous people could be expert at geometry, mathematics, astronomy, land surveying, master planning, and social organization on a massive scale. For more than a century, archaeologists had focused enormous amounts of time digging beneath their feet for artifacts in the Ohio soil. By fixing their gaze at ground level and to the heavens, Ray and Bob found something entirely new.

But the earlier work of archaeologists drew another extraordinary picture of ancient day-to-day life, and it is important to understand that too. That picture began to emerge in the latter half of the nineteenth century and, as we've seen, was greatly improved by Olaf Prufer and others after him. One crucial moment came in the 1890s when a man named Mordecai Cloud Hopewell, a veteran of the Confederate Army, came to own a farm along the North Fork of Paint Creek near Chillicothe. There he took possession of one of Ohio's largest single, Native-built earthen enclosures. The irregularly shaped parallelogram surrounded 111 acres, about the size of the walled enclave of Vatican City within Rome. Within the earthwork was the biggest mound anywhere in Ohio. Known as Mound 25, it was thirty-three feet high and five hundred feet long.

Archaeologist Warren Moorehead arrived at Hopewell's farm in 1891 hoping to find artifacts he could unveil at the upcoming 1893 Columbian Exposition in Chicago. Though his methodologies fell far short of modern standards for Native gravesites, he aimed his digging tools fruitfully, for his finds were so rich in beautifully crafted artifacts that they defined a whole new culture. Following the nomenclature of the day, the culture came to be known as "Hopewell," after the landowner. We have no way of knowing what the Native people who lived there called themselves, but the Hopewell farm became what archaeologists know as a "type site." Sadly, archaeologists like Moorehead, combined with farmers' plows, did not leave the sites as they found them. Where once there was landscape art rising with majesty now there are little more than bumps on the surface of the ground. The National Park Service protects the little that is left.

What Moorehead and others did preserve and collect was magnificent. Copper pounded and shaped into earplugs, hoops, and rings. Other copper jewelry stylized as bear's claws and bird shapes to ornament clothing. Carvings of a human hand and an eagle's claw made from thin sheets of shiny mica. Small effigy figures of beavers and a billed bird riding on the back of a fish. Elegantly curved daggers of jet-black obsidian. Extraordinary copper antlers affixed to a headdress. Other geometric shapes of pounded copper included swastikas, which were a Native American decorative motif for centuries. Pottery with elegant designs stamped into clay. There was even a panpipe, rarely found in the Americas of that era, and one can only imagine the sound of their music, combined with drums and who knows what other instruments.[1]

The beauty of the objects was arresting enough, but they told a story too. The items had chemical or organic signatures making their origin traceable. The copper and silver could only have been mined from the northern Great Lakes region. The mica must have come from the Appalachian Mountains in the distant east. Sharks' teeth, some fossilized, and seashells, from the Atlantic and Gulf Coasts. Pipestone from seven hundred miles northwest, and obsidian, a volcanic glass, found more than 1,500 miles away in today's Yellowstone National Park. These exotica were being accumulated in that

1. Ohio Hopewell, "Excavation of Hopewell Mounds."

corner of present-day Ohio, imported from all over North America east of the Rockies.[2] Was it a trading hub of some kind?

In the century since Moorehead's findings, archaeologists developed theories. They found no pattern of obsidian trade in villages between Montana and the Midwest, so someone was bringing obsidian exclusively to Ohio. Conversely, you don't see Hopewell artifacts appearing outside of Ohio—no Hopewell-style pottery, for example, and few of the unique flint arrowheads distinctive to the culture and quarries of that place and era. Precious artifacts flowed into Ohio, not out. One of two things must have been going on. Perhaps Hopewell people were traveling outward to procure raw materials and return them to Ohio. Or—and this is the more prevalent theory—something or someone was drawing great numbers of people from all over to make pilgrimages to present-day Newark and Chillicothe. And they bore gifts.[3]

Did the Hopewell culture spawn a continent-wide pan-tribal movement? After the arrival of Europeans, attempts at inter-tribal alliances came from time to time, efforts to unite people of richly diverse languages and cultures. Before people like Zitkala-Ša and the Society of American Indians there was Tecumseh's efforts to unite tribes against the colonists, and before him the Haudenosaunee Confederacy. The Hopewell movement appears to be a cross-tribal cultural phenomenon of another kind, from another millennium. While we have no written record, oral histories of the Creek Indians hint of pilgrimages to Ohio. A people that populated modern Georgia, Alabama, and Florida, the Creek had mound cultures of their own, but "in their oral history, Creeks were extensive travelers, not merely for trading purposes but also for ritual and natural pilgrimages. They traveled by boat in the Gulf of Mexico and took regular journeys north through the Mississippi Valley into the Midwest and Ohio regions," wrote Jean Chaudhuri, a full-blooded Muscogee Creek, and Joyotpaul Chaudhuri. "The Creek oral history repeatedly mentions that the Creeks traditionally went north to special mounds for pilgrimages in spring and autumn." The Chaudhuris were drawing connections to the Mississippian culture that came after the Hopewell period, but no one really knows how long such pilgrimages had been happening.[4]

⊕

2. Thornton, "Intriguing Interactions."
3. Thornton, "Intriguing Interactions."
4. Chaudhuri and Chaudhuri, *A Sacred Path,* 6–9.

By modern standards, the archaeologist Warren Moorehead broke a lot of rules. But the thousands of artifacts he unearthed, excruciating as his methods were, introduced the American public to a new vision of their own continent's rich past before European contact. From his dig site south of Columbus, Ohio, Moorehead brought his cache to Chicago for the 1893 Columbian Exposition, held a year late for its intended purpose, the celebration of the four hundredth anniversary of Columbus's vanguard of the European invasion. No shortage of irony in all of this. I was reminded of it when, at the time I was researching this story, I made a vacation trip to Malaga, Spain, and saw the city's heroic bronze statue of Christopher Columbus pointing out to sea from atop a two-hundred-foot-tall pedestal. At the base of it are bronze bas-reliefs, one of which shows Native Americans cowering at the sight of conquering Spaniards. Someone scrawled Spanish-language graffiti at that spot. "Colon Genocida," it said. "Genocidal Columbus."

Nobody knows what Moorehead himself experienced as he entered the Chicago exposition's "Great White City," but many visitors saw Native people handing out sheets of birchbark on which was printed "The Red Man's Greeting," words of protest by Chief Simon Pokagon, a Potawatomi leader. His narrative challenged the assumption that European colonization was progress over the uncivilized. "In behalf of my people, the American Indians," he wrote, "I hereby declare to you, the pale-faced race that has usurped our lands and homes, that we have no spirit to celebrate with you the great Columbian Fair now being held in this Chicago city, the wonder of the world."[5] It is a turnabout of sorts that some 130 years later a citizen of the Pokagon Band of Potawatomi would become director of the Newark Earthworks Center at Ohio State University. John Low, a professor of comparative studies, teaches history, American Indian studies, and religious studies. He now gives the Native perspective a central place in his interpretation of the mounds.

After the exposition closed its doors, a museum was created to house all the precious art and oddities carried to Chicago by delegates from around the world. There today, at the Field Museum, reside Moorehead's Hopewell artifacts, along with mummies from Egypt, hundreds of thousands of preserved bird specimens, and a tyrannosaurus rex nicknamed "Sue." As for Moorehead, his crude archaeological methodologies and descriptions of the "Primitive Man of Ohio," showed some primitive thinking of its own. But

5. Blaisdell, "Birchbark."

there was more to him than that. Shortly before his archaeological work in Ohio, in 1890, he was in the vicinity of Pine Ridge Reservation near Wounded Knee Creek. The massacre of Lakota Sioux had a lasting impact on him. "Over the next 49 years, there would be few more vocal and active advocates for Native American justice than Warren King Moorehead," writes Jeff Gill, a long-time student of Hopewell culture. "In print, in speeches, in lobbying up and down the corridors of Washington, and in exposés of corruption and mismanagement, Moorehead was tireless in his efforts to speak for Indian people without an advocate or a voice in the government."[6]

⊕

The beautiful ornaments, effigy pipes, pottery, and other items of the Hopewell culture are mostly smaller-scale objets d'art. There are no life-size or larger statues that survive, just the enormous landscape art of the earthworks, in their thousands of forms. No comparably rich cultural expression existed for a few centuries before or after these Woodlands-era people of the early first millennium. Their carefully crafted small works, combined with their grand earthworks, were a "profound and revolutionary" cultural "florescence," according to Brad Lepper. It was "a literal explosion," according to N'omi Greber.[7]

But a thing that makes this particular flowering unusual is the central seat of power and authority leading it. There doesn't appear to be any. Clearly there was substantial social organization, and there were people of higher rank, evidenced by their modestly more impressive burial treatments and regalia. But where were their cities? Why were there no population centers as there were at Cahokia later, or at pueblos that existed in the American West, with their hundreds of dwellings? Where is the evidence of kingly or pharaonic leaders, living in stately abodes, with generals lording over armies of laborers? There is none of that to be found.

Instead, as Olaf Prufer and others believe, these were people who lived in scatterings of "hamlets," as some archaeologists call them, leaving structural footprints so light that few have been found. Detailed clues of their lifestyle remain elusive, and what does exist spawns debate. In the heavily forested land of their day, the people of Hopewell made small clearings to live in and used upright logs, bark, branches, and mixtures of mud and grass to build

6. Gill, "Warren King Moorehead."
7. Lepper, *Ohio Archaeology*, 113.

small thatched-roof dwellings, twenty-to-thirty feet wide and long, room enough for ten people or so, likely members of extended families. Each forest clearing might contain just one to four such buildings. They had no large-scale agriculture, relying instead on small gardens of "weedy domesticates," such as knotweed, goosefoot, maygrass, and sumpweed, along with sunflowers and squash. Wild berries, fruit, and nuts were abundant for the gathering. Deer were hunted with atlatl—spears, launched with sticks that some have compared to the plastic arm-extenders people use for leverage to throw balls for dogs to chase. The bow and arrow did not show up until shortly after the fading of the Hopewell era. Away from their little settlements, they actively managed the landscape, removed trees, and opened larger clearings to bring deer into the open and make room for their earthwork constructions. But there is no evidence of chiefs, no monumental homages to individual leaders.

Remains of some larger timber structures have been found. The purpose of these is debated, but there is evidence they served a clan or "sodality" purpose. Were they ceremonial adjuncts to the grand earthworks nearby? Were they to the earthworks what today's Knights of Columbus halls are to the local Catholic cathedral? Or imagine, for example, a place where craftspeople gathered to reverently create the regalia worn for ceremonies: ear spools, which were ubiquitous, breast plates and headwear of copper and other special materials. There were fabrics woven and beautiful pottery shaped with delicately thin sides and decorative patterns. Was that the purpose of these great houses? Some people think the structures might instead have been for communal living.[8]

Piecing together the puzzle of Hopewell social structure has also involved investigating the way people were buried. Geometric mounds were for ceremonies, for the most part, not for burials. Other mounds—loaf shaped or conical—were exclusively for interring the dead. It turns out that some of the burial mounds were locations of honor for people of marginally higher social status. Different communities of people who otherwise lived apart from one another would share a single place of honor for their social elites. A small community might bury most of their dead in a local mound but send their elites to a place whose purpose resembled a kind of Arlington National Cemetery, the final resting place for the honored among the surrounding populations in the region. This suggests small communities lived apart from

8. Derived from Carr and Case, *Gathering Hopewell;* Yerkes, "Hopewell Tribes"; and Redmond, Ruby, and Burks, *Encountering Hopewell.*

one another but came together from time to time for an intercommunity ceremony and gathering.[9]

⊕

As a category of humanity, the term "Hopewell" covers a diverse range of populations and cultural traditions stretching across the Ohio and Mississippi Valleys and up to the Great Lakes. There were similarities in their art and earthwork constructions, but there were variations too. They thrived for some six hundred years until about 500 CE; people and habits differ over that much time and area.

In our time, archaeology has changed too. Burial sites are now better understood to be sacred and off-limits for excavation. But in the years before such limits existed, archaeologists found intriguing hints about gender roles in the clothing and body ornaments of the dead. Hopewell people in some geographic areas of Southwest Ohio bestowed on women a social status that appeared equal in importance to men. Their roles might be defined differently, but their authority seems to have been on par. Women sometimes served as shamans, for example.

In the region around Newark and Chillicothe, one study found "roles of importance were distributed more equitably among the sexes, with some male predominance in most roles and female equality or predominance in a few." Men and women wore similar metal breastplates and earspools, and bore copper "celts," heavy axe-like objects, that together served as symbols of authority or status. Either gender could apparently hold priestly roles, for both were found with "shaman-like divination items not associated with warfare or the hunt, tortoise shell ornaments and copper nose inserts . . . and conch shells used in leading public ceremony."

A few miles further to the southwest women might have held an even higher rank. "Roles of leadership and prestige . . . were exclusively or largely held by females." In addition to wearing metal breastplates and earspools symbolizing prestige, women possessed artifacts that had symbolic associations with war or hunting, and they appear to have held leading priestly ceremonial roles in preparing the dead and guiding souls on their journey to the afterlife.[10]

9. Carr, "Salient Issues," 92–98.

10. Ruby, Carr, and Charles, "Community Organizations," 112–13.

It's an overly broad generalization, perhaps, but in many Native tribes gender roles of leadership remained more equal before and after European contact and still to this day. In the nineteenth and twentieth centuries, white women suffragettes were still marveling at the way Native women exercised power within tribes by, for example, forming the councils of authority that chose or dismissed male tribal leaders. After contact, European influence might have caused some tribes to shift authority to men.

There is much more to be known about the daily life of these ancient people, but one other particular piece of evidence stands out. The war-like instruments that were found appear to have been strictly symbolic. "There is, however, no evidence for warfare during this period," wrote Brad Lepper. "There are no known human remains from Hopewell sites that bear wounds of war and there are no artistic depictions of warriors." Unlike other archaeological sites where fractured skulls and spear injuries show plenty of violence, no such signs exist among these ancient Ohioans.

And so here we have a society that appears to be living "very light upon the land," as Lepper put it, in the tiniest of settlements, free from the daily crush of population centers, self-sufficient, simple gardeners, enjoying fruits of nature all around, egalitarian, no strongman chiefs imposing their will, women in many communities as socially and politically strong as men, united in great ceremonial gathering places to mark the passage of time and of generations, adorned in regalia, welcoming from afar visitors of many languages and traditions, smoking tobacco together and living in peace for hundreds of years. All the while, prodded not by force but by ritual, they worked to shape the earth together and make their grand landscape architecture, celebrating geometry, astronomy, and heavenly wonder. It's a picture partly drawn from conjecture but supported by what we've found in, on and above the earth.

⊕

Now then, what of this fascination with the moon? Why would people of Hopewell traditions invest so much in connecting to not just the monthly phases, but the 18.6-year cycles of the moon?

There's no question that long before European contact Native people measured time and organized rituals around the phases of the moon. In fact, white Western European cultures might be the outliers for not paying closer attention to the moon, until US astronauts landed on it, that is. Two billion people celebrate the Lunar New Year throughout Asia, and crescent moon symbols are seen all over the Islamic world. The oldest known mathematical calculator, believed to be more than forty thousand years old, is the Lebombo Bone, a baboon's fibula found in Africa carved with twenty-nine notches, which might have tracked lunar phases, menstrual cycles, or both. So Indigenous people in the Americas are following traditions embraced around the world; it's the rest of Americans who seem out of sync.

Native traditions, storytelling, and oral histories hint at the moon's place in daily life through the ages. The chief of the Ottawa Tribe of Oklahoma, Charles Dawes, once said, "We still plant crops by the moon. We de-horn calves by the moon. Practically every functional daily thing we do involves the moon signs. We don't have the same thing as regards to the sun—I see the Aztec sun signs and the Hopis, and the Incas, but we don't have that in the Woodland culture."[11]

Sure, monthly lunar cycles are one thing, but the 18.6-year cycle of the moon is something else again, and that is where critics of Hively and Horn focused their sharpest skepticism. Dr. E. C. Krupp has been studying archaeoastronomy almost since the term was invented in the 1970s and edited the 1978 book that published that first observation by John Eddy that Newark's Octagon might align to the moon's longest cycle. Krupp has been the director of the Griffith Observatory in Los Angeles for an incredible 50 years. I asked him what he thought of Hively and Horn's work and I was surprised by his email response. This dean of archaeoastronomy was a skeptic.

Hively and Horn's work is "respectable and interesting," Krupp said, "but it does not prove the lunar alignment was part of the original design."

"There is no known example anywhere of confirmed interest in the moon's long-term excursion by any (ancient) culture, just suggestive alignments. . . . The 18.61-year standstill cycle has no obvious functional meaning, and people operate economically. They invest in things that matter to them and ignore things that don't matter. While the moon's excursion variation from year to year may be noticed relatively eas[ily], it has to have meaning to be incorporated into monumental architecture. We get no support from antiquity for meaning in the standstill cycle." Krupp does say the Newark Earthworks and Chimney Rock in Colorado are "evocative exceptions," that might very well be lunar markers, as hypothesized, and he fully recognizes the historic importance of the Ohio earthworks as a whole, particularly

11. "Hopewell Ceremonial Earthworks," 332.

because of the precision of their geometry. But he believes the evidence is insufficient to fully convince him the lunar alignments were intentional.[12]

Another skeptic is Dr. Stephen McCluskey of West Virginia University, an authority on the histories of science and astronomy. He visited Newark in 1999 with Clive Ruggles, a world-renowned British authority on archaeoastronomy. In an email to me, McCluskey said that what Ray and Bob did was "seek alignments marking the extreme positions of lunar rise and set (which is now often dismissed as a kind of 'alignment hunting.'). From my studies of Native American astronomies, I know of no ethnographically documented case of alignments marking the lunar extremes . . . you would have to count me as skeptical."[13]

McCluskey's mention of "alignment hunting" references the very thing that made Ray so skeptical to begin with, before he started investigating Newark.

Astronomer P. Clay Sherrod has also studied Native earthworks in North America. He recognizes the significance of the geometric arrangements in Ohio, but also notes, "People have rushed to judgement. Not everything is 'astronomical.' There is NO practical purpose in 'taming' the motions of the moon during its (18-year) saros cycle; these people needed every resource daily to simply live."[14]

Of course, Hively and Horn would be quick to agree that the deliberateness of the lunar alignments is unproven. They just say the evidence they were deliberate is too overwhelming, and the odds of chance alignments at so many locations too miniscule. And what of those who argue that Native people surely had better things to do than build giant monuments for purposes that have no apparent practical benefit? Well, whether or not they align to something, there's no denying that they were in fact built. Whatever their purpose, those people hauled mountains of dirt, clay, and stone. You might say Notre Dame Cathedral had no practical purpose. That took 182 years to construct before its completion in 1345, a time when the working stiffs involved might have been put to other uses.

The other criticism is that nobody else in antiquity did this sort of thing. Well, perhaps not. Until they did.

---

12. Krupp, email to author, Oct. 14, 2021.

13. McCluskey, email to author, Aug. 26, 2021. Parenthetical comment in McCluskey's original message.

14. Sherrod, email to author, Aug. 26, 2021.

Timothy Pauketat is the Illinois State Archaeologist and a University of Illinois professor who has studied ancient North American cultures, particularly the Mississippian culture with its pyramidal archaeological remains at Cahokia, east of St. Louis. Over the years, he has studied potential astronomical alignments at Cahokia and elsewhere, citing the work of Hively and Horn throughout his own research papers. Pauketat told me the skeptics "are wrong, oddly for the right reason. That is, it's true, watching the moon doesn't have a practical purpose if by practical one assumes a Western mindset. But the Hopewell weren't Westerners nor did they have modern sensibilities. Most precontact Indigenous Americans, much like Neolithic folks in the old world, related to the world in distinctly non-modern, non-individualistic, non-practical/rational ways. This is an old, old anthropological point that skeptics overlook. Most times the skeptics aren't anthropologists, nor are they Native.

"If they were one or the other, they'd realize that other things, phenomena, and places were understood to be alive or at least animate from time to time. Certainly the moon was. So one watched the moon to pay homage to a spirit as well as to be in alignment with the order of the universe, perhaps to understand themselves in relationship to celestial movements, etc. Probably also in the hopes that pulling heavenly order down on earth, too, would reduce the chaos on earth and in their lives. That's kinda the reason religion developed everywhere.

"In a way, that *is* practical, it's just not the western practicality (skeptics) look for."[15]

As I sought Native voices on this topic, they backed Pauketat up.

⊕

Ray and Bob explicitly made no effort to speculate about motives for building giant monuments to the moon, choosing instead to focus on the facts—the azimuths, the angles, the astronomy. To do as Pauketat recommends, to step outside the Western mindset, is hard. But the literature and guidance of Native people can help. Traditional Native beliefs and practices are rooted in a strong sense of harmony and interconnectedness with nature. We who are non-Native may not feel the same sense of discord and unease when things fall out of sync with the natural world. When chaos and disharmony are

15. Pauketat, email to Graham, July 23, 2024.

introduced—whether it is droughts or tornados, oil pipelines, or food shortages—the Native instinct is to seek restoration of balance, rhythm, and harmony. While it is wrong to think of all tribal communities as all one thing or another, many of their traditions and cultural beliefs show important commonalities.

Consider, for example, the importance of cardinal directions. North and south, east and west, are defined by the rotation of the earth relative to the sun, moon, and stars (ignoring magnetic poles for the moment). "A symbol of great antiquity found over much of North America is that of a cross in a circle," writes Jordan Paper, a professor of religious studies and student of Native traditions. "The cross symbolizes the Four Directions, meaning the entirety of this planet and the circle represents the interconnectedness of all life."[16]

"Egocentric [white] Americans perceive themselves as the center of activity, and they act upon and view others from their focal point," writes Donald Fixico, a professor of American Indian history whose ancestry is Shawnee, Sac and Fox, Muscogee Creek, and Seminole. "Traditionally, Indian people view themselves with the universe as miniscule members of a larger whole meaning that explains existence. In contrast, the Western-minded person refers to him or her 'self' as the reference point. When he or she travels, the Western-minded person turns right or left, making reference to directions in this manner. The person is the point of reference. The Wintu of California refer to left and right as the sides of the body. When traveling, the Wintu refer to the four cardinal directions to avoid confusion and becoming lost. For example, if going north, a Wintu would point out that the mountains are to the west. In contrast, some people would say the mountains are on the left."[17]

Lera Boroditsky, associate professor of cognitive science at the University of California in San Diego, has a wonderful way of illustrating a similar point. She describes the Thaayorre people, an aboriginal community in Australia. They have no words for "right" or "left," she says. Instead, one arm is the southeast arm and the other the northwest arm. Boroditsky asks her non-Native audiences to close their eyes, and then she asks them to raise their hands and "point southeast." Up come fingers pointing in all directions. "This is a big difference in cognitive abilities across languages," she tells her audiences, "where one group, a very distinguished group like you

16. Paper, *Native North American*, 58.
17. Fixico, *American Indian Mind*, 52–53.

guys, doesn't know which way is this, but in another group, I could ask a five-year-old and they would know." Likewise, she has given different people stacks of pictures showing people of different ages and asked them to arrange them by age. English speakers line them up left to right, like writing a sentence. Some aboriginal people arrange them east-west, depending on which direction they are facing. For them, the direction of time is connected to the movement of the sun.[18]

For people of the Hopewell culture, the objects in the sky must have had profoundly more meaning than we find there today. They were reference points and like other aboriginal people they probably developed a fifth sense for finding their way home after hunting or to favored branches of rivers or pastures filled with berries. It seems reasonable to think of Ohio's geometric earthworks as cathedral-like homages to the space time continuum engrained in their life—length and width, up and down, all set in time. Built to last, the earthworks were shaped to teach its lessons for generations.

Because the moon has a personality of movement all its own, a pattern more complex than other objects evident in the sky, the desire to make sense of it must have been strong. The Muscogee Creek story of the rabbit reflects this.

"Originally the rabbit was not regarded as a trickster but as a member of the little animal world. Rabbit came to the ceremonial grounds and asked the people to join their circle around a fire. However, suddenly the fire seemed to go out and it became very dark. There was some confusion and people sensed that Rabbit was running away with a large bag. They caught Rabbit, and in that process Rabbit stumbled. When Rabbit stumbled, first the moon came out again, followed by the sun. People from that time regarded Rabbit as a trickster and his stumbling created the broken separate rhythms of the lunar and solar cycles which are connected with new energies every eighteen years. But since then, we always have to be aware of the tricky rabbit when trying to understand the regularities and intervals in the cosmos."[19]

Fixico explains, "When Rabbit temporarily stole the Sun and the Moon, chaos reigned and confused Muscogee people until they realized what had happened. They captured Rabbit, and balance was restored. By observing nature and the environment for many generations, American Indians developed tribal philosophies based on the circle. By studying the changes of the seasons and observing the lives of animals and plants as a part of nature,

18. Boroditsky, "How Language Shapes."

19. Chaudhuri and Chaudhuri, *A Sacred Path*, 11.

Native logic became grounded in the central idea of a continuum of events that seemed familiar. Nature repeated itself in a continuous series of cycles and seasons of circular patterns."[20]

The ancient people of Ohio made circles everywhere. Squares and octagons, too, but there were always circles of every size. And if ever there were places where they captured the rabbit and tamed the chaos in the heavens, it is Newark and High Bank, where the wandering moon was brought into symmetry with their geometry and natural environment.

John Low, Pokagon Band of Potawatomi and director of the Newark Earthworks Center, looks at his own tribal traditions and thinks they help inform what people here were thinking millennia ago. "In our ceremonies one of the purposes is to ensure the stability of the universe, that we're living good lives, our ceremonies are being done correctly, they have efficacy, a usefulness, and all those things. Why would they have been interested in tracking the lunar movement? Perhaps, because it confirms the stability of the universe. It confirms perhaps that their ceremonies are working and the universe is in order and they were living good lives, and all those things."[21]

Black Elk was an Oglala Lakota holy man born in 1863 who, as a boy, witnessed the Battle of Little Big Horn. He said that when he was nine and very ill, he had a vision that involved a meeting with "Six Grandfathers," who represented each of the four cardinal directions plus the earth and sky. Describing his cultural traditions, he said, "You have noticed that everything an Indian does is in a circle, and that is because the Power of the World always works in circles, and everything tries to be round. In the old days when we were a strong and happy people, all our power came to us from the sacred hoop of the nation, and so long as the hoop was unbroken, the people flourished. . . . Everything the Power of the World does is done in a circle. The sky is round, and I have heard that the earth is round like a ball, and so are all the stars. The wind, in its greatest power, whirls. Birds make their nests in circles, for theirs is the same religion as ours. The sun comes forth and goes down again in a circle. The moon does the same, and both are round. Even the seasons form a great circle in their changing, and always come back again to where they live. The life of a man is a circle from childhood to childhood, and so it is in everything where power moves."[22]

---

20. Fixico, *American Indian Mind,* 49–50.

21. John N. Low, JD, PhD, Director, Newark Earthworks Center, oral presentation during Newark Earthworks tour, April 14, 2024.

22. Black Elk, *Black Elk Speaks,* 121.

Here it's worth noting the Native symbolism and mythology of the turtle, with its circular shape and its hexagonal and pentagonal "scutes." The turtle figures into the creation story of the earth diver, the animal that plunges to the water's depths and retrieves mud to place on the back of the turtle, which grows to become the earth. Native people have used turtle shells as lunar calendars because some species have thirteen scutes surrounded by twenty-eight platelets lining the shell's edges, corresponding to the moon's 27.3-day orbit around earth, and the thirteen lunar months of the year. So, for Native people throughout the millennia, the sun and the moon, the earth, the sky, the waters, and all of nature are not just an object of scientific or practical interest, but of spiritual interest too.

"We don't separate ourselves from the sky world, the surface world and the underworld," said John Low as he stood in the Newark Octagon on a sunny spring day in 2024. "All are a part of our lived experience. Thus the stars represent the fires of other tribal nations. . . . We're all made of stardust, right? We're made of the material in stars. And the Milky Way is where our ancestors are traveling to their next existence. So we're very connected in specific ways to the sky. And I think this lunar observatory was a part of reflecting the deep connection."

Many of the geometric earthworks, notably the Great Circle a mile from the Octagon, have "moats" dug to line the inside base of the mound. Accompanying Low on a tour of the Octagon was Dr. Tim Jordan, a site interpreter and college instructor, who added that "a moat like that might have been designed to hold or be reminiscent of water, which creates that connection that John is mentioning to a watery beneath-world as part of that cosmology. That is common within Indigenous belief systems."

Low, Jordan, and others further describe a common belief in a universe of three realms: a sky world, our place on earth, and an underworld. Low cautions us not to confuse the underworld with the place Westerners call hell. There are variations among tribes on this cosmology, and it is all but impossible to know what variant if any was held during the Hopewell era, but oral traditions are a strong link to the past. It is not hard to imagine how the geometric earthworks unite elements of the cosmos, reflected by the heavens, shaped from the soil of mother earth, surrounded in many places by rings of water representing the depths of the world below.

Vine Deloria and Daniel Wildcat wrote, "Much Indian knowledge involved the technique of reproducing the cosmos in miniature and invoking spiritual change, which would be followed by physical change. Hardly a tribe exists that did not construct its dwellings after some particular model of the universe. The principle involved was that whatever is above must be reflected below. This principle enabled the people to correlate their actions with the larger movements of the universe. Wherever possible the larger cosmos was represented and reproduced to provide a context in which ceremonies could occur. Thus, people did not feel alone; they participated in cosmic rhythms."[23]

Ben Barnes, the chief of the Shawnee Tribe, views the Hopewell earthworks as "artistic expressions of our positionality in the creation," using "creation" to refer not to the Biblical Genesis or Native origin stories but to the living creation around us right now, of which we humans are just one part among many. "There's this artistic expression of constellations above and metaphorical constellations below, and humans observing both the above as well as the dirt beneath their feet, and wanting to reflect their place in the creation. So it doesn't surprise me that there [are] these feelings that we have about the sacredness of these places, because they really are reflections of constellations above our heads and the passage of time, and just the wonderment that these people had in order to enter into a civic project like this."

As a Shawnee, with strong historical and cultural connections to Ohio, Chief Barnes said "a lot of different peoples of the Ohio River Valley are the descendants of the Hopewell people. So certainly the Shawnee are amongst those descendants, whether culturally or by blood. So when we see these ancient places and we look at them through the eyes of our grandparents, creating these things, these are sites of civic magnificence. . . . They came together under a civic leader to build a project, to mark the seasons, mark the occasions, also to reflect their understanding of creation. And they used soil as their medium."[24]

Jack D. Forbes, professor of Native American studies at the University of California at Davis, wrote in 2001, "Perhaps the most important aspect of Indigenous cosmic visions is the conception of creation as a living process, resulting in a living universe in which a kinship exists between all things. Thus the Creators are our family, our Grandparents or Parents, and all of their creations are children who, of necessity, are also our relations."[25] Is this a message of the Hopewell earthworks? Is what they carved from the soil of

23. Deloria Jr. and Wildcat, *Power and Place,* 25–26.
24. Barnes, interview.
25. Forbes, "Indigenous Americans," 283.

Ohio, for us to experience now, a visual-drum-beat celebration of our kinship to the rhythm of living creation and a living universe?

⊕

There is yet another way in which the Hopewell culture might have drawn connections to the moon and heavens. We learned earlier of the evidence that women held positions of leadership in some communities of the Hopewell era.

"In virtually every human culture, Earth and Sky are female and male complimentary deities, who in conjoining, create all living things," writes Jordon Paper. "In the Americas, time tends to be understood cyclically, following the course of the sun and of the seasons—there is no beginning of time. Sky and Earth are primal; there is no more powerful or earlier deity. Earth and Sky cannot be created; they are the creating forces."[26]

Often, in addition to Mother Earth, the moon, too, is thought of as feminine. In some Native traditions, an eclipse of the sun by the moon is a conjoining of female and male. "In Creek beliefs, when the 'wedding' of the moon and the sun takes place every eighteen years [at eclipse], a new set of spirits is created which invigorates the earth under the blessings of the seven *miccos* [leaders] of the Pleiades [constellation]."[27]

The male sun and female moon shape time and Creek life, write the Chaudhuris. "As in so many other societies, the moon was associated with the counting of the menstrual cycles, with changes in men's temperaments with respect to women, with the timing of some ceremonies and with other elements and events in nature. The moon has important female energy and had an important role in the timing of the lives of women. Menstruation was not 'evil' in the Creek world. Feminine menstruation is regarded as sacred, natural, and pure."[28]

Rosalyn LaPier, a University of Illinois professor of history and member of the Blackfeet Tribe of Montana and Métis, writes that "Ojibwe women historically conducted a ritual for their girls when they started their first menstruation, part of which included fasting from eating strawberry, or heart berry, known as Ode'imin, for an entire year. This was also a time to learn valuable wisdom from women elders.

26. Paper, *Native North American Religious Traditions,* 10 and 61.
27. Chaudhuri and Chaudhuri, *A Sacred Path,* 11.
28. Chaudhuri and Chaudhuri, *A Sacred Path,* 10–11.

"Indigenous people often view menstruation as a time when girls and women are spiritually powerful. . . . Historically, women built a small wooden house for a girl to live in seclusion during her menstruation each month. It would serve as a place for personal reflection as well as a space for learning from elders."

US and Canadian governments outlawed such rituals in the nineteenth and early twentieth centuries, but "today, many Ojibwe communities are reawakening such female-centered cultural practices," says LaPier. "Today, Ojibwe girls do not live in a separate house during menstruation but instead seclude themselves from family and community interactions. For the Ojibwe and other indigenous people, seclusion was seen as a special time without chores, when the girl worked on personal growth and learned from elders. At the end of the year a feast is held for the whole community to celebrate the girl's transition. At the feast the girl receives gifts from her community, and in turn she gives gifts."[29]

The Mescalero Apache Sunrise Dance is a female coming-of-age ceremony of significant spirituality, lasting four days and involving everyone in the community, during which girls become "Changing Woman."[30] Its purpose is to usher young girls into womanhood during the summer after their first menstrual period. Claire Farrer, an anthropologist and "ethnoastronomer," wrote of the careful way the Mescalero Apache time their Sunrise Dance and ceremonies to correspond to the movement of stars. Certain songs would wait until the Big Dipper appeared in its proper place, and they would then await the appearance of the Morning Star, Capella, which precedes the "pulling of the sun."[31] "To be a competent star watcher at Mescalero requires years of watching until the sky becomes as familiar as the back of one's own hand. Skillful star watchers, and there are very few of them now, can look at the sky and quickly determine their position in space as well as how far they are from known landmarks. With such knowledge, timing a girl's puberty ceremonial using only the sky becomes a relatively easy exercise."[32]

At one point in the ceremony, four crescent moons are painted on a deerskin, and each girl in turn is asked to step forward onto the deerskin. "Her left foot is placed on the first of the crescent moons, and a song is sung about infancy. Next her right foot moves forward to the second crescent while the

29. LaPier, "Native American coming-of-age ritual."

30. Arizona Museum of Natural History, "Apache Sunrise."

31. Farrer, "Star Clocks," 230–35.

32. Farrer, *Thunder Rides a Black Horse*, 99.

singers sing a song associated with childhood. Then, her left foot steps on the third crescent, and a song for adulthood is sung. Finally, her right foot moves onto the fourth crescent, and a song celebrating old age is sung."[33]

The anthropologist Thomas Buckley spent years studying the Yurok Tribe of California and wrote of rituals of isolation during women's "moontime." In 1978 he interviewed one woman who "had been instructed in the menstrual laws by her maternal aunts and grandmother, who in their times were well-known, conservative Yurok women."

"As a foster child in non-Indian homes she has been taught that menstruation is 'bad and shameful' and that through it 'women are being punished.' On her return to Yurok society, however, 'my aunts and my grandmother taught me different.' . . . A menstruating woman should isolate herself because this is the time when she is at the height of her powers."

The woman described the isolation as something the women did together. "The women said that in old-time village life all of a household's fertile women who were not pregnant menstruated at the same time, a time dictated by the moon; that these women practiced the bathing rituals together at this time; and that the men associated with the household used this time to 'train hard' in the household's sweathouse. If a woman got out of synchronization with the moon and with the other women of the household, she could 'get back in by sitting in the moonlight and talking to the moon, asking it to balance her.'"[34]

Black Elk declared, "The power of woman grows with the moon and comes and goes with it."[35]

So one might ask, if many women of the Hopewell era held positions of authority, and if Indigenous women felt so physically and spiritually connected to the lunar calendar, might that contribute in some important ways to a broader cultural relationship to the movements of the moon? Does that offer a partial explanation or suggest a contributing factor for the ancient fascination with the moon?

It's all speculative, of course, and I was cautioned from reading too much into evidence of the power and influence of women in some ancient cultures, not to mention the role puberty rites might have played. Alma Gottlieb, who with Buckley coedited a book about the anthropology of menstruation, told me different cultures generally don't invest all power in one gender or the

33. Farrer, *Thunder Rides a Black Horse*, 88.

34. Buckley and Gottlieb, *Blood Magic*, 190–91.

35. Black Elk, *Black Elk Speaks*, 130.

other, but carve out different roles and varying levels of influence. Categorizing a society as patriarchal or matriarchal vastly oversimplifies; it erases nuance. So, for Gottlieb, much more needs to be known before scholars could embrace any notion that monumental tributes to the moon were built in Ohio because of the influence of women and the monthly rhythm of their biological clocks.

Indeed, perhaps I have the order reversed. Maybe, in a culture already so invested in the movement of the moon, women might come to think of themselves as physical expressions of that culture. It's likely we will never know. But we could learn a lot from these Native traditions. Some white Americans mocked Minnesota Governor Tim Walz as "Tampon Tim" because he wanted schools to offer tampons in restrooms for girls, some of whom are too embarrassed to discuss menstruation with their parents. Imagine a world where "moontime" gave a girl pride, rather than embarrassment.

⊕

How and why did Hopewell people work in such great numbers for so large a public works project with little apparent practical benefit? If people are scattered about the countryside with no apparent reason to join together, absent any great unifying purpose or mission, like defeating a hated enemy, why would political or spiritual leaders organize collective effort in such grand fashion? Perhaps the reason was simply social cohesion and unification. Finding a great cause to rally around can have a powerful and beneficial cultural impact.

You don't have to look very far in America's own past to find a modern parallel. In fact, there's one that involves the same age-old object of human fascination: the moon. In 1961, the new president, John F. Kennedy was twice humiliated by the Soviets, first when they beat the US at launching a human into space, then two months later when an American-sponsored invasion of Cuba was crushed at the Bay of Pigs. Desperate for a way to demonstrate American power and technical prowess, Kennedy cast about for options, seeking ideas from staff for a bold initiative of some sort. If he could not immediately beat the Russians in space, perhaps there was a longer-term vision and commitment of resources that would inspire and unify Americans and the West.

"We choose to go to the moon," he announced, and do it before the decade was out. He wanted the nation-unifying effects that come with marshalling vast resources to reach a glorious finish line—the moon—always up there, always beyond reach. Privately he told aides he would rather spend money on more practical needs, like technology to desalinate seawater. But symbolism matters, so he told Congress "no single space project in this period will be more impressive to mankind." In other words, it was the "impression" Kennedy wanted, as much as tangible outcomes. The resources necessary were as astronomical as the lunar objective, all expended for geopolitical more than scientific purposes.

But remember that the tiny outposts of people in the Hopewell sphere were not known to have strong leaders. No chiefs, let alone people with anything akin to presidential or pharaonic authority. Therein lies the greater mystery. These geometric mounds were all over central and southwest Ohio, representing enormous collective human effort, with no evidence of a great leader anywhere found.

G. Logan Miller, an Illinois State University anthropologist, has a Hopewell theory he published in 2021. He argues that there might have been two forms of ritual going on. One was the ceremonial gatherings of people from near and far inside the earthen enclosures. The other ritual was the very act of building them. Like an Amish barn raising, the act of voluntarily joining with neighbors resulted not only in larger collective accomplishments, but social relationships and reciprocal benefits. The guy who didn't pitch in wasn't likely to attract much female attention or male companionship, nor would he easily find helpers when he needed a barn of his own. But one flaw in the Amish analogy is the utility of the barn. It serves an essential function. What's the utility of an earthwork?

To try to explain the Hopewell social world, Miller uses game theory, looking at how individuals behave and make choices when interacting with other people, and how behaviors and choices are rewarded or penalized. He describes a "four-Rs" framework of reciprocity, reputation, retribution, and rewards.[36] In the absence of an iron-fisted authority, these four factors were the carrots and sticks. That's one way of looking at it, and it seems helpful to a point, but it's also a bit formulaic. Can you really reduce a rich and diverse culture, including its spiritual beliefs and motivations, to "four-Rs"? Miller does more than that of course and we mustn't oversimplify his thesis, but I liked the comment by a scholar who reviewed his work and thought it bordered on "ritual reduced to the transactional." If instead we apply a

36. Miller, "Ritual, Labor Mobilization, and Monumental Construction," 164–77.

non-Western perspective, says anthropologist/archaeologist Meghan Howey, we might better appreciate cultural beliefs in which there are no "distinctions between animate and inanimate things or divides between nature and culture.

"We may struggle to explain why people would have moved so much earth without coercion, but it may have been quite obvious to them; these locations were sacred enough that they deserved to be brought into being, time of their own, and to have people who knew proper ceremony minister to them. We do not, perhaps need to look further; the being and ministering were purpose enough."[37]

⊕

Surely they did more than moon-gazing in these monumental settings, right? Archaeologists say, yes, they believe considerably more went on, and they have ample evidence of human activity, rituals, and ceremonies in and around the earthworks. Their acreage alone suggests they were large gathering places, and the objects and human remains found amidst the clusters of nongeometric mounds and earthworks tell a larger—if sketchy—story. Anthropologist Christopher Carr looked at all of the archaeology and research that's been done in recent decades, including the pioneering work of Olaf Prufer, N'omi Greber, and the many others who searched for buried clues. Carr studied the artifacts and artistic depictions of mythical figures found at Hopewell sites. He compared them to written accounts and oral histories and traditions collected from Indigenous people and their interviewers after European contact. He produced two volumes, a combined 1,529 pages, that exhaustively document and weave the data and speculation together. His two earlier books added almost sixteen hundred more pages of Hopewell research. Combined he offers insights into what might have been happening in Ohio almost two millennia ago.

Carr said that skeletal remains suggest that when people of the Hopewell culture died their loved ones buried them close to home, but there is some evidence they might later have done a curious thing. After a period of time, at an agreed upon date, people from throughout the region exhumed the remains of some of their dead. Portions of the remains—not necessarily the whole body—were then transported from miles around to a central location

37. Howey, article comment, 183.

for reburial. There they were joined with the remains of other deceased. There is evidence that periodically great gatherings would occur in which people of different communities carried the remains of the departed, so they could be reinterred in communal mortuary buildings or charnel houses at the sites where burial mounds and other earthworks were clustered. The mortuary structure was burned, destroyed, and then buried, creating a mound, where future similar ceremonies would be repeated.

These grand celebrations of final rites "probably included all of a dispersed community and/or the multiple communities buried within a charnel house, possibly along with other visitors. This would naturally have been a time for feasting, dancing, playing games, renewing and creating kinship and marriage ties, creating intracommunity and intercommunity alliances, displaying group wealth, and/or exchanging goods and ceremonial prerogatives." There may also have been rites-of-passage rituals for young people entering adulthood.[38]

Death, the great equalizer, brought people living separately and afar to one place where they could reestablish themselves as a unified people with a common tradition. It had spiritual meaning, amplified in importance by the rarity of its occurrence, but it served a practical purpose too. They were joined together like stars on a flag, *e pluribus unum.*

Carr and others have come upon another tantalizing observation. They believe these Hopewell burial traditions may have lived on for more than a thousand years, echoing across the centuries, one generation to the next, before and after the arrival of Europeans, until it reached the eyes and ears of one group of French missionaries who arrived near modern Ontario in 1636. There the French met the Wyandotte people, who they called "Huron," and witnessed what they called the "Fête des morts," the Feast of the Dead. Families dug up human remains, scraped and cleaned the bones of the corpses, and carried the bones from miles around to join in a ceremony for reburial in a common grave, with other Native communities all traveling there simultaneously for the same purpose.

A French Catholic missionary, Jean de Brébeuf, gave an eyewitness account that was retold by historian Erik Seeman. "One might assume that (Brébeuf) was horrified by this non-Christian ritual with its unfamiliar cries and chants, and by the earlier preparation of the corpses, some only partially decomposed and seething with maggots. Yet not only was Brébeuf fascinated

38. Carr, "Scioto Hopewell Ritual Gatherings," 463–79.

by the Feast of the Dead, he also 'admired' this 'magnificent ritual'." Brébeuf described their care for the dead as "heartening to see."

The Catholics and Wyandotte had surprisingly similar beliefs and rituals related to death and human remains, Seeman writes. "Both groups adhered to religions that focused on the mysteries of death and the afterlife. Both believed that a dead person's soul traveled to the afterlife. Both believed that careful corpse preparation and elaborate mortuary rituals helped ensure the safe transit of the soul to the supernatural realm. And both believed in the power of human bones."[39]

By modern standards we might think this seventeenth-century fascination with bones and decaying corpses—whether by Hopewell, Wyandotte, or Jesuit—grisly and primitive. It's worth noting that Catholics now regard Brébeuf as a martyr. Killed by the Iroquois, he was canonized in 1930, and in 2024 the skull of Saint Jean de Brébeuf, encased in a handsome glass box, toured the US accompanied by three Jesuit priests in a Volkswagen. Pilgrims came to kneel before the saint's skull in churches in Detroit, New Orleans, Nashville, Colorado, Texas, and Kansas.

Some evidence suggests the Huron/Wyandotte Feast of the Dead, as witnessed by Brébeuf, occurred every eight to twelve years, according to Carr, and "involved seven or eight days of feasting, dancing, and game-playing for prizes before the reburial of the dead. During this time, kinship ties were renewed, and clan segments displayed their wealth in a socially acceptable manner. Feasting together and burying of the dead together helped to unite the Huron, who were spread over a territory of about two or three days' walk (20×35 miles [in area])—about the size of Ross County, Ohio (home to Chillicothe and numerous Hopewell earthworks). The Huron who buried their dead together felt obliged to live in peace and support of one another because the bones and souls of their deceased relatives and ancestors were forever co-mingled and unified."[40]

"The resemblance suggests that Scioto Hopewell peoples may have also employed a logic and created an ethic similar to those of the Huron: 'We are allies, always, because the souls of our deceased ancestors and relations are buried together and thus are allies, always.'"[41]

Carr cites research explaining that the Wyandotte and Algonquin saw death as a three-part rite of passage. It was the job of the living to aid them

39. Seeman, *The Huron-Wendat Feast of the Dead,* 1–2.
40. Carr, "Scioto Hopewell Ritual Gatherings," 469.
41. Carr and Smyth, "1.6 Soul Concepts," 167.

on their journey. In the first phase, the Huron buried their dead near their village in a "rite of separation," during which they occupied a threshold to the afterlife. The "body soul" stayed with the corpse, but their "free soul" wandered "in misery and mischief, unable to proceed to the Land of the Dead." After a period of time, a "rite of reincorporation" occurred when the remains were exhumed along with those of others from throughout the region. The remains were carried to the Feast of the Dead for mass-reburial with those of others. In the third step, their liberated souls would join the free souls of others, while the body soul stayed with the bones of the deceased. These bones were comingled with those of others in a common grave or mortuary structure. Thus was created a sacred space for disparate people, united by shared grief, memory, and tribute.[42]

Carr tells us that Woodland people storytelling, as recounted to European missionaries, including the future saint, Jean de Brébeuf himself, offers another possible echo from the Hopewell past. Versions of this story varied, but in some a dead person's journey to the afterlife requires a river crossing at a bridge guarded by two intimidating figures: Brain-Taker and Ferocious Dog. Some versions of this legend have the dog itself in the role of brain-taker. As the name implies the brain-taker-dog's job was to remove and consume the brain of the approaching deceased. As migraine-inducing as the image is, the ritual removal of the deceased's brain was seen by some Native people as potentially benevolent: it erases "earthly memories and ties, the absence of which allows the soul to have a blissful afterlife."[43]

Indigenous people told Europeans these brain-taker stories starting in at least the 1600s, but they appear to have been handed down from long before European contact. In 1925, archaeologists discovered artifacts in one of Ohio's most impressive Hopewell sites, the Seip Earthworks. An enormous loaf-shaped burial mound, it was originally thirty feet high and 240 feet long, surrounded by two miles of embankment walls in the form of two giant circles and a twenty-seven-acre square. Along with skeletal remains they found some intricately carved small stone pipes depicting animals and birds. One pipe "represents a dog in the act of eating a decapitated human head, held between the forepaws."[44] The dog seems to be holding the head like a bowl. Thus, the evidence suggests the myth of the brain-taker-dog was

42. Carr, "Scioto Hopewell Ritual Gatherings," 470.

43. Carr, "Scioto Hopewell Ritual Gatherings," 720.

44. Shetrone and Greenman, "Explorations of the Seip Group," 416.

handed down for well over one thousand years before French visitors heard it and wrote it down.

⊕

We may never know if these stories and imagery are actual echoes from the Hopewell era or coincidental. Oral traditions tell us important things, but how accurate can they be over so much time? Since the fading of the Hopewell era, Native people carried their cultural beliefs into new eras, amalgamated with other tribal beliefs and practices, intermarried families and tribes, fought and made peace, and resettled wherever fertile ground, good hunting, and other tribes seemed most welcoming. The Mississippian culture arose in the Mississippi Valley sometime around 900 CE, with a more centralized authority structure, larger concentrations of population, and, apparently an inherited devotion to the sun and moon, with architecture to show for it.

Like the Hopewell era, we do not know what the people of the Mississippian culture called themselves. Their culture, too, flickered out for unknown reasons. The tribal names we know today—Miami, Shawnee, Wyandotte, and all the others—are known to us now only because they were recorded in writing and sometimes awkwardly renamed by European colonizers. While we do not know which tribes are most directly descended from those of the Hopewell culture, it is fair to say that the Hopewell influence spread across the entire continent, just as the archaeological artifacts suggest.

The Wyandotte, for example, whose Feast of the Dead in Canadian provinces so resembled Hopewell funeral practices, did not settle in Ohio until sometime after European contact. Before the eighteenth century they were primarily confined to areas along the St. Lawrence River and Upper Great Lakes. After 1701 they played an important part in the founding of Detroit, and shortly afterwards some of them resettled in Upper Sandusky, Ohio, and the Ohio Valley.[45] Although their ancestors arrived in Ohio after the Hopewell era, the Wyandotte Nation of today has joined with those tribes most involved in preserving Hopewell treasurers. Joshua Garcia, a Wyandotte cultural preservationist and historian, told me that his ancestors likely made pilgrimages to Newark and other Hopewell sites, so they now feel connected to the Hopewell culture and sense its influence on the larger

45. Wyandotte Nation, "What History Says."

Indigenous world. They were different people and tribes with divergent beliefs, yes, but the Hopewell helped fashion a common way of perceiving the world and the cosmos.

⊕

Shawnee Tribal Chief Ben Barnes compares the Hopewell culture to the Roman Empire, with its lasting influence across the European continent. "Eastern North America surely felt those Hopewell ripples throughout time, and you can see echoes of that in the religious practices of people from the eastern half of North America."

One of those "ripples throughout time" may have been discovered in a most unlikely way, the result of a chance meeting between Chief Barnes and Brad Lepper. The Shawnee tribes share one of the strongest historical connections to Hopewell geography, and at the time of European contact the Shawnee populated villages up and down the same Scioto River that was previously the main artery of Hopewell life. The interest archaeologists have in Shawnee sites in Ohio could have placed Barnes and Lepper on opposite sides of what is often a most contentious topic: Indigenous burial sites.

"We weren't destined to be friends," said Chief Barnes of Lepper. "There was an attitude with Ohio archeology that the tribal nations were hard to deal with in terms of NAGPRA policy," referring to the federal Native American Grave Protection and Repatriation Act of 1990. "Brad didn't know what he was getting into when the Ohio History Connection started getting into repatriating human remains and ancestral objects back to Indigenous peoples or tribal nations."

It was during a break at a 2014 conference on that topic, hosted by the Eastern Shawnee at their tribal offices, that Lepper wandered into a foyer and saw on display a water drum used in the tribe's traditional community circles. The leather drumhead was pulled taut using a lashing technique that piqued Lepper's curiosity. As Lepper studied it, Chief Barnes happened by and Lepper asked about it. The Shawnee leader explained that the edges of the leather are wrapped around spherical stone balls, with cord tied around each leather-wrapped ball to both hold the balls in place and also establish points for the cord to gain purchase when pulled down. The cord lashes around the ball, across the bottom of the drum and is then brought back up to the other balls wrapped in the drumhead's leather skin, pulling the skin taut.

The balls reminded Lepper of curiously unexplained archaeological artifacts found a century earlier during a 1920 excavation at Seip Mound, the same location as the brain-taker effigy pipe. Five soapstone spheres similar in size to the drum's spheres were found amidst burnt remains found with various other Indigenous objects in the presence of a cremated child. Each sphere had decorative carvings, and at the time of their discovery an archaeologist guessed they might be the child's toy marbles. Another scholar later labeled them "shamanic paraphernalia." Lepper now wondered if the spheres were all that remained of a drum that was among the burnt offerings, once lashed together like the Shawnee water drum.

Lepper told Barnes he needed to see the 2,000-year-old spherical stones.

"When I finally saw them and saw their size, it's like, holy crap. These are the exact same size as the ones we use," said Chief Barnes. "The fact that they only found five of them indicates an odd number. And we use an odd number in the way we tie our drum. The way the geometry works, as you're working the rope across the bottom of the drum, you needed odd numbers so you could finish off the knot in a particular way." He believes the ancient drum might have been carved from a cypress knee or hollowed-out stump.

Chief Barnes is dismissive of the idea that the stones might be toys or shamanic, and cites the principle of Occam's Razor, that the simplest explanation is often the best. Together, Barnes and Lepper jointly authored a paper on their findings, published in 2018 in the journal *Archaeologies*.[46]

The importance of the drum far exceeds its role as a musical instrument, Barnes explained. "Some religions have altars as the centerpiece of where worship occurs. For Indigenous peoples, the drum is the heart of that worship."

Was it stunning that so familiar an object would be buried in Ohio 2000 years ago? "Why *wouldn't* it be?" asked Chief Barnes. "Of course we're going to find echoes in those sites. So on the one hand it's *amazingly* surprising. On the other hand, it's like terribly *not* surprising at all when we really think about it. Of course, the stuff we use every day [is] going to be found in a burnt offering somewhere."[47]

⊕

46. Barnes and Lepper, "Drums Along the Scioto."
47. Barnes, telephone interview, April 7, 2025.

It was in the spring of 1768, on an evening along the banks of the Scioto, that a meteor or perhaps a comet lit the sky and the great Shawnee leader Tecumseh was born, "two arrow flights" southeast of Chillicothe. (Tecumseh's biographer Peter Cozzens tells us to ignore the Ohio historical marker that he said inaccurately places Tecumseh's birth in Xenia, some 60 miles to the northwest). That would put his birthplace not very far upriver from High Bank Works, that other spectacular circle-octagon earthwork of the Hopewell era. Tecumseh's mother is said to have been Creek and his father a Shawnee warrior who died fighting American colonists when Tecumseh was a boy. Tecumseh's name references both the celestial heralding of his birth and his father's panther clan. With his brother, Tenskwatawa, a spiritual leader known as The Prophet, Tecumseh became one of the greatest intertribal leaders of all time, uniting diverse Native tribes and tens of thousands of Indigenous people to build one of the last and greatest bulwarks against the colonizers.

The Shawnee and their confederation of tribes met a harsh end. William Henry Harrison, territorial governor and US Army commander, led attacks that included their brutal defeat of the Shawnee at Tippecanoe in 1811. One of the tribal confederation's last great stands was at Wapakoneta, Ohio, where the Shawnee had erected a legendary Council House, a place where tribal leaders convened. It ultimately was the setting for the forced signing of an 1831 treaty that exiled the Shawnee from Ohio and sent them on their hard journey to west of the Mississippi. A century after the signing of that treaty, another man would arrive in Wapakoneta who would share a most exceptional interest in the movement of the moon. Born in that small town in 1930 was the first man to actually walk on it, the astronaut Neil Armstrong.

The very last of the Native tribes to leave Ohio were the Wyandotte, forced out in 1843. At the time of their departure, Ephraim Squier and Edwin Davis were traveling along the Scioto and other rivers, scrupulously documenting the area's strange earthworks for the Smithsonian. Many of those earthworks are gone now, but the Shawnee, the Wyandotte, the Miami, and the other tribes survive. Today they are finding their way back home to Ohio and other homelands, rejoining in the rediscovery of some of America's greatest Indigenous works.

CHAPTER 10

Obscurity

I was a little square
in a round hat.
—Billy Collins, "Reflections of an Amish Childhood"

A clear vision of the Hopewell era will always elude us. But research since the 1980s has cleared away small amounts of cataract-like cloudiness. We can make out shapes if not detail. The guessing about why they followed the moon and how they used their outsized landscape art is better informed now. When Hively and Horn first published in 1982, this picture was barely formed, and for their part, the Earlham professors declined to speculate about Hopewell motivations or spiritual beliefs.

When Ray and Bob were doing their early work, all that was really perceived about these ancient people was that they lived in small hamlets and created small works of impressive artistic craftsmanship along with those enormous mounds. Their two papers showed lunar alignments at two similar sets of large geometric earthworks—Newark and High Bank—with the second set of findings essentially replicating those of the first. This was impressive and meticulous work, but the audience for their papers was miniscule. *Science* magazine and others had rejected them, and no general-audience media took their work seriously enough to write about it. Almost no one cared. Ever since Gerald Hawkins and Stonehenge, the whole field of archaeoastronomy had skeptics aplenty. The notion that there was a Stonehenge abutting the backyards of Newark, Ohio, seemed especially implausible.

At Earlham, funding for the Program for Integral Education ran out, so eventually Ray and Bob no longer taught their class on cosmology together. Peter Suber joined the Earlham philosophy faculty in 1982, having previously been one of Bob's undergrad students. It had been about seven years since

Bob was first afflicted by Guillain-Barré Syndrome, but Suber remembers that Bob had suffered a bad fall and was still struggling with neurological symptoms, requiring him to use a cane or a walker to avoid another stumble. Bob also used a cart like those used to bus restaurant tables, filling it with around fifty books and wheeling it into class. "He liked to have the book in hand that he wanted to talk about at the moment; he liked to change his mind from moment to moment about what he wanted to talk about," Suber said.

As their faculty colleagues saw Ray and Bob publish their first paper on the mounds, Suber said, "I do remember them wondering what the response would be. They did not want to be dismissed as cranks who saw intelligence behind ancient artifacts when it wasn't really there. Or when it was just their own projection. They were aware of cranks doing that with Stonehenge, for example. They were very careful not to fall into that trap, but they still wondered whether they were perceived that way. And I think it's natural to worry about that. Especially if there was scholarly silence about their work. They might have been read but dismissed as cranks. They might have been read and ignored because after all, this is not a terribly important mound."[1] At least no one thought it important then.

Marilyn Gaye Piety was one of Bob's most devoted students at the time. Bob became a mentor and friend, and they had many long and meandering conversations in his office. Bob spoke to her of his earthworks findings and frustrations. She recalled "how difficult it was for him to convince people of their significance, how bigoted people were concerning Native Americans, and how mathematically sophisticated they were willing to allow they might have been. That is, it was very clear that he felt the work that he and Ray were doing wasn't getting a fair hearing because people were unwilling to think Native Americans could have had any grasp of advanced mathematics, that most people felt they were primitive and backward."

"We talked about how the ancient Greeks had technology that was far more advanced than people had appreciated until relatively recently, and if the Greeks had it, why wouldn't Native Americans? Bob is not only brilliant," she said, "he is a man of conscience. He deplored all forms of bigotry, all forms of inhumanity toward one's fellow man."

Ray and Bob knew they could not just blame bigotry for the lack of interest in their research. Ray and Bob were not archaeologists or anthropologists, and those were the professionals whose opinions mattered most. Why would anyone in those fields expect anything useful to come from two guys like

1. Suber, interview with the author, May 28, 2024.

them? The flipside was also true. Why would astronomers and philosophers be impressed by Ray and Bob casting about in others' waters? Astronomer John Eddy's time in Wyoming's medicine circles or Newark's earthworks did not sit well with his peers at the High Altitude Observatory in Boulder. Ray and Bob could hardly expect a better reception either from their peers or from archaeologists.

In separate conversations, when I asked Ray and Bob about the poor reception to their discoveries, they both pointed me to the writings of Thomas Kuhn, the historian and philosopher of science best known for coining the phrase "paradigm shift." In Kuhn's words they found encouragement: "Almost always the men who achieve these fundamental inventions of a new paradigm have been either very young or very new to the field whose paradigm they change. . . . No part of the aim of normal science is to call forth new sorts of phenomena; indeed those that will not fit the box are often not seen at all. Nor do scientists normally aim to invent new theories, and they are often intolerant of those invented by others."[2]

Ray and Bob went back to their classrooms, aware that their Hopewell papers were gathering dust and fading further into obscurity. They respected the process of science, where ideas gain acceptance on the merits and on replication of findings. Someday, somebody might rediscover the same thing later and give them credit for documenting it first. But who could blame them for not wanting it celebrated right then and there?

Bob's slow recovery kept him frail, but Suber said Bob "had an unparalleled reputation for erudition," and he recalled that students playfully told exaggerated stories of the depth and breadth of his knowledge. He also had a reputation in philosophical circles for extraordinary scholarly insights concerning Kirkegaard, and Suber recalls there were unpublished writings of Bob's that circulated in academic circles, but which Bob strangely chose to never put into print. Rather than spend time collaborating with other Kirkegaard scholars he preferred being with students.

Marilyn Gaye Piety "spent pretty much every afternoon of my senior year in Bob's office.

"I would go there as soon as my other classes were done and sit and talk to Bob about philosophy, and life more generally, for hours and hours. . . . He was like a father figure to me, and was even more attentive to me, during that time, than my own father was. He shaped not only my approach to philosophy, but my understanding of human nature."

---

2. Kuhn, *The Structure of Scientific Revolutions*, 24.

On a campus where faculty and students alike were on a first name basis, Ray became known as "Cosmic Ray," a nickname he embraced and even used for his email address. The cosmic event of the decade was the 1985 arrival of Halley's Comet, an event that burned Ray into the memory of several students, even though Ray remembers that the view of the comet was one of the faintest in history, invisible in Richmond without a telescope.

"I had Ray when Halley's Comet came through," said one student, noting Ray was a bit of a klutz. "He would get so excited he would walk off the stage. One class someone asked a question he began to answer, then realized we needed a deeper understanding of relativity and launched into a spontaneous discussion of relativity and [its] implications. That was my wow moment with him," he said, adding, "I also have the pleasure of impressing my kid by naming all the constellations!"

Said another: "He had an ability to invite awe, wonder and curiosity." Another found his course intimidating and expected a "C" grade, but surprised himself by getting an "A," and "found a love for learning—even classes outside my discipline."[3]

The local Richmond newspaper sought his expertise when there was a solar eclipse in 1984 and again for Halley's Comet. In its 1985 description of Hively, the paper made passing reference to his other work, one of the few places outside of academic journals where their earthworks research was mentioned: "Among his research projects has been discovery in 1981 of the astronomical connection with an ancient American Indian structure. With Professor of Philosophy Robert Horn, he learned that the geometric earthworks structure built by Hopewell Indians is actually a sophisticated lunar observatory."[4] In time, Hively would help establish a new observatory near the horse stables where there was less light pollution. The Equestrian Center was an area of the campus Ray knew well because that was where he stabled his paint gelding named Zeus. He served as the Equestrian Center's faculty advisor for thirteen years.

Marilyn Gaye Piety went on from Earlham and followed in Bob's footsteps by studying philosophy in Denmark at the University of Copenhagen, in her case with the help of a Fulbright Fellowship. After further studies at Bryn Mawr College and McGill University, she has now joined the faculty at Drexel University, herself a recognized authority on Kierkegaard. Suber left the Earlham faculty and is now at Harvard University, where his many

3. Facebook posts by former students, accessed Aug. 23, 2024. https://www.facebook.com/search/posts/?q=earlham%20cosmic%20ray.

4. *Richmond (IN) Palladium-Item*, "Astronomer," 3.

noteworthy accomplishments include serving as an international thought leader among advocates for open access to information and research.

Although interest in Ray and Bob's earthworks research was scant in the 1980s, that did not stop them entirely. They visited Ohio's earthworks from time to time. But over the two decades that followed their papers on Newark and High Bank, they published nothing further. They kept their humor though. Ray gave Bob a T-shirt with the number "2.88339" printed on the front. This was a teasing reference to Bob's theory that Hopewell people had a common unit of measure—a "Hopewell Yard"—equal to 2 8839 feet. As I sat with Ray, Bob and their wives, they told me the story of the T-shirt and Bob began to explain that he came up with the number by doing a linear regression of all the measured lengths found at Hopewell sites. Not long into his discourse, Ray interjected with reinvigorated skepticism, suggesting Bob was trading in the occultist practice of "numerology." All these years later and they were still debating the "Hopewell Yard." Ray told us we needed to read Edgar Allen Poe's opening to his story, "The Mystery of Marie Roget."

"I did!" said Bob defensively.

Ray then made an admirable attempt to quote it from memory. Here's the actual quote: "There are few persons, even among the calmest thinkers, who have not occasionally been startled into a vague yet thrilling half-credence in the supernatural, by coincidences of so seemingly marvelous a character that, as mere coincidences, the intellect has been unable to receive them."

Ray and Bob were the calmest of thinkers, and patiently did the work, but patience had not given the attention due to them. Would someone, somewhere rediscover their work?

⊕

Though little-schooled in archaeology at the time, Anna Sofaer chanced to get a front row seat in the male-dominated conclave of archaeological experts who, in the 1980s, saw little reason to take people like Ray and Bob seriously. In the late 1970s, Sofaer was an artist who had taken an interest in the world of archaeoastronomy. She took a class in Mayan astronomy that introduced her to the rock art of the American Southwest, a topic that left her "completely spellbound." She visited Chichen Itza, with its famous "serpent shadow," an architectural feature that casts a snake-like shadow down the stairs of a temple, joining to a carved stone serpent's head. It's a visual phenomenon only occurring at the equinoxes. She visited Newgrange in Ireland, too, where a sixty-foot stone corridor was built five thousand years ago, so perfectly aligned that the rising sun at winter solstice shines directly down its narrow shaft to illuminate a beautiful triple-spiral petroglyph at its distant interior wall. It's a measure of her enthusiasm for the topic that the thirty-seven-year-old Sofaer subscribed to the American Rock Art Research Association newsletter where she spotted a call for volunteers to record rock art in Chaco Canyon, New Mexico.

So, in June of 1977, not long after her visits to Chichen Itza and Newgrange, Sofaer reported for duty at Chaco. "It was the second day in my life in the desert, and we all woke up and assembled to do our work," Sofaer recalled.

"'Someone needs to do Fajada Butte,'" said a project leader, referring to a daunting 443-foot-tall rock formation. "There it was in the distance. There was an experienced climber—Jay Crotty—who was ready to go and looked as if he had all the right equipment. I said, 'I'll go,' and we climbed the butte and recorded about twenty-two sites, not quite to the top but near."

Late that afternoon, "we saw a beautiful carved spiral in the shadow of three leaning large rock slabs, but it was too late in the afternoon to photograph, so we decided to return the next day. We happened to get there near noon, a week from solstice, and a dagger of light was bisecting the spiral. It was formed by one of the openings of the three rock slabs in front of the spiral." She brought an artist's eye to Fajada Butte and saw something others would almost certainly have missed, and at just the right moment in the year.

The moment changed her life. They weren't there to do archaeoastronomy that day, just record rock art, and she was mostly alone in thinking the find had significance. But the similarities to what she saw at Chichen Itza, Newgrange, and other ancient sites convinced her there was more than coincidence at work. "I went back to my artwork and worked in my studio, but I kept thinking that I needed to do something with this discovery."[5]

Like the philosopher Bob and the astronomer Ray, she was an outsider to the world of archaeology, and sometimes an outsider is what it takes. "The ancient people were combining, integrating, so many disciplines," Sofaer told me. They weren't out to impress some future archaeologist. "Their discipline was closer to astronomy, physics, architecture, art. So it seems to me, in this funny way, that it's kind of logical that we would be outside the field of archaeology but bring in the perspective that might have been closer to the people watching the sky and building magnificent buildings as incredible architects and engineers.

5. Wilder, "Interview: Anna Sofaer," 22–24.

"I brought the perspective that was also part of the ancient people's way of seeing things, which is aesthetic, organizing patterns, organizing things that have visual power."

Like the philosopher Bob Horn, Sofaer needed her own Ray Hively. She soon found a physicist who shared her interest in ancient astronomy and consulted an archaeologist and other experts too. "All these disciplines make life more interesting and more powerful. How can you create sites that we are so excited by in Ohio or Chaco or Stonehenge if you don't have all these perspectives trying to bring together a more unified vision that the ancient people had?"

In October 1979, her first paper on the now-famous "Sun Dagger" was published in *Science*, the same journal that soon shunned Ray and Bob. The slabs of light, she and her coauthors argued, not only cast a summer solstice "dagger" through the center of the spiral. At winter solstice, the slabs cast two daggers that framed the spiral's outer edges.[6]

Sofaer said, "When Alfonso Ortiz, a brilliant anthropologist of San Juan Pueblo, saw our slides of just the sun markings on Fajada, he said emphatically, 'Where the sun is so marked, so would be the moon.'"

So, three years later Sofaer published a second paper, this time in a book, edited by Anthony Aveni, the same groundbreaking archaeoastronomer who Ray Hively met at dinner with the Earlham College president. This time Sofaer and her partners made a bolder claim: the same spiral that marked solar events also captured the moon's shadow to mark lunar standstills. The spiral itself has ten carved-groove rotations, making nine grooves to the right of center, ten to the left, which she said corresponded to the 18.6-year lunar cycle. Each year in the cycle, the moon's shadow progressively touched the next turn in the spiral's left side until, after 9.3 years, it reached the outer edge. Then the shadows returned to the center over a period of a little over nine more years.[7]

That same year, 1982, the year of Ray and Bob's little-noticed first paper on Newark, Sofaer produced a film documentary, "The Sun Dagger," narrated by no less an attention-grabber than Robert Redford. It aired nationally on PBS. A spiral petroglyph smaller in size than an extra-large pizza, carved on a remote desert butte, was getting more notice than a half-mile long lunar observatory one thousand years older, sitting in the middle of a small Ohio town. Ray and Bob never expressed to me any feelings of jealousy; they are

6. Sofaer, Zinser, and Sinclair, "A Unique Solar Marking Construct," 283–91.
7. Sofaer, Sinclair, and Doggett, "Lunar Markings on Fajada Butte," 169–82.

great admirers of Sofaer. But how could they not have sensed the unfairness of it all?

According to Sofaer, the problem for Ray and Bob's original thesis was its entire focus on the moon. "They had a tougher road with the moon," she said. Her breakthrough paper of 1979 discussed solar alignments first, an impressive enough finding even if you doubted her subsequent theory of lunar tracking.

Mainstream archaeologists were then highly skeptical of any notion that ancient builders understood the moon's path. The famous Stonehenge author, Gerald Hawkins, undercut his own credibility by making claims many thought outlandish. Seen as too much the showman, at one point Hawkins said in a TV broadcast, the "circles at Stonehenge could have been used as a computer to follow the moon and predict eclipses. It is undeniably a computing device."[8] Responding to Hawkins, the leading British authority on ancient megaliths, Richard Atkinson, made his own outlandish counterclaim, saying Stonehenge builders were "howling barbarians," incapable of serious astronomy.

Sofaer said that when she attended a 1981 Oxford Conference on Archaeoastronomy, "You could not mention his [Hawkins's] name." As for Atkinson, "he managed to scandalize the whole subject of the moon."

"I think that was the end of any acceptance of the moon and then it went into everybody's controversy bin because Gerry [Hawkins] had gone a little too far and because the top dog of megalithic archeology in the U.K had embarrassed himself so much. It just became weird. It's hard to describe but at that point talking about the moon, presenting about the moon, trying to get published about the moon, was uphill. And here's Ray with terrific credentials and very, very thorough work and I understand what happened."

Anthony Aveni may have published Sofaer's second paper about moon shadows on the spiral, but he and his British counterpart, Clive Ruggles—two of the founding fathers of archaeoastronomy—were digging in their heels about ancient moon tracking. Refusing to accept just any claim that came along enhanced their own credibility.

In the years that followed, evidence mounted that ancient Indigenous people understood lunar patterns. But Sofaer remembers Aveni still stubbornly insisting at an Oxford conference: "I will never believe in a lunar finding unless there is a written record, a codex, a chronicle, an ethnographic report. Period." Taken aback, Sofaer returned to that conference the next day

8. Hawkins, "A Temple or an Observatory."

prepared to counter him. By then, new Indigenous astronomical alignments had been found in the arrangements of ancient Pueblo buildings, and the spectacular lunar alignment at Chimney Rock was discovered. As Aveni listened, Sofaer ticked off the mounting evidence. The turns of the spiral equal to the lunar cycle could be a coincidence, she said. The building alignments could be coincidences. Chimney Rock could be a coincidence.

"That's a lot of coincidences, Tony."

Remembering it decades later, Sofaer told me, "That was a pretty cool moment."

That night at the conference, she, Aveni, and others "were stumbling around, coming back after a couple of beers," when Aveni turned to her and called her "a formidable opponent.'"[9] He might have been dismissive in tone, but he appreciated the research. He had, after all, helped Ray and Bob with their article and, in Sofaer's case, even published hers.

As Sofaer's and her colleagues' work unfolded, the voices of Indigenous people offered important insights into their meaning. In Chaco Canyon they saw patterns that other Native voices would see at Hopewell sites. Phillip Tuwaletstiwa, Hopi, an earth-geometry scientist who has worked with Sofaer for years, sees in Chaco Canyon, "the desire to bring order out of chaos. Sometimes it rains too much, sometimes the wind blows too hard. Sometimes it doesn't rain. There's social unrest. There's a lot of chaos here."

The use of consistent architecture in the design of kivas, Pueblo Bonito's sun-related orientation to precise cardinal points of north-south-east-west, Chetro Ketl's five-hundred-foot wall pointing to the minor lunar standstill? "All this is set up in balance, and you can begin to see how these things complement each other," said Tuwaletstiwa. "The spiritual, the religious, the material world, the ordinary, they're all in one comprehensive mix, and it's never separate."[10]

Sofaer's achievements were deservedly celebrated in the early 1980s. It would be another decade before a respected voice in the archaeological world would consider the possibility that Ray and Bob had found something important too.

⊕

Brad Lepper began his career by "gorging himself at the archaeological smorgasbord" of the University of New Mexico, where he finished his

9. Sofaer, interview with author, Jan. 28, 2025.

10. Tuwaletstiwa, *Written on the Landscape.*

undergraduate degree just a year after the little-known artist Anna Sofaer found the Sun Dagger. She didn't publish until later and their paths did not cross then. Lepper returned to his home state of Ohio for graduate studies at Ohio State University. After life in the American Southwest, it must have been hard to imagine that Ohio could offer as many rich veins for mining American prehistory. New Mexico, after all, had Chaco Canyon and its one thousand-year-old great houses of Pueblo Bonito, Una Vida, Chetro Ketl, and others, multistory masonry buildings with hundreds of rooms that served as the economic and culture center for Pueblo people across a wide area of the Southwest. The surface of Chacoan archaeoastronomy was just being scratched.

One Chacoan feature that made a lasting impression on Lepper was its famous ancient roads, mysteriously built long and straight, no matter the topography. When the road came to a cliff, steps or ramps were built to keep it on its linear path. Their purpose remains unknown for they don't clearly connect to destinations. Perhaps they were just there to accommodate ceremonial processions. Enormous amounts of labor were required to build them and some are thirty feet wide, more than would be necessary for practical transportation.

Lepper finished his graduate work in his home state of Ohio, but he had grown up in the northeastern part of the state, some distance from the earthworks concentrated on the opposite end of Ohio. In 1988, when he was thirty-two, the Ohio Historical Society named him curator and site archaeologist for the Newark Earthworks and Flint Ridge State Memorials. He oversaw a tiny museum at Newark and consulted with other organizations in the region. According to one visitor, Lepper worked in "a windowless office smaller than the average household bathroom. The tiny, cluttered room is barely capable of containing two people, let alone the enthusiasm freely pouring from one of them."[11] Even around Newark the earthworks were an underappreciated, even unknown, historical asset. When his wife and young son went to look at cars at a dealership on the east side of Hebron Road, the salesman asked her what her husband did for a living. Their son answered for them: "He's an archaeologist!" They explained that he worked on Indian mounds in the area. "What mounds?" the dealer asked. Leppers' little son pointed across the road at the Great Circle and its walls, rising to thirteen feet above ground, clearly visible. "Those mounds!" he said.[12] The salesman had little idea.

In 1989 word of a discovery came from the owner of the Burning Tree golf course five miles south of Newark. He was in the process of expanding his

11. Schlies, "Traveling the Road Back to Prehistory," 4.
12. Lepper, interview by author, Oct. 21, 2024.

FIGURE 10.1. Brad Lepper at the Newark Octagon in 2023. Photo by James W. Graham.

course and had paid a dragline excavator operator to clean up a peat-filled watery depression in the ground to create a new water hazard for his golfers. At two thirty on a chilly mid-December afternoon, the operator hit something big and heavy. Pausing to check out the obstruction he spotted a yellowed skull and shouted, "I found a dinosaur!"[13]

Not quite, but what he did find was the skull of a 13,000-year-old mastodon. Lepper was not a paleontologist, but he was as close to one as you could find in Newark. He quickly arrived, as did the director of the local county archaeology and landmarks society. The golf course owner's lawyer told him he was under no legal obligation to preserve the find, but the owner allowed the archaeologists a chance to oversee the excavation and said he hoped they could get the job done in a day. It was twenty degrees with a blowing wind that made it feel like zero. With help from half a dozen high school students, and given an extra day to do the job, they unearthed a remarkably complete skeleton.

13. Wesley, "Mastodon Unearthed," 1.

The bones were a great paleontological find and would make a fine museum display, but there were more than bones to investigate. Elongated gouges in the rib bones suggested human butchering. There was even reason to believe that humans had relocated the carcass to the pond so it could refrigerate the meat and keep it fresher. Even more curious was what Lepper found as he focused his attention on the place in the carcass where the animal's belly used to be. He had read that sometimes evidence of the animal's diet could be found.

"I carefully troweled through the peat looking for traces of the gut contents," where he found "a cylindrical mass of vegetation that differed from the surrounding black peat by its reddish-brown color, finer texture, and pungent odor." He put the sample in Ziploc bags and set them aside and forgot about them as they scrambled to do as much as possible in the short time given them. Inadvertently, the samples froze, so a guy working at the site said he had a freezer with some deer meat in it. He could throw the sample in there. A couple of months later some scientists from Ohio Wesleyan University visited the site to collect soil core samples, and as Lepper gave them a tour of his lab he told the story of finding mastodon gut contents.

"A scruffy guy in the back said, 'If you think it's gut contents have you looked for bacteria?'"

"No, no," Lepper told him. "You don't understand, this is thirteen thousand years, there's not going to be any bacteria."

"I'm Dr. Gerald Goldstein. I'm a microbiologist, and yes there could be. What did you do with the samples?"

"Well, they froze," said Lepper, sheepishly.

"Did you keep them frozen?"

"Yes."

"That's the best possible thing you could have done."[14]

They pulled them from the meat freezer, put the samples in a petri dish, and sure enough, found bacteria that only exists in animal intestines, a finding later confirmed by a lab at Michigan State University.[15] An expert on mastodons called it "the most detailed information yet available on mastodon diet, and allows us to understand their biology much better than before."[16]

Discover magazine called the Burning Tree mastodon one of the top fifty science discoveries of 1990. At the time its gut contents were considered the

14. Lepper, interview with author, July 26, 2021.
15. Lepper, "Forensic Mystery," 22.
16. Wilford, "Mastodon Yields Living Organisms," sec. 1, p. 7.

oldest living microorganism ever found, but since then older specimens have been pulled from amber. The skeleton was eventually sold to a museum in Japan and a cast of it is now on display at the Creation Museum in Kentucky, a place run by Evangelical Christians using, among other things, animatronic dinosaurs and skeletons to put a pseudoscientific veneer on their literal interpretation of the Bible. "Creationists love science!" says their website. According to the museum's authorities, "Dinosaurs were created by God on day six of creation, approximately 6,000 years ago."[17] They lived alongside humans and mastodons and even made it onto Noah's Ark, according to the museum, but they eventually died off. Presumably, along with Brad Lepper's mastodon.

I visited the Burning Tree golf course and saw the pond. It is now renamed The Mastodon Golf Club, with a logo featuring the ancient, tusked creature standing on a putting green next to a pin flag. The exterior of the clubhouse features a wall mural of a smiling mastodon, and in front of it is a baby elephant made of fiberglass.

⊕

Lepper's mastodon findings would have been a highlight of anyone's career, but Lepper's life in archaeology was just beginning. Mastodons were not really what he was expecting from his new position in Newark. Except for the evidence related to human butchering, this was not so much about anthropology as it was taxonomy. Every kid loves extinct giant creatures, but Lepper wanted to focus on "the human connection. Where did I come from, why am I here. Where does our story begin."

Lepper returned to work he started the year before, acquainting himself with all that was then known about Woodland Native people and Ohio's earthworks. Aside from the work of people like Prufer and Greber, the information available was limited. Lepper collected every scrap of information he could. A few months before the Burning Tree dig, Lepper was invited to give a presentation at an archaeological conference, summarizing some of what he had learned, and he invited others to share with him any Hopewell resources they might know about. N'omi Greber, then with the Cleveland Museum of Natural History, approached him afterwards and told him she had recently

17. Answers in Genesis. "Dinosaurs," Answers in Genesis, accessed Nov. 24, 2024, https://answersingenesis.org/dinosaurs/.

been doing research in Worcester, Massachusetts, about ninety miles west of Boston.

"Brad, when I was at the American Antiquarian Society I saw a card catalog entry for a Newark map," she said, as he remembers it. "I don't know anything else about it, I never looked it up, and it may be one you're already familiar with."

"Ok, I'll send them a card," Lepper said, not expecting much.

Before digitized online collections, you had to physically be at such institutions and root around the dusty cabinets and shelves, or have items mailed to you. He put a note in the mail and received a letter back confirming there was a map, mentioning also a twenty-two-page manuscript that goes with it. For ten dollars they would send him microfilm copies.

"Well, okay," he thought. "Ten dollars was a lot for me back then. That was pizza money for Friday."

The envelope finally arrived. He carried the microfilm to the library, loaded it onto the viewer, and "I was just blown away."

This was a map of Newark by two brothers named Salisbury, completed in 1862, a time when much of the four-square-miles of geometric enclosures were still intact. Lepper said it was "the best map that's ever been done of the Newark Earthworks." It included not just detailed maps from precise survey work, but also data about excavations and other measurements. For more than a century, it sat on its obscure shelf in Massachusetts, hidden and unknown. It was unsurpassed by anything Squier and Davis recorded of Newark for the Smithsonian, and today is the best record we have of the graceful ellipses, squares and circles that would soon be erased to make room for Newark's little frame houses, businesses and street grids. Without the Salisbury map we could never fully verify much of what was being understood about the precise geometry and location of the walls, including exactly where they pointed. Moreover, it held a whole new set of clues to something not previously considered.

The Squier and Davis maps from the 1840s showed three "avenues" or causeways in the form of parallel enclosures, extending to the east and south from the Newark Octagon. The eastbound avenues led to the ellipsis and square a short distance away. The southbound avenue, however, extended off the map. Squier and Davis showed it following a "squiggly" path, as Lepper describes it, and they noted that it continued for two-and-a-half miles southward to Ramp Creek, with nothing more said. That's as far as Squier

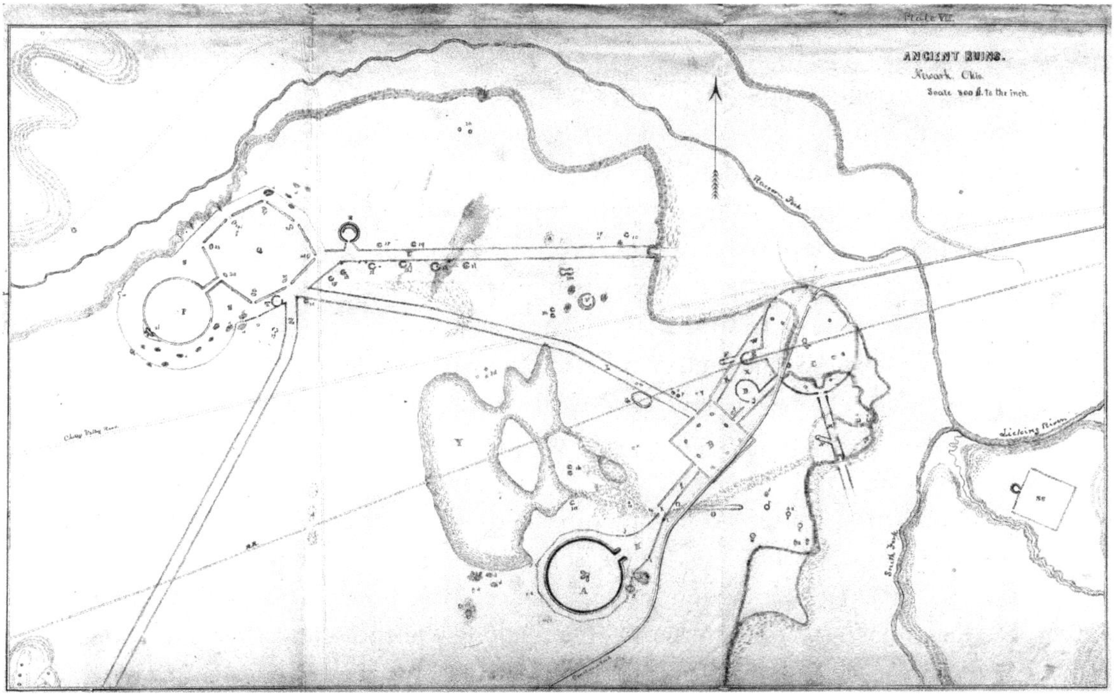

FIGURE 10.2. The 1862 Salisbury map, lost for a century, rediscovered by Lepper thanks to a 1989 tip from N'omi Greber. An "avenue" extends off the page to the lower left. Could it be the lost Great Hopewell Road? Courtesy of the American Antiquarian Society.

and Davis followed it. The parallel walls were about one hundred eighty feet apart and about three feet in height

Here is where the newly found Salisbury map made an important difference. In their map and narrative, that southbound avenue arcs gracefully away from the Octagon and then takes an arrow-straight path not just to Ramp Creek, but far beyond. Lepper combed through Salisbury's notes and found this description of parallel enclosures, "We have traced them some six miles over fertile fields, through tangled swamps and across streams, still keeping their undeviating course."

There was another earlier map from the 1820s that also described such walls, but it was generally regarded as less accurate. Its author, Caleb Atwater, claimed that parallel earthen walls might extend for thirty miles. But his speculation was based on reports he had heard of other parallel walls between Newark and points to the southwest. Maybe they weren't portions of the same walls.

Lepper had seen walls like these earlier in his career, before moving back to Ohio. As an undergrad, "we visited Chaco Canyon and they talked about the long straight roads that go dozens of miles. And I'm looking at this going, 'this sounds just like those roads in Chaco Canyon. And if it was one of those roads you know it could go for a very long distance.'"

Lepper had no room for cartography in his little office, "So I laid out quad maps on the floor of the museum and started drawing lines with a ruler and protractor. I found that if it maintained a straight course it would go straight to the heart of modern Chillicothe." Thus, such an ancient avenue would go from the Newark Octagon down a straight sixty-mile-long path to a destination very close to the circle-octagon earthwork known as High Bank. Newark and High Bank were, of course, the two places studied by Hively and Horn a decade earlier.

Lepper first presented his hypothesis of a "Great Hopewell Road" at a 1992 meeting of the Ohio Archaeological Council. His 1995 article in the journal *Archaeology* included more evidence, including a 1930s letter from a Newark businessman who flew a plane along the route and saw remnants of a pair of walls twelve miles southwest of Newark. Lepper also cited a 1993 series of aerial photographs by the Environmental Research Institute of Michigan showing remnants of walls thirty-six miles southwest of Newark and more remnants forty-seven miles southwest. Dache Reeves, the 1930s aerial photographer, confirmed earlier sightings of walls extending from the Octagon to Ramp Creek. In the years since, technology such as LIDAR has shown some evidence of circular earthwork enclosures along the proposed path of the road. The existence of a sixty-mile road remains unproven, but no one seems to doubt it is plausible. It's mostly farmland now, plowed over hundreds of times. But magnetometers and LIDAR technologies continue to improve, and every paper written about the Great Hopewell Road asks for more such investigation.

⊕

In July 2021, I decided to drive the Great Hopewell Road. That is to say, I pulled out a highway map, drew a line where the Great Hopewell Road is believed to have been and followed the rural highways that come closest to its path. I wasn't looking for remnants of ancient walls; rather, I wanted to see what kind of countryside it followed—the valleys, streams, native plants and trees. And I wanted to see how modern America had changed it all.

Running south from the Octagon, the known portions of its ancient path ran about half a mile west of a present-day Target store and the Indian Mounds Mall, a 1980s-vintage enclosed shopping center whose owner filed for bankruptcy in 2021, though it remains open. The mall weathered Covid and has reduced its vacancies since. Beyond the mall, southward, the path opens to rural Ohio. I don't know much about politics in the year 400 CE, but today the Great Hopewell Road traverses a distinctly conservative slice of America. President Joe Biden had replaced Donald Trump six months before my drive, but nobody here was taking Trump signs down any time soon. Flagpole holders were affixed to roadside fences, and American flags and Trump banners were flying on one fence post after another. The only banners featuring Biden preceded his name with the F-word. A Confederate flag featured the silhouette of an assault rifle and the words "Come and Take It" superimposed on its weathered red, white, and blue fabric.

I pulled over to the side of the road to check my map. Another car coming from the other direction slowed to a stop and a woman rolled down her window. I rolled down mine.

"You got a problem?" the woman asked in a not-so-friendly voice.

"No, no, I was just checking my map," I said.

"Oh, oh, I thought something was wrong," she said. Then she gave me a warm smile and on she went. She guessed I might be lost and just wanted to help, but you cannot ask directions to a hypothesized road.

Along the way I crossed Coonpath Road, not far from The Central Ohio Coon Hunters Association. Racoon hunting clubs dot the rural landscape of much of America, but until then I'd never heard of them. This one has the unique distinction of having an Indigenous mound on its property, listed on the National Register of Historic Places. The countryside there has gently rolling hills and old-growth trees with small farm fields tucked in wherever land was flat enough. It was hard to imagine an ancient road pointing straight through this rolling land. But in Chaco Canyon they just carved steps straight up the sides of the mesas, so the Hopewell people could have done it with greater ease on Ohio's softer soilscape.

It occurred to me that politically "red" counties like these—mostly white, rural, and working class—are the places where "Replacement Theory" finds purchase with voters. It's a theory rooted in white supremacy, though it would not be fair to put that blanket label on any large segment of these people. Replacement theory proponents argue, among other things, that white Christian family traditions are under assault, and that there is a Democratic conspiracy to populate the nation with brown-skin immigrant voters. In 2024, voters here strongly supported the Republican presidential ticket, with its rhetoric about immigrants "poisoning the blood of our country." Springfield, Ohio, about an hour from Chillicothe, is home to many Haitian immigrants who were said by certain national politicians to be eating the pet cats and dogs of local residents.

In the land where Hopewell culture thrived, then vanished, where later Native tribes thrived too, before being replaced by white colonists, the current fear of immigrant invasion and replacement comes with a thick glaze of irony. Replacement anxiety is nothing new to Southwest Ohio. Just ask the Wyandotte people. In the 1840s, a decade after passage of the federal Indian Removal Act, they became the last Native American population to be forced out of Ohio, made to travel by foot for 150 miles from Upper Sandusky, Ohio, to Cincinnati, then westward to Kansas City and beyond. In Ohio cities along the route, including Springfield, crowds gathered to watch the procession of the "last" Indians. Newspapers across the country covered the story as something both inevitable and lamentable.[18]

Now come new forms of replacement, though none so cruel and violent. As I drove down rural routes, I passed a modest white-clapboard church with a single large gothic window facing the road, three simple double-hung windows lining the side. Its steeple belfry was covered over with siding, leaving a blank-white-faced tower where once a bell rang. "Whisler Presbyterian Church," said one sign. Another that once displayed the title of the week's sermon now said

> CHURC HCLOSING [*sic*]
> LAST SERVICE 9\1
> CELEBRATION
> SEPT 8TH 2:00

It was now July. A Coldwell Banker for-sale sign was by the church door. There were other shuttered churches along the way too, built of the same white clapboard. However, two miles further south on Whisler Road and still very open for business was the lovely little Hallsville Mennonite Church. That's near where I saw the bonnets. Mennonites share with Amish people a devotion to the simpler ways, and here the two faiths lived as neighbors. I

18. Garcia, et al., "Wyandot Removal Trail."

saw a little square black horse-drawn buggy with a mother and her boy, she wearing black from head to ankles and wrists, he a little round straw hat. It couldn't be easy to divert her son's eyes from the four-letter-word political signage along the road. I saw a similarly cut dress and bonnet on a beautiful young woman on a coaster bike, fabric flowing in the breeze, but this time her dress was a bright yellow. The Mennonites sport a more progressive attitude toward color palette.

As I rounded a bend in the road and looked across a small valley, I saw speeding across a farm field an enormous wagon, pulled by a team of three large draft horses at a powerful gallop, white hair feathering above the hooves. Driving them from a standing position was a handsome and muscular Amish woman with a long dress and bonnet and a firm, confident grip on the reigns. Behind her in the wagon reclined three men in trousers, suspenders, and white long-sleeves, looking quite at ease as they raced together along the crop rows. They made a glorious sight. One wonders how mindful they are of the ancient Indigenous Ohioans who came before them. Do they feel as replaceable?

The demise of the small country churches has various causes, among them the growing popularity of Evangelical megachurches. The Solid Rock Church sits about eighty miles to the west of the path of the Great Hopewell Road. It once displayed a white fiberglass statue of Jesus as tall as a six-story building, face and arms reaching heavenward. It was an impressive sight for the drivers passing by on Interstate 75 until, in 2010, lightning struck the statue and it caught fire. The church built a new giant white Jesus, this one smiling, with arms extended horizontally in a more welcoming gesture to motorists. Another white guy replaced, but by a new Jesus of a like complexion.

⊕

For Brad Lepper, finding a mastodon and the Salisbury map, both in the same year of 1989, made for quite a start to a new job at Newark's Great Circle. As the 1990s began he started fleshing out his theory of a Great Hopewell Road, and also continued reviewing all the research, resources and reference materials he could find about the builders of the earthworks. There were academic papers to read about excavations, large and small, catalogs of artifacts, source materials in historical societies and libraries, evolving interpretations of old data and new. There was century-old data from "antiquarians," some sloppily gathered, some useful. There were academic conferences to attend, covering the most esoteric aspects of life before European contact, all the way back to the Ice Age. Lepper was also in charge of Flint Ridge, an ancient quarry and archaeological site that had been a source of beautifully crafted arrowheads, blades and drills.

Sometime around 1992 he chanced upon two academic papers that had been published a decade earlier in *The Journal for the History of Astronomy*. They were in the journal's special edition dedicated to archaeoastronomy, a field just gaining acceptance, and were written by two professors from Indiana's Earlham College, an institution not known for breakthroughs in Midwest archaeology. The authors were professors but not professionals in Lepper's world. They were a philosopher and an astronomer, and their findings were kind of, well, fringy.

He was naturally skeptical. "Archaeologists constantly have nuts coming up to us and saying, you know, 'you can draw a straight line from the Great Circle to the Great Pyramids of Egypt,'" Lepper said. "There's a lot of crap we're always putting up with. So there's a great suspicion, and someone that's not part of your discipline comes in and says wacky things, your like, 'naaah.'"

Nonetheless, "I won't say I was open to crazy ideas, but I think I was open to unconventional ideas. And this is also in the context of Stonehenge being accepted pretty widely as an astronomical thing. So why couldn't they have done it here?"

Lepper recalled that he himself received skepticism when he first proposed the idea of a Great Hopewell Road. The legendary Olaf Prufer's response to Lepper was similar to his response to Hively and Horn. "Prufer thought I was crazy," said Lepper. "He said that on a couple of occasions."

Lepper had never heard of Hively and Horn. They did not attend archaeological conferences, and they were not known for pitching their ideas to other scholars. They had just published their work and moved on.

But Lepper read their papers. "It seemed to me that their work was really rigorous and finding all these alignments, you know, it's like, if they just found one—well if they just found one they wouldn't have written a paper. Clearly from their writings, and then later when I met them and talked to them, they were their own worst critics, at first trying to falsify their hypothesis before they went with it. So when you talk to them and read their papers with a reasonably open mind, they make a really good case."

As curator at the Newark museum, Lepper was expected to bring in speakers for weekend programs during the summer. It wasn't always easy.

He had never met Ray or Bob, but Indiana wasn't too far away, so he wrote them a letter and asked if they would come give a talk.

Back at Earlham, after so many years, a letter of invitation from an archaeologist was a happy and out-of-the-blue thing. They were delighted to make the trip. The museum has no actual meeting facility, so dinner was served on folding tables and chairs in an exhibit area where they typically welcome about thirty to forty people. This was no academic conference, nor did local newspapers publicize the events; anyone could come and Lepper doesn't recall a larger than normal turnout. But the event helped rekindle Ray and Bob's waning interest in doing more research. And now they had a potential ally with expertise and credibility among Hopewell archaeologists. Suddenly Ray and Bob were talking once again about the new steps they might take, and they had encouragement from Lepper.

⊕

There were glimmerings of interest elsewhere too. Back in 1982, when Bob Horn first presented their work to the Midwest Archaeological Society, one in the audience who took particular interest was the young archaeologist, Patricia Essenpreis. A member of the faculty at the University of Florida, Essenpreis spent summers that followed at Fort Ancient and other Hopewell sites in Ohio. Fort Ancient stands apart from other Hopewell sites because here were built nongeometric earthen mounds that followed the irregular lines of hilltops and bluffs, enclosing a full one hundred acres at a striking elevation above the Little Miami River. It looked like the foundations of a fort—hence its name—but it had too many "gateway" openings to keep out aggressors, and here, as at other enclosures, a water "moat" lined the inside of the walls rather than the outside.

Essenpreis carried out excavations of various kinds, including one that revealed how Indigenous people redirected spring water into clay-lined ditches along the walls. Inside the northern section of the enclosure, the ancients built the "foursquare," contrasting with the rest of the irregular-shaped earthworks because the foursquare was so perfectly, geometrically, square. This was the same foursquare that Ray and Bob explored with students more than ten years earlier, first piquing their interest in Hopewell geometry. Essenpreis paid particular attention to that configuration, remembering Horn's presentation on Newark years earlier. She wondered if the Fort Ancient geometry hinted at astronomy the way Newark's may have.

Indeed it did. As Essenpreis wrote in an abstract for a paper she delivered in 1989 at an archaeology conference, "The [Fort Ancient] site is very irregular in form with the wall tending to follow the bluff edge. However, the northeastern portion of the work is laid out with geometric precision and contains four mounds that form a perfect square 155 meters on a side. Recent survey indicates that an observer standing on the western mound of this square could sight through particular gateways and align with the northernmost moonrise, the summer solstice sunrise and the minimum northern moonrise."

Essenpreis could have been another great ally in the search for the ingenious things encoded in Hopewell architecture. But she was diagnosed with cancer and within two years was dead at the age of forty-two. Wrote a colleague, "Pat's death followed closely the autumnal equinox, a point in the year that was surely marked by the prehistoric people whom she studied. Her remains will be returned to Fort Ancient at the time of the summer solstice."[19]

⊕

Lepper's discovery of the research of Ray and Bob was an important moment in the life of their ideas, but it would still be a long time before those ideas would creep into the consciousness of other scholars, and still longer before they would gain wider acceptance. In the early 1990s, an architecture student named Tammeron Francis arrived at the University of Cincinnati to start graduate work. He had an idea for a thesis, but it would need faculty approval. To get it, he sought a meeting with John Hancock who was then head of the university's master's program in architecture and a scholar of ancient Greek architecture, among other topics.

As Hancock recalls the meeting, Francis told him, "I want to do my thesis on the ancient earthworks of Ohio."

Hancock recalled, "There I was, the professor of ancient architectural history in Cincinnati, Ohio, and I turned to him and I said, 'the what?'"

"The ancient earthworks of Ohio," Francis repeated.

"The what?" Hancock asked again. Francis came back the next day with a copy of Squier and Davis's 1848 Smithsonian volume. As Hancock flipped

19. Reitz, "Minutes," 14.

through the pages his jaw dropped. "I had no idea."[20] Hancock was soon in his car, searching out ancient Ohio.

By 2004, after spending a decade learning about Ohio's earthworks for himself, Hancock was smitten and wrote that the Hopewell achievements "are almost equally incomprehensible as works of architecture, or as landscape experiences. As conceived by their builders, they were vast in scale, subtle in design, and both soft and complex in form." Writing about the hilltop earthwork enclosures at Fort Ancient, Hancock said, "the whole of the design could not be grasped through direct experience as an architectural idea, as a monumental spatial experience, or as a meaningful compositional whole. Like both its hilltop and geometric counterparts across the region, Fort Ancient reflects a spatial conception that is fundamentally beyond the grasp of the modern Western imagination."[21]

20. Hancock, "Ohio's Ancient Earthworks."

21. Hancock, "On Seeing Fort Ancient," 259.

CHAPTER 11

1.7 Degrees

There are no right angles in nature.
—Bertrand Goldberg, architect[1]

For the rest of the 1980s and through the 1990s, Ray and Bob published nothing further. With Lepper as an exception, their Newark work remained mostly unnoticed. Had Lepper not suddenly appeared on the scene and taken notice, they might have set the whole pursuit aside. Another noteworthy exception was N'omi Greber, much-respected as a Hopewell scholar and archaeologist, but, like Lepper, little known outside Ohio's scientific circles. With Bob's health improved, he began making trips to the area around Chillicothe.

"N'omi Greber's interest in our work kept me going to Ross County in the summers," said Bob. Ray and Bob still had unanswered questions, unsettling suspicions, and their sleuthing at High Bank told them the Scioto River Valley was the likeliest place to find more evidence.

Back in 1847, when Squier and Davis put an entire twelve-mile stretch of the Scioto River Valley on a single map, they revealed that in addition to High Bank there were more than a dozen other mound groups, with more walled enclosures, all built to the same monumental scale as at Newark and High Bank. And those were just the ones Squier and Davis could locate by river or trail. Earthworks lined both the Scioto River and a tributary called Paint Creek, practically surrounding present day Chillicothe. Though the earthworks are mostly gone now, in its day no place else had such a rich concentration of Hopewell landscape architecture.

Long before human habitation, the topography there was formed by a long-gone pre-glacial river known as the Teays. It was as big as the Ohio

1. Often attributed to Goldberg, I found no original source for this quote though his speeches and writing did express this idea, if not explicitly in these words.

River and ran from headwaters in the Appalachians north and northwest, through present-day Ohio to Illinois and Indiana. It was all destroyed by glaciers more than two million years ago, leaving behind rolling hills, deep valleys and alluvial plains. When the "first peoples" entered the area more than fourteen thousand years ago, the thick forests, wildlife, food-rich vegetation, fish-filled rivers and waterway transportation—all made it idyllic.

Bob made periodic visits to the Scioto River Valley, sometimes accompanied by Ray or Jane, sometimes on his own. "I spent much of the summers those years either working in Ross County with the county engineer's office, agriculture, forestry, soil and water, etc., to find data pertinent to our project. I collected aerial photographs from all sources I could find and digitized many. Fortunately, some archives were already digitized. N'omi was still working occasionally at Seip and we often got together for lunch or dinner."

Greber was still working with Alva McGraw, the farmer who years earlier convinced a reluctant Olaf Prufer to visit his property for what would later be some of Prufer's most important archaeological work. McGraw introduced Bob to other farmers who lacked formal training in archaeology but were willing to be coached by McGraw on how to precisely record the locations and context of Native artifacts they found. On one visit to the area, Bob's wife Jane visited a small public library in Frankfort and discovered a forgotten early map of the surrounding area. Old maps were crucially helpful to modern archaeologists.

The Scioto River meanders and snakes through southwest Ohio, but it has one odd feature south of the High Bank Works. There its winding course suddenly straightens and follows a six-mile-long line, with hills and bluffs on its west bank. The more Bob and Ray studied the positions of the earthworks, beginning with High Bank, the more they saw patterns that seemed to align not just to astronomy but to the surrounding natural landscape. Remember that the axis at High Bank sits at a right angle to Newark's axis. In other words, where the axis at Newark points to the northernmost moonrise, the axis at High Bank is almost exactly perpendicular to that line. In time, they noticed that the six-mile straight segment of the adjacent Scioto River follows a 143.4 degree bearing, matching the axis of High Bank Works. They noticed further that if you extend that axis line for 2.2 miles north-northwest from High Bank it runs straight into another Hopewell earthwork called Works East. Extending the High Bank axis line in the opposite direction, south-southeast, takes it straight through Liberty Earthworks four miles away. The river and the line through the three earthworks form a line perpendicular to the northernmost moonrise. That axis at High Bank began to make more sense as a reflection of the surrounding topography, as a link between earthworks, and as a vast architectural statement oriented to face the light of the standing-still moon.

The siting of these three earthworks, they later wrote, "suggests that these works belong to a common plan." They earlier found High Bank features that align to lunar and solar extremes, and now they saw a grander design that incorporates, "the nearly unique linear topography of a long segment of the ancient river valley."

Ray and Bob never forgot the one gnawing incongruity that made their Newark hypothesis maddeningly imperfect. All the pointers at Newark were accurate to within less than half a degree out of the 360 degrees in a circle. All but one. That wall facing north-northeast, or "E-F" on their diagram, pointed at the exact place on the horizon where the moon sets at its northmost reach over the 18.6-year cycle. The problem was the big hill about a mile away that made it impossible to see the horizon moonset from the ground. Surely they would have pointed instead to the spot on the hill where the moon visibly touched it, not to a spot you couldn't even see.

I asked Bob if there was ever an "ah-ha" moment, one revelatory instance of sudden clarity that struck them in the course of their years-long work. The moment that came to his mind was one where the meaning of the E-F wall suddenly made sense. They were always mystified about how that wall could point where it did. If they couldn't fly they couldn't spy the spot. The answer seems simple now, but it took a long time to come to them. The builders climbed the *other* hills! Surrounding hills were high enough to see both down onto the plain of the earthworks and over the hill to the horizon! These ancient master-planners laid out their four-square-miles of Newark earthworks by viewing them from hilltop vantage points.

There was archaeological evidence of small Hopewell earthworks, burial mounds and other structures on many of the hills above the Newark Octagon and along the valley of Racoon Creek. Squier and Davis reported "numerous mounds upon the hilltops and in the valley," and Lepper wrote of similar reports from multiple sources from the nineteenth century onward.[2] But the hilltops were so numerous it seemed fruitless to consider them in their calculations.

2. Lepper, "Ceremonial Landscape," 109.

One evening over dinner with me and their wives, they took turns explaining it to me.

"It was Bob who pointed out to me that from the highest mountain in Newark—if you stand on Coffman's Knob—if you stand on that highest hill, the lunar extreme setpoints align with the two valleys . . ."

"Right down the middle," Bob interjected with a jabbing finger down imaginary Sharon and Raccoon Creek Valleys.

"Then it certainly dawned on me," said Ray, "this was the perfect place to build these earthworks because of that topographical placement. If you could stand at this high point and the moon moves back and forth between these two beautiful valleys, what better, what more impressive evidence could you have that the gods and the topography were linked in a kind of sacred way in that place. That's why they built it there."

"Ray began to think about, well, what about the relation between the rest of the earthworks and the other hills. Was there any way we could choose among all those hilltops that had mounds on them? We came on the idea of tracing the alignment with the earthworks backwards to the hills." Maybe you would not need to visit every hilltop if the earthworks themselves pointed to the ones that mattered.

With this new way of looking at the problem, Ray and Bob spread topographical maps on a table and began drawing lines backwards from the Octagon. They started with the most prominent lunar alignment, the one following the axis through the Octagon and Observatory Circle northeast to the northernmost moonrise. Sure enough, going in the opposite direction to the southwest, they found a perfect hilltop backsight. They drove to the top of that hill and confirmed it made a fine view of the plain and earthworks below. More than that, if you look from that hilltop to the Great Circle, you're following a line that goes straight across it, through its "avenue" entrance and onward to the point on the horizon where the moon rises at its north minimum standstill.

"That surprised us," said Bob. "The skepticism was still there. We thought, that's too good to be true so it's probably not true." Then they found more such hilltops. At one point in their search, Ray, Bob and Brad Lepper piled into a car together and arrived at a hilltop occupied by a big house. The three pulled over to the curb and walked to the front door, no doubt making a worrisome impression on the female owner who saw them coming. What could these three men want? Their explanation was too improbable to have been made up, so she let them in. Even more, she invited them upstairs to the room with the best view, her bedroom.

From there they could see the Observatory Circle below, the Great Circle in the distance, and the way in which a line through both sites points to the southernmost moonrise at its major standstill. "We had a beautiful view . . .," said Bob. "She was delighted." She hardly imagined her property had a role to play in ancient history. Could it boost her property values?

"Much to my surprise," said Ray, "I really wasn't quite ready for this. You trace the lunar alignments in the Octagon back into the hills and you pass over four high points and incredibly those high points are connected along solstice lines. So the solar alignments finally fell into place there. There are these four peaks where the lunar alignments radiate from the peaks through the earthworks, but if you just look between the two peaks, the lines between the peaks point to the rise and set points of the sun on the winter solstice and the summer solstice . . ."

"Which means," said Bob, finishing Ray's thought, "the whole thing is laid out on the template formed by the solstices in the hills and then transferred to the valley, bringing the lunar alignments to the geometric construction of the earthworks."

Ray finally found those solar alignments that brought him to Newark in the first place, all those years ago. They just weren't where he expected them to be.

Proven true once more were those words of advice Anna Sofaer heard years earlier from the Tewa cultural anthropologist Alfonso Ortiz: "Where the sun is so marked, so would be the moon."

When they first discovered this grand valley of alignments, Bob said, "Believe it or not we still weren't ready to believe it. It looked too ingenious. Somehow or other we have got to have invented this (in our own minds)."

And what about that most annoying of anomalies, wall E-F, which, because of the hill, misses its moonset by almost two degrees? Drawing a line on the map in the opposite direction to the southeast points to "a small prominence," just the backsight hill position needed to visually follow the line of the wall to the opposite obstructing hill and over it to the exact location of the moonset on the horizon. The "prominence" was the perfect bird's eye view over the obstructing hill.[3]

If their new hypothesis is true, Ray and Bob found a valley filled with a confluence of alignments to the sun, the moon, and, as they later found, even the Milky Way. The geometry on the ground at the Moundbuilders Country Club was ground zero for what could well be an astonishing, miles-long

3. Hively and Horn, "Hopewell Cosmography," 137.

multi-dimensional version of Stonehenge, with sightlines to astronomical events through multiple alignments, on the ground, across the valley, and above from hilltop to hilltop. One writer likened it to a cat's cradle of sight-lines.

"The thing that is most striking to me about the whole phenomenon is the combination of precision and scale, which has no precedent anywhere in the world," said Ray.

⊕

As Lepper got to know Ray and Bob he was impressed by the way they would debate and collaborate. "They were always very collegial with one another, but it seemed always clear that Bob was the one sort of pushing in a direction and Ray was the one wanting to be more rigorous about testing. And I think that's kind of a best-case scenario to have colleagues like that. Somebody's pushing the boundaries and somebody saying, 'come back, let's test that, how do we test that, and let's do the hard science to test that.' And I think that's what makes their collaboration so strong."

If Bob pushed them to imagine the hilltops, it was Ray who pushed them to rigorously consider the hard data. He wanted to run a Monte Carlo analysis, which, as its name implies, asks, "what are the odds?" What are the odds that an octagon of a particular shape, drawn on the ground, would just by chance line up with not one but multiple lunar standstills? Could all of this be coincidence?

Using an Apple computer, a vintage machine by today's standard, it took days to run the Monte Carlo simulations in which billions of octagons were randomly drawn, within certain parameters, to see how many would by chance align to the moon in a similar way. The Newark Octagon had five lunar alignments that were either straight along the axis or along one of its four walls. Since three other identified alignments were a bit more conjectural, they kept the analysis more conservative and programmed the computer to try random alignments to the cleanest five.

The simulation showed the odds the alignments are accidental were about one in a million. Making the conclusion especially compelling was the existence of that sister site at High Bank, which had similar alignments. Had they asked the computer about the odds that two sites would accidentally do the same thing, the chances would have been exponentially slimmer.

To place their argument for intentionality on even firmer ground, they discovered one more nuance to consider. The compass-point alignments at High Bank are ever so slightly different from the pointers at Newark—a difference explained entirely by High Bank's different latitude, sixty miles south.

⊕

Ray and Bob prepared their latest findings for what would be their first new paper in more than twenty years. Its publication would happen close to the time of a once-in-a-generation opportunity to put their hypothesis to a test. Technically the north and south extreme lunar standstills happen at specific moments in time, but for the average earthbound viewer the extreme rise and set points repeat themselves over a couple of years and come so close to the extreme that the typical observer cannot discern the difference. Also, the moon at standstill appears to rise and set in the same place for two or three days running before moving north or south. So the year of a standstill affords viewers multiple opportunities for viewing, depending on moon phase or daylight.

An astronomer at Denison University, near Newark, was by 2004 enthralled by Ray and Bob's work and had begun working with them and other local archaeologists and academicians. Like Ray and Bob, Mike Mickelson realized that 2004–2005 was the time to test the hypothesis then expressed only on paper. Now it could be tested on the green turf of the Moundbuilders Country Club. To see it, however, would require a nighttime trespass onto the golf course.

Mickelson contacted Richard Shiels, an historian at Ohio State University's Newark campus who had a strong academic interest in race and religion. He was working to bring Native American perspectives to improve understanding of Ohio's earthworks. Mickelson said, "I twisted arms and said, 'Dick, nobody's done this yet. Nobody's made the observation. All this is on paper, it's all theory' . . . Let's go out and see this thing, see if Ray and Bob are correct. Of course, Dick told me 'I believed them from the get go.' And I said, 'but let's go look.'"

Mickelson and Shiels were joined by Brad Lepper and Jeff Gill a parish minister at the local Central Christian Church. Gill had studied archaeology in college and started informally working at Lepper's side, helping out at archaeological digs, searching the landscape for remains of the Great

Hopewell Road, and contributing to other research. They co-wrote a paper about the Newark Holy Stones. Gill started giving tours of Hopewell sites in 1990 and now gives some that are not to be missed, including a Hopewell "remnants" tour that peeks down alleys and into homeowners' backyards to find fragments of earthworks that survive.

While the golf club's occupancy of the earthworks kept the property from being subdivided for ranch homes, the club's presence still came with a cost to preservation. The Indigenous builders cleared trees to create gathering places and celebrate the moon and sky, but in the last fifty years trees were planted by groundskeepers to line the fairways and course perimeters. Now fully grown, some trees rise right on the mounds themselves, risking substantial harm, especially when trees topple in storms and large root balls tear up the earth. One mound aligned to the northern moonset is now completely covered with trees. Even if the moon rose on cue where predicted, seeing it wasn't going to be easy.

So, after darkness fell on an October night in 2004, the four arrived at Newark and walked across fairways to the tallest of the mounds—Observatory Mound. They had ample reason to believe that not for more than a thousand years did humans do what they were about to do: watch the moon rise in the eighteenth year of its cycle, seeing it as it was meant to be seen straight down the long majestic axis of the circle and Octagon.

"2004," Gill reminisced, as he stood on the same spot twenty years later, recreating the moment. "We're out here, right here. Not with permission."

"And so," continued Mickelson, "We got there at the proper time and we looked and we couldn't see anything. It was a clear sky, but there were all these damn trees along the axis. In October it occurred about nine or ten o'clock at night. The rise time changes every day . . . it might rise at five o'clock one night and the next night it rises an hour different from that. So we came out, we looked and we didn't see it. What's wrong, did I make a miscalculation?"

Gill remembered the "expectation and anticipation. We're just working off of the map, and charts and tables . . . Most of us have never watched a moon rise. If anything we've just been caught by surprise . . . But when you are intentionally planning to come anywhere, and especially here and wait, and watch, the moon does not announce itself. It gives no warning. And in fact, at a certain time you're going, 'did we check the table right? Do we have the correct time? What about the horizon?'"

"So we started walking around on the Observatory Mound" said Mickelson. The time had come so they searched for a clear view. "Then we got to a sight line where you could see the moon.

"Oh! There it is!"

"You're just waiting and watching," said Gill. "And then you get a little orange spark breaking out of the trees and the spark grows and it grows into an arc and a sphere rises up. It sends a chill down the back of your neck. It's an amazing experience."

Mickelson said, "We were off the axis however because we were on the side of the Observatory Mound. So then we decided to walk down into the flat. And then we got along the axis and then we could see it. It was the trees that were in the way." It was rising right as expected, at the tip of the axis, perfectly aligned.

"For all of us, for different reasons, it was an emotional event. For me it was, dog-gone, I connected up a model, a theory, with an actual observation. I'm an observational astronomer. I did work at Mount Palomar, at Mount Wilson, Maunakea. So, you know, going out and taking data was something I did. So for me that was my position. For Brad and Jeff and I think for Dick, it was emotional in the sense of, you know, we just connected the sky with this earthwork. You know it was, I think, spiritual for them. I'm putting words in their mouth, but that's kind of the way I think of it."

Said Gill, "It will always be one of the most remarkable experiences of my life, to stand out here with friends," and see the moon in timeless alignment with the architects' ancient dream.

Mickelson later wrote about that night: "Words fail to adequately describe what we observed and felt. The moon rose directly along the Octagon's main axis. Hively and Horn's hypothesis was correct! We experienced what the builders of the Octagon had so many centuries before. It had likely been hundreds of years since anyone had purposely observed this phenomenon. Brad Lepper, Dick Shiels, Jeff Gill, and I experienced what those ancients saw, for us, a very emotional event. In my case, as an astronomer, I confirmed the hypothesis proposed by Hively and Horn, however the experience was quite a different one for the others."

Ray and Bob were not there that day. But they have seen the place on other moonlit nights and wrote about it.

"Even today when one stands inside the Newark Circle-Octagon earthworks (especially under the light of a low altitude full moon when the

FIGURE 11.1. A digital recreation of an ancient moonlit night's shadows, which Hively and Horn believe created striking visual effects intended by the Hopewell designers. Image courtesy of the IDIA Lab: Institute for Digital Intermedia Arts at Ball State University.

Octagon walls cast dark bold shadows across the softly illuminated interior) one cannot help but be stirred by the stunning expenditure of physical, cultural, and intellectual energy involved in their construction. They stand today as impressive testimony to what a culture can achieve when motivated by ideas with sufficient power to inspire its collective imagination, intellect, and courage."[4]

"The only thing that would have made it better," said Gill, "would have been to bring more people out here to see it with us. We were not able at the time."

⊕

By the following year, Ray, Bob, Brad Lepper and a growing circle of academicians had exposed enough people to the idea of an earthwork moon marker that many more were taking notice. It was time to bring them together. In Newark, a "Moonrise Committee" was organized to plan a conference, timed

4. Hively and Horn, "Hopewell Cosmography," parentheses in original, 161.

to coincide with another good early-evening moonrise while it was still striking that northern-most standstill and creating the longest moon-lit nights of the Hopewell calendar.

Shiels led the coalition that organized a full day of educational events slated for Saturday, October 22, 2005, with sponsorships from local universities and the Ohio Historical Society. John Hancock, the University of Cincinnati professor who only a few years earlier had never heard of Ohio's ancient sites, was now fully immersed in them. At one session he planned to premiere a new video of Ohio's earthworks created by the Center for the Electronic Reconstruction of Historical and Archaeological Sites. Mickelson helped them identify the right day for a moonrise and planned a lecture on lunar alignments. Naturally, the gifted educator-archaeologist Brad Lepper, would speak. There were even to be poetry readings that included Allison Hedge Coke, an emerging Native American artist who would go on to win a number of literary awards for works that celebrated Native culture, many of them on themes related to mounds.

This was not an academic conference, though academicians were in full force. This was for the wider audience of non-scientist Ohioans who wished to better know earthworks in their midst. This time the local Newark Advocate newspaper more than made up for its scant earlier attention. The day before they ran a page-one article and a two-page inside spread featuring artist renderings of the lunar alignments found by Ray and Bob more than twenty years earlier.

Ray and Bob were given the three o'clock time slot, to be immediately preceded by a singing and dancing exhibition by the Native American Indian Center of Central Ohio. This was by far the biggest audience to ever hear their presentation. By one estimate more than one thousand attended the conference, including students and local residents. Ray and Bob started by explaining the hypothesis for which they were coming to be known, the lunar alignments of the Newark Octagon and works at High Bank. Then they addressed new findings for the first time, hidden since ancient times in the surrounding hills. This was unpublished work.

"I remember this very vividly because Ray was describing our discovery of places in the hills and then discovering that those points themselves were solstice markers," Bob said. Like a great unveiling, Ray displayed on a huge screen an illustration showing that the points across the whole valley, including the surrounding hills, were visually connected and aligned. The implication, though Ray did not explicitly say it then, must have been apparent:

the valley surrounding them might well constitute one of the greatest, most ambitiously conceived astronomical observatories in the ancient world.

Suddenly, as the audience collectively grasped what was being said, "There was a great AHH-AHHHH from the audience. It was breathtaking—literally!" said Bob. "The atmosphere at that point was electric."

Afterwards, Lepper was elated by the response. "Brad's attitude was: this is the opportunity to take advantage of the presence of journalists and get this out."

But as much as he enjoyed the audience response, Bob insisted to me that this was not the kind of publicity they most sought. It "ran against" their instinctive desire to secure acceptance by scholars who understood the rigor of their work and the merits of their evidence. They weren't looking to create a media sensation.

"That 'ah-hah' was coming from a lay audience," agreed Ray, "not an audience of skeptics."

Bob said "We wanted to get this out in a way that it would be appraised by archaeologists, then it might be time to say something" that truly warranted acceptance by the public at large.

The Moonrise Committee planned a highlight for the evening: a 10:18 p.m. moonrise viewing over the Octagon, weather permitting. They hoped the view would be as good as the "secret" one Mickelson helped organize a year earlier. Buses and porta-potties were arranged, and a good crowd was expected. But then the clouds thickened and rain fell. A rain date had been agreed upon for the following day, Sunday, when the standstill would be equally impressive. But unexpectedly the country club refused to allow people onto their fairway. The crowd would damage the wet sod, they said. When the Moonrise Committee tried to reschedule it for November 18, the club refused that too. The committee had been working for months with the country club, municipal officials, and others. Now the moon would make its spectacular rise without them.

An angry Shiels told a reporter "The most prominent people in town belong to this club, and they are using their power to keep the public off this important site."

Club General Manager, Ralph Burpee was having none of it: "Everyone would love to portray us as rich fat cats. Well, this is Newark, Ohio, which pretty much precludes rich fat cats."[5]

5. Maag, "Ohio Indian Mounds."

FIGURE 11.2. Posters featuring this digital recreation of a Newark moonrise promoted a 2005 conference where a moon-viewing event was canceled at the last minute by the Moundbuilders Country Club, which said its rain-soaked grounds would be damaged by foot traffic. Courtesy of the University of Cincinnati Center for the Electronic Reconstruction of Historical and Archaeological Sites.

If Ray and Bob disapproved of publicity stunts, publicity came nevertheless. The brouhaha with the country club received media coverage not just locally but in the New York Times and other major daily newspapers around the country.

Although the Saturday and Sunday moon viewings were cancelled, the clouds subsided Saturday night, and despite the no-trespassing order from the club and the presence of two police officers, about 100 people slipped onto the darkened fairways of the Moundbuilders Country Club. Members of the club were having a charity "Monte Carlo" night at the nearby clubhouse, so a few members wandered out too, cocktails in hand, themselves curious about the moonrise. Though the ground was wet, the sky was now clear. At the expected moment, the moon shot its first gleaming white light over the horizon and through the tree leaves, edging above the Octagon's most distant corner. It must have been stunning, but there doesn't appear to be much recorded about the evening. It was an odd gathering for a moonrise, a random collection of people with differing perspectives, astronomers, golfers, archaeologists, police officers and a few random others, looking eastward at the sight of that evening's Hopewell moon, a moon they've seen before, but a sight like none other.

⊕

About two years later, in 2007, the author John Sugden traveled to Ohio State University to give a talk about that great Ohioan, Tecumseh. Sugden was an Englishman whose 1999 book was considered the definitive biography of the great Shawnee leader. In the audience was a self-described "Sugden junky," Glenna Wallace. Wallace had been an instructor of English composition and world literature at Crowder College, a small school in Missouri just across the border from Oklahoma. She became responsible for the college's travel program and accompanied students to the world's great destinations: the Acropolis, the pyramids of Egypt, the Roman Coliseum, Stonehenge. She also happened to be a member of the Eastern Shawnee Tribe of Oklahoma, and more recently had taken up study to learn more about her own tribal history. That led her to become more involved with her tribe, so much so that by 2006 she was elected the first female chief in the tribe's history.

Continuing her Shawnee self-education, she jumped at a chance to travel to Columbus to hear and meet Sugden. After his lecture, his Ohio State faculty hosts, including Dick Shiels, asked Sugden and the others to travel with them to their Newark campus to see the great earthworks of that city. Wallace had heard of the famous Serpent Mound, but knew nothing about Newark. She wasn't particularly interested in other mounds, and knew little about them, but she joined the tour group anyway to get more time with Sugden.

On the drive to Newark nothing was said about the mounds; the conversation was all about Sugden and his work. On arrival, the Newark Octagon first looked like nothing more than a golf course. A tournament was on and the paved path was busy with golf carts moving spectators and players. Cart drivers complained about the visitors from Ohio State.

"One screamed out 'you're in the way, you have to get back, get back further than that," recalled Wallace. "'We have to get by. Why don't you leave and come back another day? We're having a golf tournament. We're busy. You don't belong here.'"

Then the group climbed the steps of a wooden platform built to give non-golf visitors a better view of the earthworks. It was a sunny October day with a clear view and leaves changing color. "I could not believe what I saw," said Wallace. "It was totally unexpected but absolutely beautiful. All you had to do is take one look and it was impossible to fathom how much work went into creating those mounds, and how many people it would have taken and how many years it would have taken. And I knew from all of the world heritage sites that I had been to that it was as vast and as monumental as any I had seen."[6]

She wondered, how could she not have known about this place? The experience brought on waves of conflicting emotions.

"At first I was excited, I was so elated, I was overjoyed. It's not Shawnees who built that. I'm not saying that. It's Native Americans . . . They had to be brilliant. They had to be knowledgeable. They had to be mathematicians. They had to be astronomers. They had to have so many skills I can't begin to imagine and they had to have dedication and perseverance. One basketful of dirt at a time."

"And then I became angry," she continued. "Not because I was a chief but because I was a Native American. Our ancestors did this and I'm not even permitted to go and to walk on this land, or to see it, or to have time on it . . . I remember the scripture that I said that day. And I said 'Father forgive them for they know not what they do.' And that day it became a commitment to me that that was a legacy that I wanted to make sure that survived."[7]

Wallace, or Chief Glenna as she likes to be called, dedicated the years afterward to advocacy on behalf of Ohio's earthworks. She often tells the story of her first visit to Newark. Always in her telling she repeats the complaint of the golfer who shouted, "you don't belong here."

⊕

The Shawnee who were one people under Tecumseh are today divided into three branches, one of which is known simply as the Shawnee Tribe. Its chief today is Ben Barnes, who made his own visit to the Newark earthworks some years after Chief Glenna's revelatory arrival. Compared to Chief Glenna's first glimpse at the Octagon, Chief Barnes was somewhat better prepared for what to expect. He was no less impressed.

---

6. Glenna Wallace, interviewed by the author, April 21, 2024.
7. Glenna Wallace, Speech at Rededication Ceremony.

His visit occurred under much different circumstances. "It was raining like hell the day I went there. There was nobody there." He walked the site undisturbed, accompanied by Jeff Gill and another local Hopewell expert, and "got to walk the whole thing, and nobody bothered us. It was raining cats and dogs."

"I remember feeling a little bit of mirth." The golfers were rained out, left with "discomfiture that I was getting to walk those mounds on a golf day. Mother nature wouldn't let them play. I do confess to a little bit of schadenfreude."

"They didn't know who I was, what it represented, me being there. But it's certainly amusing."[8]

---

8. Ben Barnes, interview with the author, April 9, 2025.

CHAPTER 12

The Modern War on Indigenous America

> The destruction of heritage is inseparable from the persecution of people.
> —Irina Bokova, UNESCO Director-General, 2016

> What then is, generally speaking, the truth of history? A fable agreed upon.
> —Napoleon Bonaparte

As Ray and Bob's bold interpretation of the earthworks slowly gained acceptance, would a new awareness of it contribute in some small way to a change in the way Indigenous people are perceived by Americans as a whole? Would a larger portion of America's non-Native supermajority begin to acknowledge that more than a thousand years before the European arrival, our continent was already the sweet home of an exceptionally gifted and sophisticated culture, fluent in astronomy, geometry, land-use planning, surveying and, of particular note, the art of government by consent of the governed? Two guys from Earlham College were not going to accomplish that much change that easily. The history of displacement, erasure, and nonsense narratives was too ingrained.

Consider the amount of time and energy so earnestly devoted over centuries to devaluing Indigenous achievement. Here's an interesting example. Seven years after Ohio became the seventeenth state in 1803, its legislature established Pickaway County, north of Chillicothe, not far west of the location of the hypothesized Great Hopewell Road. The county's commissioners needed to establish a new town to serve as county seat. They knew of one local ancient landmark, hidden in a densely forested area, that might make a nice feature for their new town. It was a pair of adjoining Native earthworks—a circle and a square—that had already attracted interest from antiquarians and others with an interest in science and ancient history. The

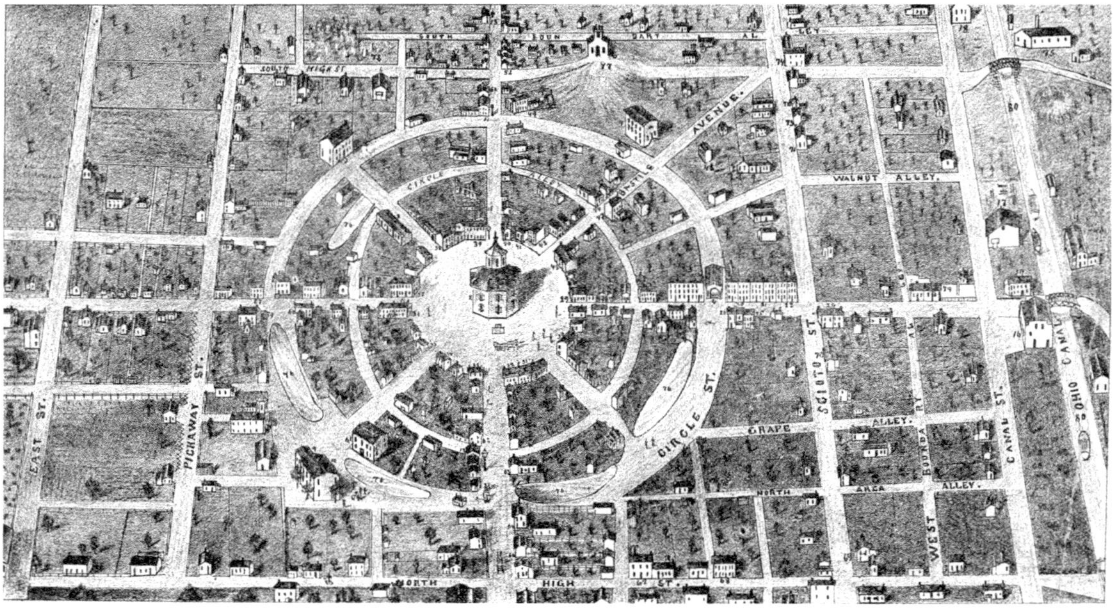

FIGURE 12.1. Birdseye view of Circleville as it appeared around 1836. Credit: Library of Congress, Geography and Map Division.

circle had the same 1,050-foot diameter as circles at Newark, High Bank, and two other earthworks in the region, though in 1810 the symmetry with other sites wasn't yet understood. The other adjacent enclosure was 900 feet square and had eight earthen segments, two per side, separated by openings to the inside. So, even though it was a square, it had eight segmented sides.

Rather than tear down the earthworks, the founders of the Pickaway County seat chose to embrace them in their own curious way. They used the ancient structure as a basis for laying out the new town's street grid: circular and radial streets within the Indigenous circle, linear streets in the adjacent square. In the middle of the circle they placed their county courthouse, built in the shape of an octagon. They named their town "Circleville," and it attracted the curious, including President James Monroe, who visited in 1817.

This use of a Native site might seem sacrilegious to Indigenous people today, but the town founders weren't thinking of these places as sacred, and in its day it was a quaintly novel city plan. It paid homage, at least, to the area's ancient past in a way that future land developers would not. The city was built and prospered. But in time the circular design and oddly shaped lots were deemed "peculiar," more trouble than they were worth. In 1837, at the request of local leaders, the Ohio State Assembly established the Circleville

Squaring Company and the town spent the next twenty years straightening the circular streets and realigning buildings, giving the whole town a square grid just like any other nondescript little town in the Midwest. State historians said with some pride it was "the earliest known example of urban redevelopment in the United States." That was fine, but now the town is known not for its lost earthworks but for its annual Pumpkin Show, with pies, giant gourds, and a Miss Pumpkin Show Queen and Court—tiaras, sashes, and all. Oddly, it has streets, a park, and a cemetery named Hitler, because a man by that name was a founding father long before Adolf was born. Circleville calls itself "The best little town around!" But it's not round anymore.

The city of Newark did a better job of preserving its earthworks, but in doing so they repurposed them in ways that fell short of honoring Indigenous culture. Before the Octagon became a golf course, the Great Circle across town served as a Civil War training facility for Union troops, and afterwards it was the venue for a "Grand Reunion" of veterans, attended by fifteen thousand to twenty thousand people, family and friends included. In attendance were President Rutherford B. Hayes, General William Tecumseh Sherman (named for the famed Shawnee leader, incidentally), and General James A. Garfield, future president. It was an impressive assemblage, to be sure, until the speaker platform, built next to the Eagle Mound in the Great Circle's center, began to collapse. Hayes and Sherman "only saved themselves by springing forward out of their chairs, which tumbled back into the ruins," according to a report in *The Cincinnati Enquirer*. Sherman is said to have remarked that a drunken carpenter almost achieved in an instant what the rebels failed to do in four years. A few years later, William F. Cody brought his Buffalo Bill's Wild West show to the Great Circle, featuring, as advertising boasted, the "largest delegation of wild Indians ever brought east." Cody featured horseback stunt riding, rifles firing blanks, live buffalo, and even a guest appearance by the Lakota Sioux Chief Sitting Bull.[1]

The Great Circle also served as county fairgrounds for almost eighty years, until 1933. It was known as the "Old Fort," since, like Fort Ancient, it was mistaken for a defensive structure. During its last decades as a fairground, an amusement park called Idlewilde Park was operated there, featuring a Ferris wheel, casino and billiard hall, bowling, shooting galleries, and a roller coaster. It had a track variously used for racing horses, bicycles, motorcycles, or automobiles.[2]

1. Pickard, "A View Within the Circle."
2. Lepper, "Newark's Great Circle."

Elected officials needed to satisfy both those who favored preservation of the earthworks and those who wanted to put the real estate to other uses. Elsewhere, thousands of mounds and archaeological sites have been ruined or obliterated, a process continuing even today, and preservation efforts are needed still. The Octagon remained a golf course up to 2024, despite its historical and spiritual meaning. And even with the findings of Ray and Bob, it is alarming to discover that many white Americans still wage rhetorical war on the accomplishments of the Hopewell, and by extension, Native Americans in general.

⊕

In 1980, while Ray and Bob were diligently gathering evidence for their upcoming publication on Hopewell astronomy and geometry, another professor was busily constructing a counternarrative regarding the Newark earthworks. Go back with me now to the story of David Wyrick, the discoverer in 1860 of the Newark Holy Stones, carved with Hebrew letters, uncovered at an archaeological site along with Native relics of the Hopewell era. Wyrick died, his reputation sullied, his Holy Stones called a hoax and long ago stuffed in a forgotten drawer at little Johnson-Humrickhouse Museum in Coshocton, Ohio.

Until 1980, that is. A biology professor at Ohio's Denison University with side-interests in history and the Bible, rediscovered the long-forgotten story of the Newark Holy Stones and made a trip to Coshocton to have a look. Gathering as many pieces of the story as he could find, Professor Robert Alrutz concluded that Wyrick's critics rushed to judgement, that a great injustice might have been done, and that the stones may in fact be authentic evidence of Hebrew-speaking people in America many hundreds of years before Columbus. His 1980 paper on the subject was published in an academic journal called *The Journal of Scientific Laboratories*.[3] Alrutz's status as a scientist—albeit a biologist—gave him a measure of credibility. Lepper and Gill have suggested that the late Alrutz may have been a "young earth Creationist," despite his training in biology. He was a leader of a local Evangelical Lutheran church, which doesn't tell us much about how he personally interpreted the Bible.[4] Two of his contemporaries at Denison told me they

3. Alrutz, "Newark Holy Stones."

4. Corporate records had Alrutz on the board, according to https://opencorporates.com/companies/us_oh/251103.

could not confirm he was a believer in creationism, but one of them suspects he "probably was."[5] A handout Alrutz distributed at a 1989 Denison faculty lecture lists various dates "in Ancient and Medieval American History," such as "Carthaginian trade" in America as early as 325 BC, and "Jews settle Kentucky and Tennessee" in 69 AD.[6] If he did believe in young earth creationism, holding that the earth is no more than 10,000 years old, that might help explain his embrace of the Holy Stones as having possible authenticity as Hebrew in origin.

Whatever his personal beliefs, Alrutz's paper caused a big stir among people on the religious fringe. Taking Alrutz's work seriously were not just groups of Christian Bible literalists, but factions within the Church of Jesus Christ of Latter-Day Saints, or Mormons. By 1991, requests to see the Holy Stones became so frequent that the museum put them on display for the first time. Now a steady stream of pilgrims visits, making the charming, small historic town a popular stop on bus tours. On my own visit there I asked the museum director what kind of people come to see the stones. "Evangelicals? Mormons?" I asked.

"Yes," she answered.

David Wyrick, so quickly dismissed by experts in his own day, now has a whole new set of admirers some 120 years after his death. In recent years, someone among his admirers paid to erect a shiny new marble headstone for his grave. There the monument stands, its crisply carved letters contrasting with the weathered original lying flat and in pieces on the ground next to it, grass creeping over it, a taunting remnant of the elaborate trick said to have been made at Wyrick's great expense, possibly perpetrated in part by the original gravestone's carver himself.

Less than a decade after Columbus breathed his last, the myth of the Lost Tribes in America was circulating. It so persisted that in 1912, when the Society of American Indians held its second meeting—like the first, in Columbus, Ohio—a society founder was asked if he believed the Native people descended from ancient Hebrews. A journalist cited as evidence the similarity of certain Native words to Hebrew.

"Why there are 59 Indian languages," replied Arthur C. Parker, though today we know of many times that number. "It can just as readily be proved

5. Juliana Mulroy, biology professor emeritus, Denison University, email to the author, Dec. 19, 2022.

6. Robert Alrutz, handout for Denison faculty lecture, Nov. 20, 1989, collection of Denison University Library archives.

that Indians came from the Greeks. . . . I belong to the Seneca tribe. Does that prove that I am a Roman?"[7]

⊕

The Lost Tribes narrative is not the only lie that won't die. Another centuries-old myth is of the "white Indians," descendants of colonists of European origin who arrived long before Columbus. As the first Europeans made their way slowly westward across North America, reports of "bearded, light-skinned Indians," some with "blonde" hair, always placed them just a little further west than colonists had reached. Keep going and you'll find them. They were supposedly descendants of early Welsh or Viking explorers. George Catlin, who otherwise created a marvelous collection of paintings that created an invaluable historical record of tribes and cultures, thought he saw signs of whiteness among the Mandan of the Upper Missouri River. But numerous other explorers, including Lewis and Clark who spent a whole winter with the Mandan made no mention of "white Indians." And by that time there were plenty of French and other Europeans intermingling and having children with Native people.[8]

Robert Silverberg wrote a long and detailed exploration of these false narratives, which he subtitled *The Archaeology of a Myth*. In his 1968 book *Mound Builders of Ancient America,* he bemoaned efforts to attribute Ohio's mounds to anyone other than Indigenous people. In addition to dismissing theories about Lost Tribes and white Indians, he introduces us to John Wells Foster, author of an 1873 work called *Pre-historic Races of the United States of America*. Foster opens with a promising homage to the earthworks of Newark, Ohio. "I confess that, as I traced out the labyrinthine system of earthworks here displayed with its great circles and squares, its octagons, gateways, parallel roads, and tumuli, the whole spread over an area of several square miles, and as I speculated upon the purposes of their construction, and on the origin and extinction of the people by whom they were reared, I was profoundly impressed."[9]

That reference to "extinction" of the builders hints at the dark path his book takes after that. He goes on to a lengthy examination of the shape of the skulls taken from Indigenous burial sites. Ten years before the term

7. *Ohio State Lantern,* 1.
8. McLaird, "The Welsh," 245.
9. Foster, *Pre-historic Races,* iii.

"eugenics" was coined, he argued that Native people lacked the cranial capacity to create such sophisticated landscape architecture. To say they built Ohio's geometric earthworks, Foster wrote, "is as preposterous, almost, as to suppose that they built the pyramids of Egypt."[10] Foster concludes, a superior, now extinct race must have directed the construction of the Ohio earthworks. That race, in turn, must have been wiped out by Indians.

Of Foster and countless other mythmakers, Silverberg wrote: "The discovery of the mounds of North America provided a link to Herodotus and Homer, to Rome and the Vikings, to England's barrows, to all the mounds of Europe and Asia that had been known so long. . . . If the Israelites had built mounds in Canaan, why not in Ohio? Learned men came forth to suggest that our land had been visited in antiquity by Hebrews, Greeks, Persians, Romans, Vikings, Hindus, Phoenicians—anyone, in short, who had ever built a mound in the Old World. The silent structures along our rivers were credited to many nations; and then, of course, it became necessary to determine what had become of those ancient immigrants to America. The answer was obvious: they had been exterminated at some past date," most likely by Native people, who for centuries continued to cause, "so much trouble for the Christian settlers of the New World."[11]

Silverberg's take down was mostly aimed at white racism from centuries past. Despite his ambitious effort to document and discredit such thinking, the assault on Indigenous achievement still rolls relentlessly on, like wagon trains through Indian country. Now, however, the deniers of Indigenous achievement have new information to misconstrue: the findings of Hively and Horn.

⊕

In 2010, Fox News personality Glenn Beck, whose showmanship made him exceptionally popular, stood in front of a news graphic. Behind him on the right: the Great Pyramid of Giza. On the left: the Newark Octagon.

He then described what he said were inexplicable mathematical similarities between the two.

"If you take the angle of the Great Pyramid of Giza, the slope is 51.8 degrees. Let's go back to the earthworks," said Glenn, pointing to the Newark Octagon. "If you measure the line that goes straight through the center of

10. Foster, *Pre-historic Races,* 300.

11. Silverberg, *Mound Builders,* 6.

the structure. Right here. And then you go true north, it's 51.8 degrees. That angle is exactly the same angle as the Pyramids of Giza. It's the same math, the same calculations as ancient Egyptians." Beck also illustrated measured dimensions of the side of the pyramid and compared them to squares formed by lines drawn in the Newark Octagon. The same unit of measurement was employed by builders of both monuments, he claimed.

He then showed images of the Newark Holy Stones and their Hebrew engravings. He described Wyrick and his survey of earthworks. Pointing to the Holy Stones, he said, "This, by the way, is *sitting* in Ohio," as though it were the Holy Grail right under our noses.

"What is that about? Where is that history?" According to Beck, "Science was colluding with government because of commerce. And religion was involved," implicating the Smithsonian Institution as well. "Why do I tell you all this stuff. Not because I'm an Indian expert or anything else. You gotta do your own homework." Beck describes it all as a wide-ranging scheme to deprive us of any knowledge conflicting with their portrait of these ancient people as hostile Native people.[12] Apparently, if nineteenth-century white Americans knew the genius behind the design of the earthworks, it would have contradicted the nation's belief in its "Manifest Destiny" to conquer the West and banish the Indians. This sounds sympathetic to Indigenous people until it became apparent that the conveyors of this narrative really want to credit the earthworks to the presence, influence, and design of the Hebrews of the Lost Tribes of Israel. They, not Indigenous Americans, were the geniuses behind Hopewell mathematics, geometry, and astronomy, long before Columbus.

Beck credited as his source a documentary called "Lost Civilizations of North America" released the same year. The documentary included interviews with numerous scholars with excellent credentials. Not only was Brad Lepper featured, but it also offered professors of anthropology from Indiana University, the University of Texas at Austin, Central Connecticut State University, and Marquette University, and a history professor from Eastern Illinois University. As it turned out, none of them who agreed to be interviewed really knew what they were getting into. Their statements were taken out of context and their rejections of the film's conclusions were not aired. Beck had given the strange documentary so much publicity that the scholars whose statements were misrepresented felt it necessary to denounce it in a joint statement:

12. Beck, "Native Americans Wrote in Ancient Hebrew."

"We want to make it clear that we do not support the theories presented in *The Lost Civilizations of North America* DVD. In our opinion, there is no compelling archaeological or genetic evidence for a migration from the Middle East to North America a few thousand years ago, nor is there any credible scientific evidence that Old World civilizations were involved in developing Native American cultures in pre-Columbian times. Many of the artifacts used to support the film's claims, such as the Newark 'Holy Stones,' have been proven fraudulent based on convincing scientific evidence and historical documentation."[13]

Beck, as it happened, had converted to the Church of Jesus Christ of Latter-Day Saints (LDS) about ten years before that broadcast. Many of his church brethren were embracing these new theories as validation of their version of American history, which regards Native Americans as Lamanites, one of two "groups that began as the descendants of two Israelite brothers." Lamanites abandoned the gospel of Jesus, but Nephites hoped to win them back. In his broadcast, Beck didn't mention his Mormon connection, but there is an unmistakable link between Beck, the *Lost Civilizations* video, and the Mormons.

The LDS Church's official position on Native Americans, as articulated on its website, leaves open the question of whether Native people were descended from the Lost Tribes of Israel. "The Book of Morman invited readers to consider other peoples, notably the native people of the Americas, as lost sheep of the house of Israel." But the church "does not take a position on the specific geography of the Book of Mormon or claim complete knowledge about the origins of any specific group in the Americas or the Pacific."[14]

Whatever the official LDS position, there are today active factions among Mormons who strongly suspect that the earthworks of Ohio are described in the Book of Morman. In fact, there's a whole cottage industry devoted to it, with books, videos, magazines and a "Book of Mormon Evidence Conference," boasting "70+ speakers and 130+ presentations, on 5 total stages, over 3-days, and 60+ vendor booths." There are at least two guided tours, including the "Book of Mormon Evidence and History Tour," where you'll visit traditional Mormon historical sites such as Navoo, Illinois, before moving on to Ohio to see its earthworks, including the Newark Octagon, Great Circle and, of course, the Newark Holy Stones in Coshocton.

Through these media offerings you will enter the world of a Mormon subgroup that calls itself "Heartlanders." You'll learn that Ohio is what the Book

13. Atalay et al., "Lost Civilizations."

14. Church of Jesus Christ of Latter-Day Saints, "Lamanite."

of Mormon was referring to when it described the Land of Bountiful. According to one account, "Nephi, the Son of Nephi," saw a vision of Christ at the Newark Octagon "at 6:29 p.m., Tuesday, April 4th, 1 BC," under a full moon, foretelling the birth of the Christ child in Bethlehem the following day. Years later, "the moonrise for Saturday, October 3rd, AD 33 was in alignment (with) the central line of the Newark Earthworks," and the next morning the just-crucified Jesus descended from heaven at or near the Newark Octagon "in His resurrected glory."[15]

How does one dissect the mind of Glenn Beck or understand the views many Mormon people have of Indigenous Americans? The tragedy is the thievery of a rich Native culture, bent to the purposes of non-Native religious extremists, and their twisted interpretations of the books of the Bible or the Book of Mormon.

There's one particularly interesting character tied to all of this. Wayne May, a long-time convert to the LDS Church, has made a business of selling books, videos, magazines, and his own guided tours—including one of Hopewell sites—with much of his content dedicated to pre-Columbian America and the earthworks of Ohio. He speaks to Mormon audiences, and his videos are featured online at websites such as one hosted by the Joseph Smith Foundation, which, it must be said, is not sponsored by the LDS Church. On his website you can buy books such as *The Ten Tribes of Israel,* and the classic from 1873, discussed earlier, *Pre-historic Races of the United States,* with its quack conclusions about the cranial shortcomings of Indigenous people. Also for sale are books by a fellow named Frank Joseph, who was also editor of May's magazine, *Ancient American.*

Frank Joseph's book *Advanced Civilizations of Prehistoric America* argues that people of the Hopewell culture were actually Japanese immigrants, and the people of the related Adena culture were "Keltic" (with a "k"). He gives admiring descriptions of Adena stone carvings that looked like swastikas, which he claims are "identical" to the Irish *Crosóg Bhríde,* or "Brigid's Cross." Hopewell mounds he likens to Japanese constructions of the same time period. He claims both the Hopewell and Adena cultures bore no genetic similarities to "Plains Indians," and that over time Indians "obliterated" both the Hopewell and the Adena, leading to an era of several hundred years when "the lamp of civilization went out in North America." Likewise he mourns the loss of the ancients of Chaco Canyon, with their astronomy

15. Lefgren, "The Newark Earthworks."

and architecture. Like the fated Hopewell and Adena, "civility was proportionately replaced by savagery." The author concludes that the defeat of the Adena and Hopewell by the cultureless hordes is a cautionary tale we should heed today.

"Future archaeologists sifting through the remains of a late nineteenth-century church building, abandoned one hundred years later, on Chicago's south side will be no less challenged than today's excavators trying to puzzle out the mysteries of Pueblo Bonito," writes Joseph.[16]

The dark references to swastikas, savagery, replacement, and a Black neighborhood of Chicago starts to make sense when you learn that Frank Joseph is a pen name. His real name is Frank Joseph Collin. He gained infamy as the Chicago leader of the National Socialist Party of America who, in 1978, planned a Nazi march through Skokie, Illinois, home to thousands of Jewish residents, many of them refugees from Nazi death camps. His plan to march was scrubbed, but he led other demonstrations, including one that opposed Black integration of the mostly white Marquette Park neighborhood of Chicago. Collin started falling out of favor among white supremacist groups when it was reported his father is Jewish. His leadership aspirations were further quashed when police caught him picking up young boys on his motorcycle, offering them ten dollars for oral sex and then taking them to his apartment above Nazi headquarters in Chicago. He had pictures too, and his conviction on multiple counts of taking indecent liberties with a child, and his subsequent ejection from the Nazi organization, showed there is only so low even a Nazi will go.[17]

After release from prison he reinvented himself and wrote several books on "ancient America." Wayne May, now gaining some acceptance as an interpreter of Mormon history in ancient America, was his publisher, so I sent May an email. I wanted to make sure I had the right person, so I asked May if "Frank Joseph is a pen name for Frank Joseph Collin, who you probably know was a controversial figure in the 1970s."

May responded, simply: "He is the same person from the 1970s."[18] Give May credit for transparency.

⊕

16. Joseph, *Advanced Civilizations,* 262.
17. Enstad, "Ex-Nazi," sec. 1B, p. 7.
18. Wayne May, email to author, Aug. 17, 2022.

"There is only one thing in the world worse than being talked about," said Oscar Wilde, "and that is not being talked about." As painful as it is to hear the rantings of Glenn Beck and the rest, at least Ray and Bob's work was becoming known. And, sadly, people who are either charlatans or just "doing their own homework," continue to gain audiences, no matter how wild they may be.

Joe Rogan and Tucker Carlson were two of the top-rated podcasters on America's charts in 2024, and their influence is such that their interviews with—and subsequent endorsement of—Donald Trump were considered pivotal to his 2024 reelection. Both Rogan and Carlson have featured on their shows a self-described "renegade scholar" named Randall Carlson, whose bushy gray beard, shoulder-length gray waves, and body type bring to mind Jerry Garcia of The Grateful Dead. He speaks with an air of authority about glacial epochs, lost civilizations, and ancient architecture, including the Ohio Earthworks, but his professional background appears to be limited mostly to homebuilding and remodeling in Decatur, Georgia.

In videos, podcasts, and seminars with titles like "Sacred Geometry" and "Squaring the Circle," Randall Carlson argues that a cataclysmic event 12,000 years ago—an asteroid collision, perhaps—suddenly dropped the planet's temperature, spiking mass extinctions and a "resetting" of global human civilization. Advanced civilizations were all but obliterated, except for fragments of knowledge that somehow were passed on to descendants across multiple continents. This, he maintains, helps explain why the earthworks of Ohio, pyramids in Egypt, and other monuments exhibit similarities of geometry and mathematics. In other words, the earthworks were not wholly Indigenous American inventions, but rather the work or inspiration of a long-lost "advanced" culture that predated them. It's all poppycock according to serious scholars.

On one program, with Tucker Carlson engaging approvingly, the two agreed that Indigenous people couldn't possibly have built the earthworks with their simple tools; that skeletal evidence in Ohio showed that "giants" up to eight feet tall might have helped with the construction; and that people were found in burial sites who had no genetic resemblance to Native Americans. There were also references to conspiracies suppressing the evidence.[19] None of it true.

19. Randall Carlson, interview with Tucker Carlson.

Another lost-civilization-theorist is Graham Hancock, producer of many books and a Netflix program. He and Randall Carlson promote one another online, and more than once they appeared together on Joe Rogan's podcast. Hancock, too, argues that a great advanced civilization was all but destroyed in a cataclysmic event of some 12,000 years ago, but in his telling they were a seafaring people who still managed to spread their knowledge across continents. He believes they might be connected to the lost civilization of Atlantis. Hancock credits Ray and Bob with important contributions and wrote at length about the astronomical alignments and geometry they found. He credits Native people with constructing great mounds of the Midwest, but not with the independent invention of the geometry and mathematics embedded in them. The likes of Randall Carlson and Graham Hancock have a talent for blending fact and pseudo-fact; the true stuff becomes the sheep's clothing hiding their wolf-pack of truth-ravaging nonsense.[20]

⊕

The Serpent Mound, about thirty miles southwest of Chillicothe, is considered the largest effigy mound in the world. Carbon dating has been inconclusive about its age. That it is an effigy—that is, shaped like an animal–suggests it is not the product of Hopewell artistry. More likely it was built by the Adena culture of 800 BCE to 100 CE, or it was made by the Fort Ancient Culture around 1000 to 1500 BCE. That wide expanse of time shows how perplexing it is to archaeologists. The absence of artifacts buried within it contribute to uncertainty. The one sure thing is that it is a masterpiece of Indigenous art, one of the most gracefully executed and beautiful aboriginal creations anywhere.

At less than fourteen hundred feet in length, it is smaller in scale than the largest of the Hopewell geometric mounds, so the curves and coils of its snake-shape can be appreciated at lower elevations, such as the one offered from the viewing tower erected next to it. The snake's head is said to align to the sunset at summer solstice, with other features pointing less convincingly to the winter solstice.

Its sinuous shape and alleged astronomy have captured public imagination, and groups of people with divergent, sometimes conflicting, perspectives pay it homage. That was why sheriff's deputies were summoned to

20. A debunking of the "lost white race" theory is in Colavito, *Mound Builder Myth.*

FIGURE 12.2. Dache Reeves's photo of Serpent Mound, 1930s. National Museum of the American Indian, Smithsonian Institution (P13211).

Serpent Mound during the winter solstice of 2020. Dave Daubenmire, who leads Pass the Salt Ministries, formed, "to encourage the Body of Christ to step into the cultural war," organized a trip there with the aim of "praying down [the] Satanic serpent mounds." Daubenmire was reported to have said on Facebook that "he believed Ohio's earthworks were built by Nephilim, a race of giants some say are the offspring of fallen angels and human women."[21]

Philip Yenyo, executive director of the American Indian Movement of Ohio, got wind of the minister's plans and met his group in the parking lot. No fists were thrown, but they had words and there was a moment when

21. Kruzman, "Ohio's Indigenous Sacred Sites."

one stepped aggressively into the path of the other, and an intervener had to separate the two.

"Don't tell me to get out of the way on my own land," Yenyo told one of them. "It's our birthright. It's our sacred site."

"It's public land," replied a church member. "This land will be taken in the name of Jesus."

"This land was already taken a long time ago," Yenyo said. "You people keep taking it."

One prayer group member walked on top of the mound and was asked by park facility staff to get off.

"I'm not calling the Indians dark," Daubenmire told a reporter. "This has nothing to do with the Indians. We went there because we believe dark energy is released there."[22]

It wasn't the only time the sheriff was called in. In 2012, a group called Unite the Collective, some wearing T-shirts that said, "Light Team," were caught burying muffin-sized objects in the soil of the mound itself. A video they posted said the buried "organites" were intended to "lift the vibration of the Earth so we can all rise together."[23] In 2011, another group brought thirteen crystal skulls, falsely claiming they were of Mayan origin. The Serpent Mound site has interested New Age followers since at least 1987 when people all over the world gathered for mass meditation events there and at other "energy centers," including Stonehenge, Chaco Canyon, the Great Pyramid of Egypt, and Sedona, Arizona. That two-day event was timed to coincide with a particular planetary alignment propitious for world peace.

And, of course, there are those who see in large earthworks evidence that aliens were their builders. In 2013, the History Channel's *Ancient Aliens* placed Serpent Mound, the Nazca geoglyphs in Peru, and crop circles in England into a category of possible alien creations, perhaps meant to point to the presence of iridium as spaceship fuel.

Ray Hively and Bob Horn found something magnificent in the designs and knowledge of the Hopewell culture, findings that were ignored for years. Now their discoveries are not only widely accepted but also turned on their head for bizarre purposes. It reminds me a bit of astronaut Buzz Aldrin, who put his life on the line by taking the first steps on the moon with Neil Armstrong. He's an American hero, but there were skeptics. When Aldrin

22. Knight, "Native Americans, 1.

23. Johnson, "Desecration of Serpent Mound," C4.

was seventy-two he was confronted by a man who claimed the landing was faked. So Aldrin punched him in the face.

Ray and Bob advanced science in Ohio, but to reach acceptance, they had to paddle against the scientific mainstream, only to then find a back current of pseudoscience and racial animus. Like the Lost Tribe theories Europeans brought to America centuries earlier, the new mythologies are a hard-to-control invasive species of fictional narrative, some of it merely silly, but sometimes rising to the level of cultural genocide.

They are frustrating setbacks, yes, but they are increasingly outnumbered by signs of true advances in science and Indigenous cultural embrace. The actual and wonderous story of Native American achievement is increasingly speaking for itself.

CHAPTER 13

Rediscovery

> Our people were canoe people. Until they made us walk. Until our lakeshore lodges were signed away for shanties and dust. Our people were a circle, until we were dispersed. Our people shared a language with which to thank the day, until they made us forget. But we didn't forget. Not quite.
>
> —Robin Wall Kimmerer, *Braiding Sweetgrass*

Maya Lin, born in 1959 in Athens, southeastern Ohio, remembers the topography around her home "was hilly and wooded. Behind our house were three ridges separated by streams—my entire childhood was spent playing in these woods and on these hills. I called the middle one the 'lizard's back' because it started up from the creek bed, like a tail. It grew into a long winding ridge, and ended in what to us looked like the head of a lizard. That image and the presence of Indian burial mounds—the effigy mounds and the serpent mounds—were a profound influence on my work."[1]

Her father, a ceramicist, left China in 1948, and her mother, a poet, had to be smuggled out of China after the Communists took over in 1949. They met in the US and together joined the faculty at Ohio University, where they had accomplished careers but did not talk much about their earlier life. It wasn't until Lin was in her thirties that she gave much thought to her own Chinese ethnicity. She was a loner in high school, had no close friends, wore no makeup, did not go to prom.[2] But she pursued an interest in art and emerged from anonymity to be covaledictorian, later earning acceptance into Yale, where her love of art and math led her to focus on architecture. During a junior year semester in Denmark, she visited an enormous cemetery that doubled as a popular park. It was the burial place of Søren Kierkegaard and

1. Lin, *Boundaries,* 6:02.
2. Menand, "Maya Lin."

other noteworthy Danes, and Lin appreciated the way a place for enshrining the dead could also enrich the lives of the living.

In her last year at Yale she learned of a design competition for a Washington war memorial. Funereal architecture remained an interest of Lin's, so she took the competition on as a class assignment. She went to work and visited the site in Washington.

Lin said her idea was "first brought to shape in mashed potatoes at the dining hall," later calling it, "an earthwork."

"Walking through this park-like area," she wrote of her proposed design, "the memorial appears as a rift in the earth—a long, polished black stone wall, emerging from and receding into the earth. Approaching the memorial, the ground slopes gently downward, and the low walls emerging on either side, growing out of the earth, extend and converge at a point below and ahead. Walking into the grassy site contained by the walls of this memorial we can barely make out the carved names upon the memorial's walls. These names, seemingly infinite in number, convey the sense of overwhelming numbers, while unifying these individuals into a whole."

It was reminiscent of the burial mounds she knew from Ohio. "I imagined taking a knife and cutting into the earth, opening it up, an initial violence and pain that in time would heal. The grass would grow back, but the initial cut would remain a pure flat surface in the earth with a polished, mirrored surface, much like the surface on a geode when you cut it and polish the edge . . . it would be an interface, between our world and the quieter, darker, more peaceful world beyond." She knew nothing of the alignments Bob and Ray were discovering that same year, but her design of the long V-shaped walls included alignments of her own: one to the Lincoln Memorial, the other to the Washington Monument.

It was a blind competition, so entries were assigned numbers and the designer's names hidden. Hers was one of fourteen hundred.

In 1981 she received a call. Representatives from the design competition wanted to meet with her. She assumed she was one of many selected for meetings and that they would discuss mundane details, things like drainage. On a spring day in 1981, three officers representing the Vietnam Veterans Memorial Fund, arrived in New Haven, entered Lin's Yale dorm room and sat down. Lin, five-foot-three, black hair down to her knees, listened as the officers calmly informed her that she had won the competition.[3] "Competition entry No. 1026" was, in fact, the jurors' unanimous choice. The jury said

3. Lin, "Making the Memorial."

FIGURE 13.1. Maya Lin, influenced by Ohio's ancient earthworks, said of her design of the Vietnam Veterans Memorial in Washington: "I imagined taking a knife and cutting into the earth." Library of Congress, Prints & Photographs Division, photograph by Carol M. Highsmith (LC-DIG-highsm-04921).

her work "created an eloquent place where the simple meeting of earth, sky, and remembered names contains messages for all who will know this place."

The aftermath of the design selection is well known. It did not sit well in Washington, DC. How did it happen that a young Asian American college student was the designer of a national memorial to soldiers killed in Southeast Asia? A leader among the veteran critics compared her design to an "open urinal." Ross Perot, a financial supporter of the memorial who later ran for president, fought vigorously to stop it. He was joined by leading Republican Congressman Henry Hyde, novelist Tom Wolfe, conservative leaders Pat Buchanan and Phyllis Schlafly, and many more.[4] But the aftermath of its completion and dedication is also well known. It's now a beloved and sacred place. Visitors routinely shed tears, and hesitant hands reach to gently touch names. People leave things. A Purple Heart. A postcard the soldier sent home. Army boots. A care package with cookies and Kool-Aid, returned to the sender, marked KIA. A mom left her son's baby sweater.

4. Menand, "Maya Lin."

Lin has gone on to have a stellar career as a creator of landscape art, one of which in Sweden bears an intentional likeness to Ohio's ancient Serpent Mound. Of that design, Lin wrote, "When European settlers first encountered the ancient midwestern effigy and burial mounds of Hopewell and Adena tribes, they were convinced that the forebears of the present-day Native Americans could not have been sophisticated enough to produce them. They conjectured that a more advanced culture from Europe had visited the Americas much earlier and created the works. Perhaps it was that early history and false assumption about the origins of these works that drew me to create a piece that links Europe and North America. The early burial mounds of both places have a formal similarity that was of great interest to me."

"I am very drawn to landscape," she said on another occasion, "and my work is about finding a balance in the landscape, respecting nature, not trying to dominate it."

Further echoing a Native American hungering for harmony with nature, she said, "All of my work is about slipping things in, inserting an order or a structuring, yet making an interface so that in the end, rather than a hierarchy, there is a balance and a tension between the man-made and the natural."[5]

People thought a twenty-one-year-old daughter of Chinese immigrants could not create so perfect a symbol of American valor and loss, just as some still question Native authorship of the earthworks.

Maya Lin wasn't alone among modern landscape artists in being inspired by Ohio's mounds. Herbert Bayer's *Earth Mound,* a 1954 landscape art installation in Aspen, Colorado, looks barely distinguishable from any of hundreds of Hopewell small circular enclosures in Ohio. Yet it is modern art, by a leader of the Bauhaus movement. Bayer's work is considered quite influential among modern land artists, but I was taken somewhat aback when I saw on the Cultural Landscape Foundation's website that his *Earth Mound* "is considered by many to be the first instance on record of landscape as sculpture." Forgive the writer; perhaps the intent was to say, "first *modern* instance."

If the modern era of land art had defining moments, one would probably be 1968 when the Dwan Gallery in New York held an exhibition called "Earth Works." Another came the following year when the exhibit "Earth Art" was held at the Andrew Dickson White Museum of Art at Cornell University. Also

5. Wiles, "Maya Ying Lin."

in 1968 three young artists collaborated on a film about a journey they took together to Mono Lake in California, an otherworldly, ancient lake with limestone pillars. They were Robert Smithson, Nancy Holt, and Michael Heizer. Afterwards, working separately or together, they helped change the landscape of modern art in a quite literal way. The ancient Ohio influence is unmistakable with all three. They show you just how *modern* ancient art can be.

Robert Smithson is among the greats in the modern era of land art, and you may know his *Spiral Jetty,* an arrangement of black basalt rocks that extends 1,500 feet out into the Great Salt Lake of Utah. Built in 1970, the work was inspired by Serpent Mound, and you can see that when you look at the ancient work's spiral tail.[6] Before he died at age thirty-five in the crash of a plane he was using to survey one of his other earthworks, Smithson married Nancy Holt, who became noteworthy in her own right. Nancy Holt's *Sun Tunnels,* installed between 1973 and 1976 in Utah's Great Basin Desert, are not mounds, but concrete cylinders that align to the summer and winter solstices. Sunlight and moonlight streaming through holes in the sides of the cylinders create patterns matching four constellations. Her *Up and Under* in Finland is a snake-shaped earthen mound with horizontal tunnels that align with the North Star. Round pools of water remind one of the Hopewell pools that some believe connected spiritually to the underworld. Holt died in 2014, but New Yorkers hope to build her proposed *Sky Mound* on a reclaimed landfill four miles from Manhattan. Along with mounds arranged in a geometric pattern, *Sky Mound* would feature gravel paths aligning to solstices, a pond, and a concrete sphere representing the moon.[7]

Among Native-inspired living land artists still working today, none achieve the scale of Michael Heizer. "Since the late '60s," wrote Klaus Kertess in *ArtForum* magazine, "Michael Heizer has pushed Modernism toward the ancient builders of megaliths and carvers of the earth's surface—simultaneously backward and forward." In the 1980s, at Buffalo Rock State Park in Illinois, he brought bulldozers to an abandoned coal strip mine and created *Effigy Tumuli,* which Kertess said, "is specifically engaged with the much-neglected earth mounds left by Indians throughout the Midwest and Southeast—many of them circular, oval, conical, or, especially along the lower Mississippi, roughly pyramidal burial structures," as well as effigies of animals. There, on a bluff above the Illinois River, now reside a 770-foot-long catfish, a 140-foot-long frog, and a 2,070-foot-long snake. There's also a

6. Golbert, "Face of the Earth."
7. Holt/Smithson Foundation, "Artworks of Nancy Holt."

similarly large water strider and turtle. Like ancient effigies, these are horizontal bas reliefs, hard to make out at eye-level but readily recognizable from the air.

As big as they are, Heizer's Illinois earthworks are modest compared to his *City*. Constructed over fifty years in a Nevada desert, an hour's drive from the nearest blacktop road, it is a mile-and-a-half-long and half-a-mile wide area of sculpted mounds, embankments, walls, depressions, and concrete geometric shapes. Only six visitors are allowed per day. Heizer wants it to be experienced on foot as a relatively solitary engagement. His work "is inspired by Native American traditions of mound building and pre-Columbian ritual cities of Central and South America," according to Gagosian, the Los Angeles gallery that represents his works. I've never been to *City*, but I suspect that walking it will bear some similarity to a walk through Newark's Octagon or Great Circle.

⊕

As the art world has taken ancient mound building into the modern era, so too have new generations of archaeologists taken recent learnings from Ohio to new places. Did other Native cultures show similar astronomical sophistication before the European encounter or was that a skill honed along the Scioto River, then forgotten? What traces of Hopewell culture are still to be discovered?

Jarrod Burks, whose early career included collaboration with N'omi Greber, is now a leading practitioner in the use of new technologies to find traces of the past. LIDAR, satellites, magnetometry, ground-penetrating radar—he uses them all, and the technologies continue to improve. Much of what we know of Ohio's earthworks comes from the simple process of going back to the nineteenth-century surveyors like Squier and Davis and looking at the places they mapped for us. But what if the only things they mapped were what they knew about or could easily travel to? As it turns out, they missed a lot.

In the early 2000s, the daughter of an aging landowner happened to notice survey work happening at an archaeological site called the Junction Earthworks. The site was near an area where residential development was quickly sprawling outward from the edges of Chillicothe, and the daughter and her siblings, whose mother had died, were contemplating the future of their property. She contacted the state's historic preservation office and asked about the man doing the survey work. They had an "Indian ring" on their land, the daughter said, and wondered if the surveyor would be interested in seeing if anything more of archaeological interest might be on their property.

"It was the first time I'd ever had anyone call me and invite me to survey at their property," said Burks. "I knew she had an earthworks site on her property." In the 1840s, Squier and Davis had noted two there on a map of the larger Chillicothe area, but they did not show them in any detail. Burks had only a handheld magnetometer and these sites are routinely much too large to make a complete survey. But he promised the daughter he would follow up.

Sometime later he was working on an aerial survey on an unrelated property and asked his helicopter pilot to fly over the daughter's farm. It was June and winter wheat was maturing.

"That's the perfect time to take aerial photographs on farm fields if you want to look for earthworks. The wheat everywhere but the earthworks is turning yellow, but where the ditches are, it's usually still green because it's wet there and so the wheat is still growing, it's not drying out yet. I could see the two that Squier and Davis had mapped and I could already see that one of them wasn't a circle. One of them was a different shape. So we had already changed the Squier and Davis map in twenty seconds."

At that point the helicopter pilot was running low on fuel. "So I just took three photos as we were sort of turned over the site. And when I got home I opened up the files and was looking at them and it was like, wow I see some obvious other enclosures there in the weeds and then some possible ones too that were a little more subtle."[8]

He returned with magnetometer equipment that spots soil disturbances and found several more enclosures, including one or two with unusual shapes, and postholes arranged in a circle, what archaeologists call a "woodhenge." In all, Burks discovered the site had eleven enclosures, making it the highest concentration of small earthworks ever found in Ohio until that time.[9] That site, known as the Steel Earthworks, was combined with the previously discovered Junction Earthworks, and conserved with the help of private and state funds and the Arc of Appalachia, a privately funded conservancy.

Southern Ohio, it seems, might be one of the world's vastest palimpsests, acres of land like medieval parchment scraped clean to be reused, but not irrevocably erased, images and shapes secreted just under the top layers.

8. Jarrod Burks and Alan Tonetti, interviewed together by the author, May 20, 2024.

9. Archaeological Conservancy, "Preserving Steel Earthworks."

Al Tonetti, a retired state archaeologist, has worked with Burks and others to search for and conserve more places like the Steel site. It is hardly unusual for them to find similar earthworks where none were previously mapped, and they can only look on private land where owners are willing to allow them. He and Burks told me of a golf course in the Columbus area that has a well-preserved and identified "Adena sacred circle." Aerial LIDAR data showed strong evidence of another one on a nearby fairway. But the country club declined an initial request to do a ground survey of the site. Perhaps, the experience of the Moundbuilders Country Club told them what trouble mounds bring.

Tonetti is now a leading figure behind the Heartland Earthworks Conservancy, a nonprofit group dedicated to finding and preserving such earthworks. There's a growing appreciation for Ohio's Indigenous heritage, and people are willing to donate money and volunteer to preserve it. But it is a race against time. Tonetti and Burks believe there are many thousands of undiscovered earthwork sites, but the open spaces and riverfront properties that are ripe for exploration are too rapidly being developed in ways that destroy evidence of the past.

"The biggest threats are sand and gravel mining and construction of data centers and solar farms," said Tonetti. "Columbus is now the fourteenth largest city in the United States, and it's growing in all directions, especially to the east where the Intel microchip factory is being built. That's another huge [development]—thousands and thousands of acres. And none of the archaeology that's being done out there, at least as far as I know, is using geophysics to identify not just earthwork sites but any kind of archaeological site."

I asked a spokesperson for Intel whether they planned to use technologies such as magnetometry, ground penetrating radar, and LIDAR to identify archaeological remains at their construction sites. In a statement emailed to me the company said it is committed "to cultural preservation at all our sites," adding, "we comply with all local, state, and federal regulations regarding archaeological preservation at the site." They said they are working continuously with the Ohio History Connection and wish to "meet all requirements." Left unsaid was a commitment to use the best technology available. Not all that is required is enough to save the past.

As Tonetti said, "There's all sorts of archaeological sites out there that you'd never find unless you're using the magnetometry and ground-penetrating radar and other forms of modern instrumentation to detect these things."

⊕

And within and beyond Ohio, there is more being discovered at other archaeological sites. Prior to Ray and Bob's discoveries, Indigenous North American lunar astronomy was practically unheard of. Since then, scientists have found more evidence.

About five years after Ray and Bob's first paper about Newark, a University of Colorado Boulder astrophysicist named J. McKim Malville began a similar investigation of archaeoastronomy at Chimney Rock, a Chaco cultural site in Southern Colorado. He theorized that an observer standing at the site's nine-hundred-year-old Great House Pueblo would be perfectly positioned to watch the moon rise at its northernmost standstill, framed precisely between two monolithic, natural pillars of rock. The pueblo itself was built of timbers with visible tree rings where it was cut down, allowing him to date the structure's construction in two phases, one in 1076 CE, the other in 1093 CE, both of which fall within years in which the moon was making its northernmost standstill. Malville proved his alignment hypothesis right when, in August 1988, he stood at the Great Pueblo and watched what must be one of the most spectacular lunar standstill views in all of archaeoastronomy. There are those who say it's a coincidental alignment, but as Anna Sofaer and others have shown, Chaco Canyon holds evidence of other such astronomical knowledge by the same people in the same era.[10]

Back in the Midwest, working in the early 2000s, was Dr. Timothy Pauketat, the archaeologist and anthropologist at the University of Illinois, a leader among scientists investigating Mississippian cultural sites in the Cahokia area of Illinois, across the Mississippi River from St. Louis. The Chacoan culture was thriving almost one thousand miles away, but something strangely similar was happening in the same eleventh century timeframe in Cahokia. Monks Mound, a giant, flat-top, pyramidal earthwork, is the largest and most prominent ancient feature of this, the largest pre-Columbian Native American site in North America. Pauketat took particular interest in a smaller site fifteen miles east of Monks Mound, a place he calls the Emerald Acropolis. It is an earthwork that, like its Athenian counterpart, is set on a natural hilltop, a setting all the more dramatic because the surrounding farmland is so flat.

It turns out that the platform mound on the hill and conical mounds at a lower elevation together form a line pointing northeast 53 degrees, where the

10. Malville, "Chimney Rock," 20–28.

moon rises at its 18.6-year northern extreme. That is, it points within about a degree of the direction of the Newark Octagon. Just as interesting are the remains of smaller buildings there and at the nearby Pfeffer Site. These small pole-and-thatch structures might have been places for prayer or temporary shelter for pilgrims. They show signs of being built, torn down, then rebuilt a few years later to realign by a few degrees in another direction. One direction points to the north maximum moonrise, the other rebuilt shelter to the north minimum. Pauketat speculates that the building and rebuilding might be separated by nine-year intervals, the time between minimum and maximum moonrises. One building he found most convincing as evidence of lunar alignments was found to be pointing to the lunar minimum alignment, but in its floor was a trench aligned to the maximum standstill. Inside the trench was evidence of rituals and offerings of objects such as flint blades and spear heads.

Structures in the Cahokia area around Monks Mound, by contrast, do not seem to align so much to lunar events. Structures there do however commonly point in the same direction—5 degrees east of due north. The intent is unclear but might have been to frame a view of the Milky Way at a time when the moon appeared to pass through it.[11] Other Cahokian sites, such as Angel Mound in Southwest Indiana,[12] and another far up the Mississippi River near Trempealeau, Wisconsin, also seem to point ancient viewers to the moon. Like the Emerald Acropolis, Angel Mound has numerous small structures aligning with a central monumental axis that points to the moon, and a paper about it published in 2021 nods to the work of Ray Hively and Bob Horn.[13]

Pauketat speculates that it's more than coincidental that built homages to moonrises were happening at Chaco and Cahokia at the same time. He believes it's possible there was cultural interchange and pilgrimages between the two sites. Though he hasn't found artifact evidence, he thinks the timing and the lunar constructions are evidence enough to suggest connections.[14]

Pauketat noted that the moon still has cultural significance for Native people today, "But knowledge of the long lunar cycle was lost, probably somewhere in the 13- or 1400s. Maybe not lost, but put away. So you don't see these lunar alignments in major ceremonial sites after that time." Long-cycle

11. Pauketat, "Lunar Twins."
12. Pauketat, *Archaeology of the Cosmos*, 156–57.
13. Malouchos, "Mound to the Moon," 7–9.
14. Pauketat, "Lunar Twins."

moon ceremonies seem to disappear in both Chaco and Cahokian cultures at around the same point in history, he says, adding that dislocation of populations would change how you observe lunar movement, based on latitude. So a major movement of people could create an obstacle to preserving cultural traditions.

Sofaer at Chaco Canyon, Malville at Chimney Rock, Pauketat at Cahokia, Hively and Horn at Newark—the evidence of pointers to the moon and sun preponderates. For years, Anthony Aveni supported the research but doubted the conclusions. Going all the way back to that Earlham president's dinner with Ray, he remained stubbornly skeptical, waiting not for proof but something closer to it. By 2005 it was time to give in. "I have always been highly skeptical about lunar alignments," Aveni wrote, noting he found none in his vast work in Mesoamerica, nor had a colleague found any in Mediterranean tomb sites. "In the Hopewell case I give ground only grudgingly to Hively and Horn's conclusions regarding Newark."[15]

⊕

Even as others build on their work, Ray and Bob themselves are not to be counted out. Some months after I started interviewing them, Ray and Bob were at work on a new paper, published in 2023, a full forty-one years after their first paper about Newark. This time they looked at Hopewell achievements from multiple new angles.

Their ongoing search for Newark alignments to the sun took them to Wright Square, an earthwork once located more than a mile east of the Octagon, north of the Great Circle. Mostly gone now, nineteenth-century maps showed it was a prominent construction, connected to other earthworks not only by multiple walled pathways, but by important geometric relationships. The area of Wright Square closely matched the area of the circle adjacent to the Octagon. Its perimeter measure matched that of the Great Circle. This was known, but now, in their newest paper, Ray and Bob reported their "rediscovery" of Wright Square as a solstice observatory. They found that by standing on its north corner and looking southeast, the winter solstice sun rises with remarkable precision from directly behind the highest hilltop summit in the area, known as Coffman Knob. "It is as perfect an alignment as could be achieved," they wrote.

15. Aveni, "An Assessment of Studies in Hopewell Astronomy," 252.

Back at the Octagon, they found another new solstice view. Again, it relied not on alignments within the earthwork, but on a view outward to a nearby hilltop. Standing where the Octagon meets the avenue to the circle, an observer will see the summer solstice sun set directly over the closest hilltop, a feature they called H2, just eight-tenths of a mile away. "The spectacle of watching the sun set directly over this flat-topped overlook would have been riveting," they said. They found more solstice alignments too, but these two stood out.[16]

Their other 2023 findings returned to the topic of lunar alignments and here they tried a new way of imagining how humans first experienced the light of the moon in those places, and of the geometry of that experience, especially at Newark. They introduced the concept of "orthogonality," a word that describes the relationship between two lines perpendicular to one another, forming a "T" shape.

"The concept of orthogonality was the most fundamental principle of Hopewell geometry," said Ray. "They must have experimented for generations in developing the skill and technology for producing right angles of great precision on a monumental scale. All of their figures including squares, rectangles, and octagons can be formed using orthogonal structures."

Their earlier papers showed walls that pointed straight to moonrises and moonsets. What if the experience of the viewer had more to do with the nighttime play of moonlight and shadow on the walls of the octagon and circle? They realized that the shape of an octagon means that for every wall pointing to the moon, there are two other walls perpendicular to it. The perpendicular wall closest to the moonrise casts a long wide shadow inside the octagon, growing shorter as the moon rises. Likewise, the opposite wall interior becomes illuminated by the moonlight. At a lunar standstill, a pole erected along a wall perpendicular to the moonrise would throw a shadow at a near-perfect right angle. You could stand anywhere in the octagon and see the play of moonlight and shadow.

Finding those right angles to the moon recalled the very first exposure they had to Hopewell geometry decades earlier when they and their students were so intrigued to find at Fort Ancient a nearly perfect square formed by four distantly arranged small mounds. Those right angles continued to impress.

16. Hively, Horn, "Unification," 83–85.

The concept of orthogonality had another important implication that involves the illusion you get when you walk perpendicular to the direction of the moon and see it appear to "follow" you. Ray told me he and Bob had near identical childhood memories: "Bob said he had the same experience as a child when he was running through the woods and noticed that no matter where he was or how fast he ran, the moon didn't change its position relative to him. And he got the impression, as I did as a child, that the moon was following him, and it established a kind of personal connection."

In their paper, Ray and Bob departed from their lengthy discussion of angles, azimuths, and orthogonal lines to recount those childhood memories and note that in the Octagon, the following-moon illusion could have been an important part of the lunar standstill experience.

Covering no small amount of new ground, their 2023 paper went on to introduce yet another important astronomical element: the Milky Way. Scholars have found multiple examples, dating to the era before European contact, of Native American cultures that viewed the Milky Way as a "path of souls," guiding the journey into the afterlife. The Milky Way's presence in the sky was much more pronounced in the time before electricity, and its visibility lessens year by year as light pollution obscures it more. Ray found it startling that most of his students had never even seen the Milky Way. A group called the International Dark-Sky Association (now DarkSky International) was formed in 2001 to identify and preserve the beauty of the starlit sky, and has certified only about 200 "dark sky places" around the planet. What the ancients regularly experienced as a magical feature of the heavens is today all but lost to most of us.

Given the sacred place of the Milky Way in Native traditions, could the Hopewell have connected those star-views to their landscape art, as they did the moon and sun? A challenge to answering that question is the changing sky over millennia. The moon's transit over its longest cycle doesn't change its 18.6-year course much, but two thousand years ago the Milky Way's position in the sky was different. So Ray and Bob had to find its place in the Hopewell era sky. Using planetarium software on a computer, they traveled back in time to view the night sky over Newark in the year 100 CE.

The Milky Way paints a fuzzy but majestic band of light from horizon to horizon, drawing a rough line across the sky that is at its brightest and most impressive at its zenith, touching the horizon in one direction, then arcing across the sky, overhead, to touch another location on the opposite horizon. Those touch points move north and south with the seasons, making two extremes on one horizon and two on the other, like the sun's annual back-and-forth. When Ray and Bob compared the ancient position of the Milky Way to the transits of the moon they made another discovery. In 100 CE, all four extreme horizon touch points corresponded with surprising accuracy to the four major standstills of the moon. On clear, moonless nights in the spring or summer seasons of the Hopewell era, you could stand where the avenue enters the Octagon and see a truly glorious display of starlight aligned to the central axis of the Octagon, stretching from the same place the moon rises at its northern-most point at a major standstill, arcing overhead, and descending over the Observatory Mound, touching down near the spot of the moonset at its southern-most standstill. During the fall and winter months, the display shifted, and if you stood in the center of the Observatory Circle when the Milky Way was directly overhead you could see it reach from the place on the southeast horizon where the moon rises at its major southern standstill, stretching across the sky until it reaches the opposite spot on the horizon, to the northwest, where the major northern standstill moon sets. So on moonless nights, the star display would be both spectacular and a regular reminder of those momentous times to come, and the path the moon will take, when it returns for its greatest displays every 18.6 years.

As recently as 2025, Ray and Bob were at work on one of their boldest propositions yet. They looked anew at the geography of the area transited by Lepper's hypothesized Great Hopewell Road, with Newark at the north end, and High Bank Works to the south, near Chillicothe, almost sixty miles away. High Bank was a site that they earlier found aligns with extraordinary precision to two other earthworks along a six-mile stretch of the Scioto River, by itself a major feat of large-scale planning. Now they considered whether Newark might align to other works over even greater distances. Ignoring, for the moment, the path taken by the Great Hopewell Road, they instead drew straight lines on a map, as a crow flies, from the center of the Observatory Circle at Newark to the center of the circle at High Bank, fifty-eight miles away. Then they drew lines from Newark to the centers of corresponding circles at other Scioto River Valley earthworks.

Three lines stood out. Not physical lines on the ground, of course, but lines Ray and Bob drew on a map. For reasons we may never know, three lines had inexplicable but undeniably geometric relationships to astronomy. That is to say, orthogonal relationships. A forty-one-mile line drawn straight from Newark to Circleville was perpendicular to a line pointing to the major

FIGURE 13.2. An artist's view of the Milky Way above the Newark Octagon in the year 100 CE, an alignment described in a 2023 paper by Hively and Horn. The illustration, not drawn to scale, is by Betsy Wallin.

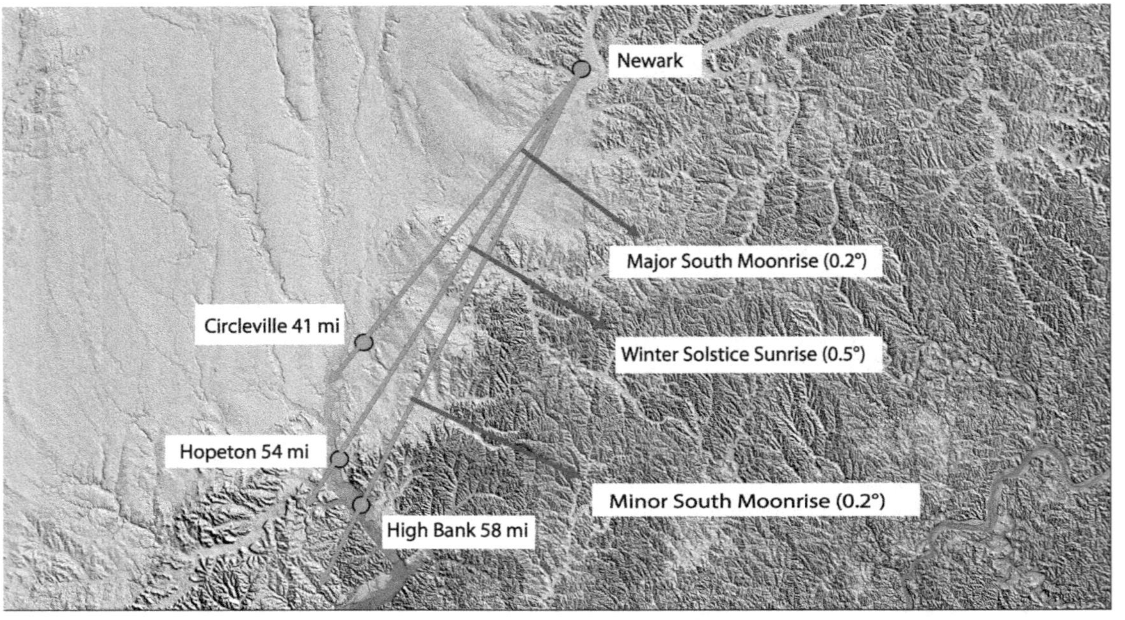

FIGURE 13.3. In 2025, Ray and Bob offered an as yet unpublished hypothesis that lines between Newark and three earthworks may have been intentionally designed to align orthogonally to the three extreme southern rise points associated with the sun and moon. Margins of error are shown in parentheses. Illustration by Ray Hively.

south moonrise, to within two-tenths of a degree. A fifty-four-mile line drawn straight between the Newark and Hopeton Earthworks is perpendicular to the winter solstice sunrise, to within half a degree. A fifty-eight-mile-long line to High Bank was perpendicular to the minor south moonrise, within two-tenths of a degree. "All three extreme southern rise points associated with the sun and moon are orthogonally aligned," said Ray. It was already known that the four earthworks involved were connected in another way too: all had circles of 1,054 feet in diameter, although Hopeton's is slightly smaller, and each is paired to an octagon or square.

"The startling nature of this hypothesis is twofold," he explained. First, "it suggests that all four earthworks were conceived together as part of a regional plan extending about 60 miles from Newark." Second, "that Hopewell designers and builders could successfully survey and extend straight lines over sometimes rugged terrain for up to fifty-eight miles."

I found it hard to wrap my head around this one. Why would they build something like that? What's the point? Could it all be coincidental? It's a massive connecting of dots that seems too good to be true. And yet, that is the data that Ray and Bob found.

Asked why the people of the Hopewell era might build something of a scale dwarfing other ancient monumental works, Ray told me he "speculates that Hopewell observers and architects believed that they might succeed in connecting with the celestial powers represented by the sun and moon by imprinting their knowledge of their motions on an even larger scale than that of Newark alone."

Some months earlier, when they wrote of that Hopewell masterwork at Newark, they made a similar interpretation: "Their plan to construct these earthworks on a scale where their geometrical and astronomical knowledge was only visible to the celestial beings traveling high above the valley floor is poignant evidence of their probable purpose. We believe the architects were attempting to connect and communicate with the Upper World and the ever moving 'gods' in that world. The combination of scale, precision, and sophistication of their achievement has no known peer anywhere in the prehistoric world. It is gratifying and instructive to recognize that a culture that has been so long ignored and underestimated did achieve such a wonderful and inspiring feat."[17]

Were the Hopewell constructions intended for what ancient people believed were "celestial beings traveling high above"? Or was it, as others speculate, a desire to bring order to chaos, to harmonize with the heavens above and the soil underfoot. Was it a conceptualization or metaphor for timeless creation? Maybe it was all of the above. Hively and Horn always cautioned against speculation in the absence of hard data, but they also understood that in order to demonstrate intent one must find motive.

In late 2025 Ray and Bob learned that the *Journal of Skyscape Archaeology* had accepted some of their newest findings for publication. They regard the journal as one of the world's most respected in the field. It was a level of validation that had been eluding them for more than forty years.

⊕

As artists, archaeologists, and astronomers usher us into a new era of Hopewell understanding, other disciplines are joining the exploration in fascinating ways. One of them is a rethinking of American history from an Indigenous perspective, yielding new ways to think about the origins of democracy and the so-called "rise of civilization." It isn't enough to call out the racism rooted in the old notion that Indigenous cultures are less

17. Hively and Horn, "More Topography," 42.

"civilized." We need to think about Indigenous social organization and ask ourselves what else we can learn from ancient and contemporary Native Americans. What does the word "civilized" mean, and how does it demean?

The people of the Hopewell culture built their monuments, lived healthy and peaceful lives, and invented new forms of artistic expression, all without an apparent central authority as we know it. What does that tell us about our "civilization"? What does it mean to say society "evolved," and if it did evolve, was it all for the better? What can be learned about giant collective accomplishment by people living independently in small hamlets scattered across surrounding forests? Is a "city" a prerequisite for civic achievement? Asked about the Hopewell life in disbursed hamlets, Shawnee Chief Ben Barnes encouraged me to think in a different way about the idea of "city."

"We're basing it on a paradigm of our understanding of what a city is," he said. "You don't ask blackberries on a vine if they're fruit, just because they don't clump like grapes. So these berries, those little communities, are scattered out for a reason: to not tax the resources of the lands. So maybe they were these interconnected civic organisms. We just don't understand them as cities in the way we understand cities today."

David Graeber and David Wengrow also tried to shift the paradigm in their influential 2021 book with a title that was, to say the least, ambitious: *The Dawn of Everything: A New History of Humanity.*

Graeber, who died in 2020, was a professor of anthropology at the London School of Economics, known in part for his association with the Occupy Wall Street movement. Wengrow, an archaeologist, had positions at the Institute of Archaeology at University College London and at New York University. I would not do their sprawling narrative justice by trying to distill it here, but one thing it does is ask us to rethink our preconceptions about cultural advancement. Does society really improve and advance in a linear fashion, moving over time from primitive to advanced? They critiqued mid-twentieth-century "neo-evolutionists" who "argued for the existence of discrete stages of political organization successively: bands, tribes, chiefdoms, states—and held that the stages of political development mapped, at least very roughly, on to similar stages of economic development: hunter-gatherers, gardeners, farmers, industrial civilization."[18] Should we not think instead of human history as a long period of experimentation with different forms of social

18. Graeber and Wengrow, *The Dawn of Everything,* 109–10.

organization, some of which worked very well even if they did not survive intact? As an example, they point to ancient cultures that tried agriculture, tried hierarchical social structures, then abandoned them, and lived happily in their absences. If the landscape was full of food to gather and fauna to hunt, why centralize around big farms and be dependent on others' systems of food distribution? Who needs central authority when small groups of people are independently doing just fine? Perhaps, Graeber and Wengrow argue, those social structures that seemed primitive were actually more civilized than ours. Maybe there is much to learn from the people of the Hopewell era.

The authors describe the fading of the Hopewell culture after 400 CE and the rise of the Mississippian, centralized around Cahokia, after 800 CE. Cahokians were a hierarchical society that pulled its population into city centers, developed agriculture, and ruled with violent authority. Graeber and Wengrow say it appears that people eventually rejected such authoritarian rule, either by open revolt or by simply walking away, and the Native cultures that emerged afterwards largely reverted to decentralized tribes and clans, and a form of rule by the consent of the governed. That oversimplifies of course. But they also argue that as Europeans arrived and were exposed to the freedoms enjoyed by Native peoples, liberated from kings and unjust laws, it helped spark the Enlightenment in Europe, leading eventually to new conceptions of how people might be governed. They point to a seventeenth century Wyandotte chief named Kondiaronk, a gifted orator and critic of European society, who traveled to Europe, visited the salons of intellectuals, and gained wide influence through writings based on his dialogues. The European Enlightenment then came full circle and influenced thinkers and revolutionaries in the American colonies, even if they did not fully appreciate the Indigenous origin of the democratic institutions they would create after 1776.

And so, Graeber and Wengrow see the Hopewell as part of an Indigenous American continuum in which societies are organized by consensus. The Hopewell culture had wide influence across the continent, attracting cultural pilgrimages and offerings from afar. Perhaps their influence involved more than just knowledge of the heavens and geometry. Perhaps they modeled a more democratic society, too, and all it could accomplish.

These authors connect Hopewell success to both democracy and pluralism. "The unity of Hopewell lay in the celebration of difference. To take one example: while later North American societies would distinguish entire clans and nations by characteristic hairstyles (so it was a simple matter to distinguish a Seneca, Onondaga, or Mohawk warrior at a distance), it is difficult to find two figures in Hopewell art—and there are quite a few of them—that have the same hair. Everybody appears to have been free to make a spectacle of themselves, or to obtain some dramatic role in the theatre of society, and this individual expressiveness was reflected in miniature depictions of people sporting what seem to be an endless variety of playful, idiosyncratic styles of haircut, clothing and ornamentation."[19]

Graeber and Wengrow found elsewhere in the world other cultures—like the Minoan Crete in the Mediterranean—that modeled similarly enviable lifestyles. In their concluding paragraphs, Graeber and Wengrow wrote, "Perhaps if our species does endure, and we one day look backwards from this as yet unknowable future, aspects of the remote past that now seem like anomalies—say bureaucracies that work on a community scale; cities governed by neighborhood councils; systems of government where women hold a preponderance of formal positions; or forms of land management based on care-taking rather than ownership and extraction—will seem like the really significant breakthroughs, and great stone pyramids or statues more like historical curiosities. What if we were to take that approach now and look at, say, Minoan Crete or Hopewell not as random bumps on a road that leads inexorably to states and empires, but as alternative possibilities: roads not taken?"[20]

And perhaps we can now look at Native American traditions of self-governance as echoes from an ancient Hopewell past, like water drums, carried across generations to the Indigenous cultures that the colonialist Europeans encountered, emulated and then tried to extinguish. The Iroquois Confederacy, it turns out, influenced the founding fathers of these United States, though the extent of that influence is open to debate. Perhaps the Iroquois were an echo of a Hopewell past. Perhaps the Hopewell are among our modern democracy's distant forebearers? The men who gathered in Philadelphia to form a democratic government were influenced by the Greeks and Romans, to be sure. But some say they also appropriated, without attribution, from Indigenous traditions. Perhaps the people of Hopewell and the tribes that followed are Founding Fathers too. And Mothers.

⊕

19. Graeber and Wengrow, *The Dawn of Everything*, 462–63.

20. Graeber and Wengrow, *The Dawn of Everything*, 523–24.

More reasons to think anew about words like "primitive" and "civilized." "Prehistoric" and "literate." The invention of writing, as Western people think of it, becomes an artificial dividing line. We call people preliterate if they had no alphabet, as the West thinks of it. But wasn't the geometry, design and abstract knowledge imparted in Ohio's earthworks, written as it was on the land, a form of writing, writ large? Couldn't the Indigenous unwritten knowledge handed down to Franklin and Jefferson bear a kinship to seminal writings like the *Magna Carta*?

In his essay, "Devine Blindness," N. Scott Momaday, the Kiowa writer, said, "In America there is something else, a continuum of language that goes back thousands of years before the printing press—back to the times of origin—an indigenous expression, an utterance that proceeds from the very intelligence of the soil: the oral tradition."[21]

Through her writings and documentaries like "Written on the Landscape," Anna Sofaer sees how much is communicated through abstract symbols across the desert floor of Chaco Canyon. She told me, "Generally the establishing, paradigm-setting academia does not look with respect at those people without writing, pre-writing, or non-literate people, because it's a different kind of ontology. It's a different kind of relationship with the landscape and the sky . . . [academia doesn't] take the time or the willingness to enter another Gestalt, another way of looking at the world. And I think I've given up even caring about it as a serious debate. And I think Horn and Hively have too, which is really smart. Show it! Show what's there! Share it with the people who understand it, and try to bring it out as much as you can in science and in film or any other exhibit where you can. I think's it's glorious what [Hively and Horn] achieved in doing that."[22]

⊕

Slowly, there is growing appreciation of not just the intelligence but the sacredness of Indigenous monuments and burial sites. In the 1990s, my old boss, Illinois Governor Jim Edgar, working with representatives of various tribal nations, closed a museum display of Native American unearthed skeletons, in situ, at Dickson Mounds, associated with the Mississippian culture. That happened shortly after Congress enacted the Native American Graves Protection and Repatriation Act, which was a start, but still has not achieved

21. Momaday, "A Devine Blindness," 84–85.

22. Sofaer, interview with author.

FIGURE 13.4. In Jacksontown, Ohio, south of Newark, Fairmount Church and its graveyard surround and protect an ancient Native burial mound. Photo by James W. Graham.

its goals of gaining for Indigenous Americans the dignity and respect that Native burial sites deserve.

To truly take hold, the change will have to extend beyond museums and into rural areas, like the ones in Ohio where so much remains to be found and preserved. Fairmount Presbyterian Church is about six miles south of the Newark Octagon on the outskirts of Jacksontown, population 402, named for President Andrew Jackson. In 2010 the congregation invited the Native American Indian Center of Central Ohio to come to their church and help guide them through a religious ceremony they wouldn't be able to do very well without help. It was a hot July day when sixty people gathered. In 1833, the church was built right next to a large burial mound that is either Hopewell or Adena, which puts its origin pretty much shortly before or after the birth of the Man the church celebrates. The mound is eighty feet across and reaches about as high as the small church's rain gutters, and when I visited in 2024 I could find no historical marker. Driving by you might think the mound is nothing more than a debris pile. But the congregation, to its credit, preserved it, and for almost two hundred years has buried its own loved ones in a graveyard surrounding the burial mound. And now church and mound stand tall above the surrounding gravestones of early settlers and more modern arrivals. There are other churches and cemeteries where the same phenomenon occurred, settler burials joined to ancient Native ones. Working on this story, I was surprised to discover that my own father is buried a short walk from a Native burial mound adjacent to Oakwood Cemetery in Joliet, Illinois, although most visitors do not know the mound is there. Vandals removed its historical markers, so now bare metal stands convey only that yet another narrative of Indigenous history has been robbed.

Back in Jacksontown, in 2010, the church asked Mark Welsch, a local Native leader of Dakota heritage, to lead them in a "re-blessing" of the mound. The ceremony "concluded with participants creating a prayer circle around the mound and offering individual prayers in turn," according to the local newspaper, *The Buckeye Lake Beacon*. "Following the ceremony, participants had a potluck dinner featuring Native American foods."[23]

23. *Buckeye Lake Beacon*, "Mound Re-blessed."

CHAPTER 14

World Heritage

Beneath the pinholed heaven, the night was God-dimensioned and monumental before electric light.
—Niall Williams, *This Is Happiness*

On a Saturday morning in late June 2002, Barbara Crandell, a woman claiming Cherokee ancestry, decided to visit the Observatory Mound at the Newark Octagon. She was seventy-three years old, with twelve grandchildren, and had snow white hair, which she wore in a single long braid. In a small town just south of Newark, her family raised horses for harness racing. She needed a cane, so it wasn't easy climbing the side of the mound, there by the tenth hole. She had visited before and prayed on the mound, once for a son who was sick in a nearby hospital, another time for people out West afflicted by wildfires. Moundbuilders County Club didn't allow the public on that or any other mound, saying they might get hit by a stray ball. There was an elevated wooden platform installed for visitors nearby at a safer distance from hard-hit golf balls, but Crandell didn't like it. "When I go there to pray, I need to touch the earth," she said.[1]

Two golfers told her to leave. She ignored them. Club President Skip Salome, alerted to the intruder, walked over to tell Crandell she wasn't allowed on the property. She ignored him too, so a short time later Salome returned with two police officers. Sharp words were exchanged about who did and did not belong there. According to the local newspaper, "After arguing with Salome and the officers, Crandell threw her cane at Salome when she feared she was in danger but did not strike him. Salome said he was struck on his leg by the cane."[2] Crandell was arrested and charged with fourth-degree misdemeanor disorderly conduct and criminal trespassing.

1. Associated Press, "Woman arrested," 7.
2. DeMauro, "Cherokee wants trial," 1.

Despite the presence of police who saw everything, she pleaded innocent and would not wave her right to a jury trial. She wasn't going to make this easy. After a full day of testimony, a jury of eight found her guilty of criminal trespassing and the judge fined her $250 plus court costs, a total of more than $800. "I'm not going to pay a dime," she told the judge. She preferred jail.

A local group called "Friends of the Mounds" came to the rescue. The incident was widely publicized and donations flowed in from across the country, so Friends of the Mounds paid her fine for her, much of it in Sacagawea dollar coins.

Friends of the Mounds was founded two years earlier by Richard Shiels, Brad Lepper, and Jeff Gills. Shiels called Barbara Crandell "the Rosa Parks of the Newark Earthworks,"[3] and, like Parks, Crandell put a sympathetic public face on those who take no back seat to country club golfers when it comes to transiting the sacred ground at Newark. What first got the Friends of the Mounds agitated and organized was the country club's earlier plan to disturb if not wreck portions of the archeological site in order to build a new clubhouse. The Friends stopped that project but didn't stop there. Next they pushed for expanded public access, with the ultimate aim of removing the golf course entirely. Three months before the Crandall arrest, the country club tried to appease adversaries by ever-so-slightly loosening its rules, saying it would periodically crack open the door to public visits. They would grant public access four times a year on days of their choosing. Of course, the days chosen were not conducive to travelers, two of them falling on Mondays, when weekly lawn maintenance restricted golfing anyway.

That public access was restricted at all is hard to understand, given that the Newark Earthworks were and are owned by the nonprofit state historical society, entrusted by the state with caretaking responsibility on behalf of the people of Ohio. For vaguely understood reasons the society signed a 1998 renewal of its lease to the club, allowing the golf course to stay put until 2078. Shiels says the lease renewal was approved behind closed doors, with little discussion, on the recommendation of the historical society's staff.[4] During those years and afterward, Shiels, the Eastern Shawnee Chief Glenna Wallace and others pushed the historical society to better preserve and celebrate the cultural value of the earthworks. Shiels said it was hard enough to get phone

3. Shiels, "Shiels: Remembering."

4. Shiels, Dick, interview with author, July 12, 2021.

calls to the society returned, let alone formally make their case.[5] But in time the society's old guard was replaced and it even changed its name to something that sounded less at home on a dusty shelf. By 2014 the Ohio Historical Society was rebranded the "Ohio History Connection," and it wasn't just window dressing.

In the meantime, except for four times a year, visitors could only see the earthworks by climbing the stairs of that short wooden viewing stand Crandell eschewed, or by walking a short asphalt path outside of the earthwork wall, one shared with golf carts. Access was somewhat easier during winter months and on Monday mornings.

Shiels found another way to do an end run around the country club. Along with fellow history professor Lucy Murphy he proposed the establishment of the Newark Earthworks Center at Ohio State University's Newark campus. When the Center launched in 2005, Shiels became its founding director. Soon, Friends of the Mounds, the Center, the Ohio History Connection, and others were at work on their boldest objective of all: they wanted Ohio's earthworks added to UNESCO's list of World Heritage Sites. At that time, only twenty US sites had made the list, places like Yellowstone, Mesa Verde, the Grand Canyon, and the Statue of Liberty. Cahokia and Chaco Canyon sites were added in 1982 and 1987. Now, they believed, it was Newark's turn.

But wait. A golf course? They expected UNESCO to recognize a golf course as a World Heritage Site? The first step was getting the US Department of Interior to agree to put their nomination forward, an effort begun in 2009. Shiels and others, working with the Ohio History Connection, believed that UNESCO World Heritage status would so shame the golfers that the country club would soon go away.

"We saw World Heritage as important but also as a way to remove the country club. We assumed we would get World Heritage and the world would come and want to see this site," Sheils said. That would force the issue of the country club.

The Department of Interior had a list of fifty-five US sites which it planned to winnow down in order to put forward the most credible nominees. "The Department of Interior put together a list of ten of them that it provided to UNESCO saying we would make our nomination from this list of ten," said Shiels. Ohio made the first cut. "Then the Department of Interior invited us to come to Washington periodically, and we got to know people from the

5. Gaitten, "Why the Ohio History Connection."

other sites. But they seemed to only be working with four or five sites, and the others all went forward and we were wondering 'why not us?'"

"To our surprise, when we met with people from the Department of Interior and asked, 'why are the others going forward, why are we not going forward?' their answer was 'we're not about to nominate you until the country club is gone.'" It was a matter of cart and horse.

That put pressure back on the Ohio History Connection to negotiate an end to golfing on the Octagon. They would need to use the state's eminent domain authority, not to seize the property because they already owned it, but rather to buy out the country club's lease. Negotiations over the buyout price dragged on for five years. At one point the golf club was pointing to a study that said it would cost $26 million to build a new course. Later, the Ohio History Connection said the value of the lease was $800,000.[6] The state took the country club to court in 2018, and the litigation dragged on for years, eventually landing before the state Supreme Court.

⊕

While the Newark properties were a state concern, other earthwork sites to the southwest, around Chillicothe, were a federal one. The Hopewell Culture National Historic Park, previously known as Mound City, occupied land that had once served as a US Army base. In 1923 the US Department of Interior designated it a National Monument, and in 1990 the park was expanded through the purchase of the nearby Hopeton Earthworks property. By 2001 more Chillicothe-area land was acquired to preserve remnants of geometric mounds around the enormous Seip burial mound, the Hopewell Mound Group property, and High Bank Works, that crucial second circle-octagon that resembled Newark's. Though some of the newly acquired National Park Service sites had suffered from farming and development, magnetometers and LIDAR provided valuable documentation of barely visible mound remnants and the locations of lost earthworks. Authorities began planting tall grasses and prairie flowers, sculpting the plantings in a process called "interpretive mowing," which leaves taller plants where the earthworks once stood. Visitors can thus visually imagine the grand geometry and scale of earthworks that once covered such wide acreage.

But none of them were as well preserved as the Newark Octagon and the Great Circle, a mile away. The Octagon needed the courts on its side.

6. Gaitten, "Why the Ohio History Connection."

⊕

Aside from putting an end to golf at the Octagon, Shiels had another objective: to better engage Native Americans in all aspects of the earthworks. Among the academicians, Shiels stood out as an advocate for the Native American perspective.

"I was part of a small group that wanted to find out what the Indians think," he said. "I was the guy pushing to work with Indians."

Indigenous Americans often showed up for tours of the Great Circle and of the Octagon when it was free of golfers. It was around the year 2020 that Shiels tagged along to help Jeff Gill lead his "remnants tour" through the side streets and alleys of the city of Newark, a walk that takes half a day, allowing plenty of time for conversation along the way. On this tour was a Native man of Dakota heritage, accompanied by two sons who looked to be in their twenties. With Gill leading the way, Shiels stuck close to the Dakota man and heard his story.

He told Shiels of his childhood on a North Dakota reservation. "He said he grew up believing that Indians are descended from 'savages,'" recalled Shiels, "Consequently, he had believed about himself that he was much less intelligent than people of other races."

He spoke to Shiels at some length about a meeting he had with his teachers in the weeks before high school graduation. They gave him a dose of "reality." Set your sights low, they told him. The life of a professional is not for you. He spent a lot of his life not expecting anything of himself, letting himself go physically and otherwise. But about fifteen years earlier, in 2005, something happened that changed his life. He attended the very first Newark Earthworks Day at the Ohio State campus. Shiels was stunned. The man had no idea he was talking to the person who was the principal organizer of that long-ago event, the one that was supposed to end with a viewing of a moonrise until the country club said the grass was too wet. The man also didn't recognize Jeff Gill as a speaker at that conference.

But otherwise, the man's recollection of what he learned was richly detailed. The geometry, the astronomy, the moon. Most of all, he said with a big smile, he learned "we were not savages." When he looked in a mirror, the man said, he saw someone different. He lost weight, took better care, and "changed the way I raised my sons."[7]

7. Shiels, "Shiels: The Life-changing potential."

Brad Lepper, who has given as many Hopewell tours as anyone, had a similar experience. Like Shiels, he too was interested in building more bridges to Native Americans. In the early 2020s, he gave a tour of the Great Circle and as his flock of followers disbursed, Lepper stuck around to spend more time with Brett Barnes, an elder in the Eastern Shawnee Tribe of Oklahoma. A pain from a back injury forced Barnes to use an electric scooter, so it was a surprise when he pushed himself up from his scooter and declared a need to say something. Instead of turning to Lepper to say it, he turned away and faced the mound in the center of the Great Circle—called Eagle Mound because of its shape. The words came out but they were in Shawnee. Lepper waited and wondered whether it was a prayer. No, Barnes explained, he was speaking to his ancestors. Lepper hesitated, then he asked what he had to say to them.

"We are still here," said the Shawnee elder.[8]

⊕

In 2019, Licking County Common Pleas Court Judge David Branstool issued a ruling. The Ohio History Connection could use the state's eminent domain authority to cancel the golf club's lease. The club had argued that it served public purposes as important as those pursued by the OHC, and that it had invested enormous sums to maintain the property over the decades. "Regardless of how long the Country Club has occupied the site," wrote Branstool, "or the number of fundraising events it hosts, its current use of the property as a private, members-only country club, contradicts its suggestion that it operates the site for a public purpose. . . . At the end of the day, one hundred years of manicured lawns does not immunize the Country Club from eminent domain to restore public access to a site of prehistoric earthworks."[9] He told the parties to settle on a fair amount to compensate for the broken lease. But the country club wasn't giving up; they took it to the Ohio Supreme Court.

It took three more years, but in 2022 the high court ruled. "The Newark Earthworks are the largest remaining complex of earthworks in the world," noted Justice Michael P. Donnelly. "These earthworks were built at the dawn of the Common Era using little more than sticks and deer bones but with a sophisticated understanding of soil engineering that allowed them

8. Lepper, "Lepper: Descendants of builders."

9. Mallett, "Judge Rules OHC Can Reclaim."

to withstand thousands of years of erosion. The Octagon Earthworks align with the 18.6-year cycle of the moon's orbital path around the earth with unparalleled geometric precision at a scale that dwarfs the Great Pyramid of Giza. Of all known prehistoric earthworks in the world, they offer a unique example of human ingenuity and the perennial desire to understand the universe and its celestial bodies. The historical, archeological, and astronomical significance of the Octagon Earthworks is arguably equivalent to Stonehenge or Machu Picchu."[10]

The six-to-one ruling for the state sent the matter back to Licking County Judge Branstool's court for a jury trial to decide the value of the lease. The country club tried yet another appeal to the high court, but that too lost, and in time the jury trial would begin.

⊕

Meanwhile, with court decisions going the way of public access, the US Department of Interior became sufficiently confident that the country club's days were numbered. They agreed to move forward on the nomination of Ohio's earthworks for UNESCO World Heritage status. UNESCO scheduled sessions for 2020 and 2021, but the COVID-19 pandemic generated postponements, delay, and a backlog of nominations. The US-Ohio team went into the year 2022 with some confidence, but a different sort of complication arose. The unfortunate choice of host nation for that year's World Heritage Meeting was the Russian Federation. Four months before the meeting, Russia invaded Ukraine. Leaders of forty-six countries signed a letter declaring that in addition to Russia's destruction of human lives and entire cities, "fifty-three cultural buildings (historical monuments, places of worship, libraries, etc.) had been damaged or destroyed by 31 March." The list included Kharkiv, a UNESCO Creative City, Chernihiv, on Ukraine's list of World Heritage nominees, and more. Referring to World Heritage selection criteria, the letter said, "It is impossible for the forty-fifth session of the World Heritage Committee to be held either in Kazan or under Russian presidency while the latter is destroying 'outstanding universal value' in Ukraine."[11]

No one in Ohio was going to quarrel with postponement on those grounds.

10. State ex rel. Ohio History Connection v. Moundbuilders Country Club Co., 171 Ohio St. 3d 663, 2022-Ohio-4345.

11. United Kingdom Foreign, Commonwealth & Development Office, "Open Letter."

UNESCO chose a new host nation, Saudia Arabia, and scheduled its World Heritage meeting for Riyadh in September of 2023. The Ohio team had been working in earnest since at least 2016 to build the voluminous documentation necessary for World Heritage designation. John Hancock, the architectural historian, had emerged to chair the group leading the UNESCO effort, later called the World Heritage Ohio Ambassadors. Co-leading the effort on behalf of the Ohio History Connection was Jennifer Aultman, recruited in 2016 to be World Heritage Director in charge of coordinating the nomination effort and assembling and organizing the mountains of papers and support documents that would be needed. By 2023, Aultman was director of historic sites and museums for the Ohio History Connection. She had come to Ohio from Virginia where she had been curator of archaeological collections at Thomas Jefferson's Monticello, itself a World Heritage Site. Aultman said that between 2018 and 2021 Ohio's final 332-page World Heritage Ohio nomination document required the support of ten writers and editors, two graphic designers, one mapmaker, several reviewers, and many supporting team members.[12]

Crucial to the nomination was the raw material collected over decades of research by Brad Lepper and Bret Ruby, the leading expert for the National Park Service's Hopewell cultural sites. Both had central roles on the team from the beginning. Phyllis Ellin, also of the National Park Service, had advised other World Heritage applicants and now coached the Ohioans on the nuances of UNESCO scrutiny. Other key contributors over the years were Dick Shiels, Jeff Gill, John Low, and Marti Chaatsmith, a woman of Comanche and Choctaw heritage who was crucial to the team's engagement with Indigenous tribal leaders. Chief Glenna Wallace had long before become an unofficial chief spokesperson for Indigenous people, but she was far from alone among tribal representatives working for the nomination. Others joining the official effort came from the National Congress of American Indians and the Inter-Tribal Council of Northeast Oklahoma, which included the Eastern Shawnee Tribe, Shawnee Tribe, Miami Nation, Wyandotte Nation, Seneca-Cayuga Nation, Quapaw Tribe, Peoria Tribe, Ottawa Tribe, and the Modoc Nation. Ray Hively and Bob Horn might not have been on the writing team, but the team's documentation contained numerous references to their research.

⊕

12. Aultman, "Aultman: A World Heritage fledgling."

In the Islamic world, where time is measured on lunar calendars, months begin when a crescent moon is first seen with the naked eye. Moon observation committees are given the task of declaring sightings of the crescent, and sometimes they disagree, causing differing committees to start the month a day apart. In 2023, in Saudi Arabia, the first sighting of the month of Rabi' ul-Awwal was on the day that Gregorian calendar-followers call September 17th, and on that day Ohio's delegation was on its way to Riyadh. The Ohioans had reason for optimism, but they also knew to expect the unexpected. Would the committee raise the question of the still-unsettled legal fight with the Moundbuilders Country Club? The legal wrangling hadn't concluded, and the golfers still controlled the site. Another concern was Clive Ruggles, a Brit and a world authority on archaeoastronomy, who for decades was skeptical about Hively and Horn's claims of lunar alignments. Now Ruggles was on the very World Heritage committee evaluating the nomination from Ohio. In fact, according to Hancock, the Ohio team knew Ruggles had been principal author of two reports for the World Heritage Committee, one of which pointed out that no ancient civilization in the world had demonstrated knowledge of the entire long lunar cycle. Ruggles even questioned why such a lunar monument would be worth the effort. The reports also outlined the stringent and precise criteria that would be necessary to show that any ancient monument tracked the moon's 18.6 year path. The Ambassadors believed they met the criteria, but at moments like this you prepare yourself for all possible obstacles.

To serve as the delegation's principal spokesperson before the World Heritage Committee, the Ohio team chose Chief Glenna. Several others made the trip to Riyadh with her, including Lepper; Aultman; Megan Wood, their boss at the Ohio History Connection; Bret Ruby and Chris Alford of the Hopewell Culture National Historical Park; and representatives of the Seneca Nation, Wyandotte Nation, Miami Nation, and the Pokagon Band of Potawatomi Indians.

The Hopewell nomination encompassed eight Ohio sites in all. It listed Newark's Octagon and Great Circle first, followed by Hopeton Earthworks, Mound City, High Bank Works, Hopewell Mound Group, Seip Earthworks, and Fort Ancient. UNESCO said that for sites to be considered, they "must be of outstanding universal value and meet at least one out of ten selection criteria." Lepper argued that Hopewell sites might well qualify under all ten criteria, but some criteria involve natural phenomena, like the ones that put the Grand Canyon on the list. Making that argument would be a stretch.

Ultimately, the Ohio team decided the best bet was to focus on two qualifying criteria:

- "to represent a masterpiece of human creative genius"
- "to bear a unique or at least exceptional testimony to a cultural tradition or to a civilization which is living or which has disappeared."

Ohio's nomination went into great detail over hundreds of pages, but its central arguments focused on a few things. "Huge squares, circles, and octagons are executed with an astonishing precision of form, technique, and dimension, consistently deployed across a wide geographic region," they declared. "There are alignments not only with the sun's cycles, but also with the far more complex rising and setting patterns of the moon. These earthworks served as ceremonial centers, built by dispersed, non-hierarchical groups whose way of life was supported by a mix of foraging and farming, and who developed sophisticated knowledge of astronomy, geometry, and earthen construction."

It went on to describe, "highly complex masterpieces of landscape architecture . . . geometric precision . . . astronomical breadth and accuracy (such as encoding all eight lunar standstills over an 18.6-year cycle). . . . They remain tours-de-force of landscape architectural design and engineering; their scale, precision, complexity, and extent is [*sic*] unmatched anywhere in the world . . . bears exceptional testimony to the unique characteristics of their builders, who lived in small, dispersed, egalitarian groups. . . . The continent-wide reach of this culture's interactions is evident. . . . The quantity, diversity, and aesthetic quality of these artifacts have few equals in the history of American Indian artistry."[13]

They made their case convincingly, beautifully even, but would the committee see it the same way? Would a collection of people intimately familiar with every kind of wonder of the world find wonder in Ohio?

The committee convened at noon. It was four in the morning in Newark, where the sky above the Octagon was clear, windless, and moonless. In Riyadh, Chief Glenna took her place at the table facing the committee with the US Ambassador to Saudi Arabia, Michael Ratney, at her side. Dr. Abdulelah Al-Tokhais, who chaired the World Heritage Committee, entered the

13. "Hopewell Ceremonial Earthworks – Nomination." UNESCO World Heritage Convention, 2023. https://whc.unesco.org/en/list/1689/documents/.

expansive Riyadh conference hall in a flowing white robe, a red-and-white checkered ghutra on his head. The first speaker was to be a representative speaking on behalf of the International Council on Monuments and Sites (ICOMOS), the organization charged with evaluating proposals for World Heritage designation.

Influenced by Ruggles, ICOMOS had published a warning to applicants against "gratuitous and random astronomical alignment hunting." Such claims must come with "clearly identifiable principal axes or other major structural orientation." Anticipating that, the Ohioans included some context in their filings: "Indeed, with respect to these stringent criteria, it is significant to note that the pioneering scholars of Hopewell-era astronomy, Ray Hively and Robert Horn of Earlham College, began their investigations with great skepticism. Beginning at Newark's Octagon Earthworks, they expected to demonstrate that it would be easy to find random solar alignments. This only added to their astonishment at finding none of the six key solar alignments, but instead all eight of the lunar ones."

Dr. Al-Tokhais opened the proceedings by declaring, "ICOMOS you may have the floor," not bothering to identify its spokesman by name. The speaker delivered his assessment of the nomination in an unemotional monotone, speaking in English with what sounded like a German accent. He repeated much of the same evidence employed by the Ohioans, but in the measured language of a diplomat. He expressed concern about the number of different agencies, private owners, and communities involved. And of course he mentioned the golf. "Follow up has to be insured concerning the acquisition of the leasehold on the Octagon earthworks component part." But they let that slide for now.

Early in his short presentation, sounding like a structural engineer, he told the committee, "ICOMOS considers that the methodology for the comparative analysis is sound and the rationale and criteria for selecting the component parts for the serial nomination are justified. The nominated property demonstrates criteria one and three." Then, at his conclusion: "ICOMOS recommends that the Hopewell Ceremonial Earthworks, United States of America, be inscribed in the World Heritage List on the basis of criteria one and three."

The chairman invited public comment. Any of the Ohio team's tableful of people could have spoken in the proposal's favor, and Chief Glenna was prepared and eager to share their story. She had done her homework; she could handle anything. She had traveled twenty-two hours, overcome difficulties with passports, and waited anxiously for visas, which arrived with just days to spare. Despite all of that, the team knew to hold their tongues. When you've made the sale, stop selling.

It was almost a letdown. Hearing no comments or objections, the chair wrapped things up, declared the recommendation adopted, and said, "Congratulations to the United States and the entire Hopewell committee." The entire proceeding lasted five minutes.

As happy as she was, Chief Glenna still wanted to give Indigenous America its moment on the world stage. Iran's presentation earlier in the day involved two hours of discussion with plenty of opportunity for that country to plead its case and showcase its heritage. Here was a global forum and she wanted to take advantage of it. "I just sat there thinking there's so many people in this building and they haven't discussed this nomination at all. They don't even know what we're talking about. . . . And so I was just disappointed in not being able to tell that to the world and to have that broadcast everywhere."

But at that moment their place on the World Heritage List was secured, there was applause from across the hall, from people around the world, with broad smiles and many handshakes. They had done their homework *too* well. Logan York, there on behalf of the Miami Tribe of Oklahoma, said he was overwhelmed to hear one of the longest standing ovations given to any of the nations presenting that day.

After the decision was rendered and the US ambassador expressed thanks to the committee, he invited Chief Glenna to say a few words. Though her remarks might have felt more meaningful had they happened earlier when they could influence the outcome, Indigenous America would get its shot at a world audience after all. So she took it:

"After more than twenty years working towards this goal, my immediate reaction is to shout, and to shout with joy. But at the same time, my eyes are moist with tears and my lips, my chin, and my voice tremble. My exhilaration is coupled with reflection, as I am so humbled, so honored, and so thankful for the world at long last recognizes the commitment, the spirituality, the knowledge of astronomy, mathematics, art, geology, and aesthetic vision, resulting in the imaginative thinking used by our ancestors to create these magnificent earthworks. They were not just geniuses, they were uncommon geniuses. Their genius lives on today in many descendant tribes, including the Seneca Nation, the Miami Nation, the Pokagon Band of the Potawatomi, and the Wyandotte Nation, who have also sent representatives here today."[14]

14. "Summary Records of 45th Session," UNESCO, 597.

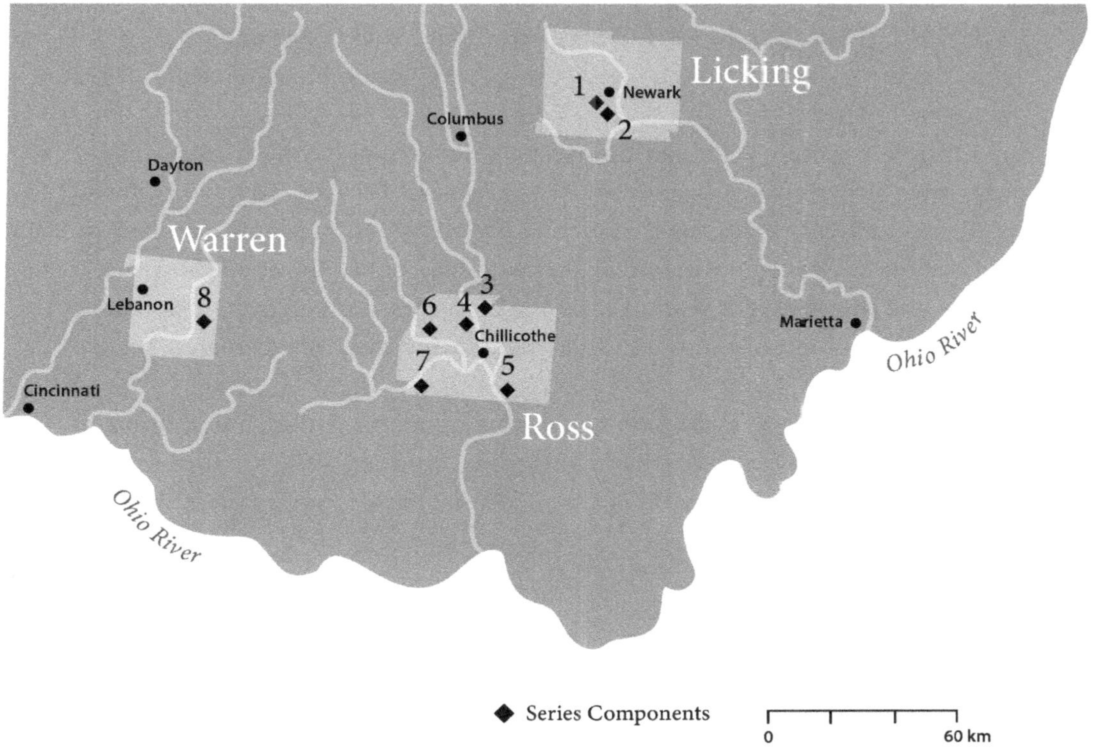

FIGURE 14.1. Eight sites in three Ohio counties are now on UNESCO's list of World Heritage Sites. Image courtesy of the Ohio History Connection.

Seated nearby, York wore a gorget, a silver-colored metal crescent across his chest that traditionally was a symbol of power, but he liked to wear it as business attire, like a necktie. The glint of it shined from beneath his pinstriped suit coat.

"I tried not to cry on world television," York told me. "I think I mostly managed it. It was elating. Finally, these things that our ancestors built are being recognized on the world stage by world leaders and historians. . . . Listening to Glenna Wallace's speech while we were there was, you know, equally tear jerking. I swear they're all just trying to make us all cry. But it was pretty amazing. You know, it's hard to describe that feeling of your ancestors going through all of that. And, you know, finally it's maybe not done but you know it's being recognized that they did this amazing thing. They did it and nobody else did. The giants didn't do it. Aliens didn't do it. And that the world is recognizing that. Elation, it's hard to explain. It's a very good feeling. I was very proud to be there. I can't imagine how Glenna felt, you know, it's twenty years of her life and it finally happened."

Joshua Garcia represented the Wyandotte Nation and, like Logan, remembered the emotion of it. Most struggled to hold back tears, some failed. "I was having to bite my tongue or bite my cheek to not make myself cry," he told me.

"There's nothing you can do except be overcome with joy and understanding how significant an event like that was," he said. To have a world audience telling Americans that Native people weren't "running around in loin cloths . . . it helps people realize how intelligent we have been for thousands and thousands of years. That's one of the reasons I enjoyed it so much, to finally have it on paper . . . that [the earthworks were] created before colonization."

As the committee moved on to the next item and nation, a line formed. About one hundred people from many other countries waited in turn to congratulate and shake the hands of Chief Glenna, the US Ambassador, and the National Parks representative.

⊕

When I woke up the next morning and heard the news, I called Bob Horn and Ray Hively. I missed Ray, but he later left a voice message:

"I think Newark in particular represents a kind of prehistoric prayer to the gods that appeared to order the sky and the earth. While the prayer may not have been answered during the Hopewell's time, in a sense it was answered today by the UNESCO decision, because that decision means that the earthworks will be preserved in the future where all can appreciate the fact of what the Hopewell accomplished. Indigenous prehistoric cultures have been ignored and underestimated for far too long. . . . When I see the Newark Earthworks, I get the same sensation that I got when I saw the first space shuttle launch. It's an example of how, even with the imperfections and shortcomings of individual humans, when they are motivated collectively to do something great they can achieve it. And anyone who doubts that can just come to the Newark Earthworks and be inspired. It's a wonderful legacy now that those earthworks will be preserved to inspire future generations as well."

Later Ray told me by email, "The significance of the Hopewell achievement is that it represents an intellectual and cultural achievement which has an importance which transcends any connection to ethnic identity. Euclid, Galileo, and Copernicus, and even people like Bob and myself have an

FIGURE 14.2. Jane and Bob Horn in 2015. Photo by Mary Horn.

intellectual (and perhaps a spiritual) kinship to the observers, architects, and builders responsible for the Newark Earthworks. I feel a much stronger connection to the people who conceived and built the earthworks than I do my German ancestors."

When I talked to Bob Horn, he was taken back to the day he and Ray first saw the large black-and-white photo of the Octagon and circle, taken by Dache Reeves in the 1930s. "The geometry was just startling, but Ray and I seemed to be the only people who were startled. I found that very hard to account for."

Bob was reminded of Dick Shiels's observation that textbooks until that time began American history by telling about Cahokia, which was built some one thousand years after the Hopewell culture flourished. "Now it's set back to where he thought it ought to be, with Hopewell," and might get pushed earlier as more is learned about places like Poverty Point in present-day Louisianna, built more than one thousand years before the Hopewell. Bob

FIGURE 14.3. Ray Hively in his office at home near Atlanta in 2022. Photo by James W. Graham.

was thinking of all there was still to learn, and believed that a great benefit of UNESCO's action was that it would attract more research into the Hopewell culture.

He recalled his trip to Denmark as a young man, seeing ancient stone megaliths illustrated on Danish currency because Danes view them as a part of their own ancient heritage. By contrast, "European Americans don't claim what Native Americans have done as a heritage. But now we've got *World* Heritage designation of this site and many others. So the complicated issues of what inheritance is, and how we estimate it, and what goes into claiming it, I think it is very interesting." Those Americans who have ignored Hopewell achievement might now find it harder to ignore, given international attention. "The fact that Hopewell is being claimed as a world heritage puts us in this country, vis a vis the Hopewell, in a different position from where we've ever been before."

Ray and Bob are not resting on laurels. Both were still thinking about the Hopewell in new ways, still looking for new things to learn about the era.

"I think we will find Newark is not only the Rosetta stone for Ohio Hopewell," Bob told me earlier by email. "It has much more to tell us about monumental construction on this continent both before and after Hopewell, perhaps from –3000 to +1600."

Before six o'clock that morning, Bob received an email from Lepper, writing from Riyadh. "Today the Hopewell Ceremonial Earthworks have been inscribed on the UNESCO World Heritage list," wrote Lepper. "Your research on the astronomy of the Hopewell earthworks has been instrumental in demonstrating the outstanding universal value of this amazing earthwork architecture. Without your work we would not be where we are today. Many thanks and congratulations. Brad."

I asked Bob to compare this day to the day in 1982 when he and Ray published their first paper about Hopewell astronomy, and nobody noticed. He replied, with a laugh, "As David Hume said of his Treatise on Human Understanding, 'it fell dead-born from the press.'"

"Paradigm changes take a while. In fact, the adage is, 'the holders of the paradigm just have to die.'"

⊕

It was just a matter of time before the question of golfing would be answered.

Barbara Crandell, the woman arrested for praying on the mounds, said, "They built these things so we would remember who we are. Don't lose track of who you are! When I go to the mounds, I feel a great welling up of pride and love for my people. I love my ancestors. I love their bones. That's the way I was brought up. I have great reverence for them. And every one of those mounds, I know their hands lovingly gathered the dirt and put it there. And I can feel their hands patting me, when I go there. So that's why I think it was left as a trail for native people to follow. Go there and connect with your ancestors, so you can walk a good path. It is terrible that people are not allowed to go to these places. I mean, they're not just for Indian people. I mean, I connect with them, maybe in a different way. But all peoples should be able to go there. They should be able to go there and see this wonderful sight. And I'd like to have it open for everybody."[15]

⊕

15. Ancient Ohio Trail, "Octagon's Modern History."

The day Ohio's Hopewell earthworks became a World Heritage Site, Bob Horn called his daughter Mary. She was delighted by the news, proud that her father had an important hand in it. She now lives in Wisconsin on the Menominee Reservation, with the community into which she was born before her adoption by Bob and Jane. She is now an enrolled member of the tribe, which regained federal recognition in 1976. Her apartment, surrounded by huge trees, is near the sawmill of Menominee Tribal Enterprises. Her people have harvested trees there for 170 years and their business serves today as a global model for sustainable forestry. When Mary was born there in the 1960s, Native children had no tribal schools of their own to attend. "The Menominee reservation has its own schools now and they are teaching the Menominee language," said Jane.

"They had that thing for vowels on the wall," Mary said of one of the new schools. "They had everything labeled in Menominee, like they have it written on the door and you have to say it in Menominee, and the windows. You have to use Menominee. I'm working on it." In 2024, a new high school opened too. It was to be called the Menominee Indian High School, but before it opened students successfully petitioned to change its name to Menominee Nation High School. A school youth program called Medicine Fish is finding unique ways to reacquaint a new generation with its Indigenous past, including its past relationship with the buffalo, an animal considered sacred to Menominee people. A new herd is being established nearby. As a trailerful of buffalo arrived to join the herd, a radio journalist described the scene:

"Before the buffalo thunder onto the landscape eleven Medicine Fish members quietly form a circle. They break into a song of thanks to their buffalo relatives, their voices soaring," with lyrics in their native tongue. "Four years ago, there was no circle. There were no buffalo. Now Menominee youth—young men and women—are finding their voice and community in traditional ways."[16]

Despite growing up far from Wisconsin, Mary's circle of Menominee friendships has grown after years of attending powwows, first with her parents and then with her own daughters. Once Mary herself sponsored a powwow in Richmond, the town that seemed so strange when Bob and Jane brought her to their home. Now Mary's grown daughters are members of the tribe too, but they live near their grandparents in the house Bob and Jane lived in before they moved to a place that's easier for an aging couple to manage. They all stay in close touch.

16. Bence, Susan, "In Wisconsin, Menominee Nation."

Mary's brother Jonathan lived in West Virginia with his wife, who is part Cherokee, and they went to powwows too. Jonathan died of natural causes in January 2025. For Bob and Jane, their life journey has taken them deep into the Indigenous cosmology and science of a most distant past, while they traveled a parallel path, in the most personal way possible, with children of their own, experiencing through them the modern blessings and burdens of American Indigeneity.

⊕

In 2024, Zitkala-Ša—the young Native American woman whose nineteenth-century journey from reservation to Richmond preceded Mary and Jonathan Horn's own journey to Richmond—was featured by the United States Mint on the reverse side of a quarter that features George Washington on the obverse. For most of the twentieth century she was all but forgotten. Like Hopewell and so much other Indigenous achievement, she too is now rediscovered.

But a year after the minting of that coin a new president took office and introduced a new and bitter assault on "wokism." In the summer of 2025, President Trump declared on his Truth Social network, "The Washington 'Whatever's' should IMMEDIATELY change their name back to the Washington Redskins Football Team. There is a big clamoring for this. Likewise, the Cleveland Indians, one of the six original baseball teams, with a storied past." The president added later, "Indians are being treated very unfairly. MAKE INDIANS GREAT AGAIN (MIGA)!" The Washington and Cleveland teams were renamed the Commanders and Guardians, respectively, in 2022.

Two days after Trump's comments, the White House deputy press secretary declared, "President Trump has decided to withdraw from UNESCO—which supports woke, divisive cultural and social issues."[17] This was not expected to affect Ohio's new designation as home to World Heritage Sites, but it surely put a chill on the warm feelings many Ohioans had for their recently bestowed global recognition. For Indigenous America, it was another of many moments when a step forward preceded steps the other way.

⊕

17. Anna Kelly (@AnnaKelly47), "NEW: President Trump has decided to withdraw from UNESCO," X, July 22, 2025, https://x.com/AnnaKelly47/status/1947626672188231707.

In August 2024, news broke of a plan by the Moundbuilders Country Club to acquire another golf course called The Trout Club on the north edge of Newark. The owner had been renovating the old club for several years. Trout Club owner Brent Dewey was sympathetic with the plight of the golfers across town and willing to help them find a way out of their dilemma. "We're doing the best thing for the club, the community and the employees," said Dewey. "We look it as a win-win for all sides. They got shoved out of their land," he said, referring to the golfers. "Now they have a home secure."[18] When the final deal was announced, the Ohio History Connection said that an undisclosed sum of money would help the Moundbuilders Country Club acquire the Trout Club. They would move there and turn the Octagon over to the people of Ohio, to Native people, to all the world. Plans immediately were announced by the Ohio History Connection to "open the Octagon Earthworks for full public access on January 1, 2025."

As good as this news was, there was one small complication. The moon was scheduled to make a nighttime standstill appearance down that central axis on October 21, 2024, at 9:44 p.m. There would be other times that season when the moon would rise there, but not when the moon was two-thirds full and at a not-too-late hour. It was the best viewing opportunity in a generation. The guys with the golf clubs still controlled the site, however, and I had been wondering since August if they would open it for so perfect a viewing. I asked somebody in-the-know if the public would be allowed in, and he responded by email. "If you were to show up at the Octagon on October twenty-first sometime before around 9 p.m., no one would tell you to leave. Though we are not to advertise that fact."

I wasn't telling a soul. That afternoon of the twenty-first, during a club-sanctioned open house, I walked the Octagon and met a member of the World Heritage Steering Committee, Bill Weaver, a warm and friendly man, who seems to love anyone who loves Ohio's ancient history. We chatted about various things and eventually he made a vague inquiry about my plans for the evening. I'm not always quick on my feet, but I could tell he was probing to see if I knew the secret about the moonrise viewing. It was like swearing not to reveal the undisclosed location of a rave party and not knowing what to do when somebody makes a winking reference to it. There was nothing rave about a moonrise, but we both were cagey in our awkward way and eventually admitted we were both in on the "secret."

18. Mallet, "Moundbuilders Reaches Deal."

FIGURE 14.4. Time-lapse image of the northernmost moonrise that occurred on October 21, 2024, where Chief Glenna Wallace and other Native leaders were given the front row for viewing. Photo by Timothy E. Black / Newark Earthworks Center.

As secrets go, this one wasn't closely held. About two hundred people showed up including representatives of several Native American tribes. Through the darkness I made out Chief Glenna, three of the Native delegates who were in Riyadh, and others. The "first peoples" among us were encouraged to enter the golf course first and set their lawn chairs up in front of the rest of us, for an unobstructed view. The clubhouse lights were out, except for the parking lot. A golf course is very dark at night—you couldn't see your feet—but dark is what you want for a moonrise so we gingerly made our way onto the fairway. The golf club's parking area had some too-bright streetlights, but otherwise the darkness revealed a beautiful star-lit night. It was jacket weather, and we all faced down the central alley to the octagon and the trees in the distance, to where the ancients taught us the moon would rise.

The star Cappella was slightly to the north of the axis of the earthworks, Jupiter shined brightest in the sky, just to the south, waiting to be soon outshone. Familiar faces in the darkness: Lepper, Hancock, Gill, Tonetti,

Aultman, and more I couldn't make out. The moon would inch over the horizon at 9:44 p.m., but it would be another fifteen minutes or so before the moon's aura would fill the darkness above the tree line. We waited and waited. Slowly, the glow grew and then we thought we saw a spark. Then more spark through the thick distant trees. With branches as points of reference, you could see the moon move. The crowd was almost completely silent; we were in church after all. Soft whispers to guard the precious quiet. Crickets were louder than people. Reverence. Respect for those most deserving of the view, the Indigenous, seated in front like the family closest to the nuptials or the wake. People were careful with their phone cameras; not a flash happened. Most just watched the slow rise and growing light. As the moon rose above the trees, I saw a meteor mark a trail toward the north edge of the Hopewell alley, like a welcoming smile.

I left knowing it would be a few months before I would return. By then the careful process of removing the sand traps and tee boxes will have begun. Care will be taken because the soil below might hide more traces of Newark's Indigenous past. A few trees will be removed to clear the view back to how the original builders intended it. The grass on the grounds and on the walls will be allowed to grow more naturally, without the golf manicure. Lines of sight to the heavens will be reborn. It will be open to all, all day, seven days a week, including certain moonlit nights like this, where the moon stands still.

ACKNOWLEDGMENTS

This story is framed by the decades-long collaboration of Bob Horn and Ray Hively, but the third figure in the framework is Brad Lepper. To the three of them I am in great debt. None bear any responsibility for whatever flaws reside here, but they all contributed in crucial ways both direct and indirect. Professors Ray Hively and Robert Horn were supportive from the moment I sent them unsolicited emails in the spring of 2021. In meetings, over meals together, by phone and in email they shared all they could remember and all they wrote down. They explained astronomy, topography, archaeology, family experiences, personal challenges, and more. They enlisted Jane Horn and Susan Hively in the effort too, and both made important contributions to my narrative. As the serious academics and truth-seekers they are, Ray and Bob didn't worry so much about how they were portrayed. Mostly they just wanted me to be accurate, fair to all the people who worked on Hopewell scholarship, and willing to credit others for what they contributed. I'm grateful to Mary too, daughter of Bob and Jane Horn, for the important experiences and perspective she shared.

Brad Lepper patiently and skillfully educated me, as he does for so many, from tourists to scholars. The time he gave me personally was invaluable, but even more important were his scholarly works and writings for wider audiences, which informed many, many pages of this book. Without him and his writings, this story could not have been told. Brad Lepper is also an exceptionally gifted educator and speaker, and I can't imagine how many tours he has given, telling the Hopewell story with infectious enthusiasm. Sometimes he teams up with Jeff Gill, another who helped me and has volunteered his exceptional expertise, enthusiasm, and efforts to scholarly research and education. Lepper's colleagues at the Ohio History Connection are a treasure to anyone wishing to learn more. Thank you to OHC's Neil Thompson, who answered questions, introduced me to important interviewees and assisted with images for this book.

A number of others helped me improve my understanding of Indigenous peoples' perspectives. I'm grateful to Glenna Wallace, chief of the Eastern Shawnee Tribe of Oklahoma, who has been a powerful advocate for Hopewell site preservation, global recognition, and public access. My interview with her was a highlight of my research work. An equal highlight was my interview with Ben Barnes, chief of the Shawnee Tribe and President of the National Native American Boarding School Healing Coalition. Joshua Garcia of the Wyandotte Nation Cultural Center and Museum, and Logan York, tribal historic preservation officer, Miami Tribe of Oklahoma, both worked effectively to represent Native American interests during the effort to secure UNESCO World Heritage Site recognition. They helped me too. Dr. John Low, current director of the Newark Earthworks Center, Ohio State University, specializes in American Indian studies and related topics, and is an enrolled citizen of the Pokagon Band of Potawatomi. He offered useful insights into the possible meaning of the earthworks to their original builders.

Ohio is filled with scholars whose Hopewell work extended far beyond classrooms. Mike Mickelson, J. Reid Anderson Professor of Physics and Astronomy, emeritus, Denison University, patiently taught me about lunar orbital dynamics. He's been part of the Hopewell archaeoastronomy team for decades. So has Dick Shiels, emeritus associate professor of history and founding director of the Newark Earthworks Center, The Ohio State University, who I interviewed and who has been a long-time advocate of the interests of Native American people. Thanks also to John Hancock, professor emeritus of architecture, University of Cincinnati, and chair of the World Heritage Ohio Ambassadors; Al Tonetti, president of Heartland Earthworks Conservancy; Jarrod Burks, PhD, Ohio Valley Archaeology, Inc.; John Fillwalk and the team at the Institute for Digital Intermedia Arts (IDIA Lab) at Ball State University; Jennifer Bush, director, Johnson-Humrickhouse Museum, in Coshocton, Ohio; and Tyler Swinney of the Cincinnati Museum Center. Although I did not interview him, recognition must be given to William Romain, an important figure in Hopewell research and archaeoastronomy around the world, especially in Ohio. His research has influenced many scholars.

Anna Sofaer, known for finding the now-famous "sun dagger" in Chaco Canyon, and for her wonderful documentaries, gave me invaluable insights into many topics, including the challenges faced by those who make the case for ancient Indigenous knowledge of the complexities of the moon and sun.

At the University of Illinois, two who generously shared their renowned expertise are Timothy Pauketat, archaeologist, professor of anthropology and director of the Illinois State Archaeology Survey; and Alma Gottlieb, professor emerita, department of anthropology. At Arizona State University, Christopher Carr, professor emeritus, School of Human Evolution and Social Change, has published voluminous work that I found exceptionally enlightening.

Tribute must be paid to the Newark (Ohio) *Advocate*, a daily newspaper that has covered news about earthworks and published numerous articles by experts on archaeology and Native culture. They are exemplary of what we stand to lose as local journalism struggles to survive and reinvent itself. Larger institutional resources that were helpful to me included the Smithsonian's National Museum of the American Indian, the Newberry Library in Chicago, Clements Library at the University of Michigan, Franklin County Genealogical and Historical Society, and the wonderful reference staff at the Winnetka-Northfield (Illinois) Public Library, for whom no academic journal article is too obscurely hidden. Friends Barbara Hermansen, John Montgomery, and Jeff Zilka were dependably there for me and lent a hand along the way.

Thank you, Tony Sanfilippo, my editor at the Ohio State University Press, who saw potential in my work, encouraged me, and steered me in better directions. Tony recruited the aid of scholars in the fields of Indigenous studies and archaeology, all of whom read this book and provided invaluable guidance and editorial advice.

My wife, Linda Kingman, was infinitely patient and supportive as I worked on this. Her suggestions and insights always make my work better. My son Spencer inspires me for a lot of reasons, but one of them is simply because he's such a great writer himself and is a good role model for his dad. Lastly, there is my mother, Virginia P. Graham, to whom this volume is dedicated, because she loved books right up to her death on April 17, 2025. By example and in words, she encouraged me to think that writing is a worthy pursuit, and books an honorable contribution.

BIBLIOGRAPHY

Adair, James. *History of the American Indians.* London: Edward and Charles Dilly, 1775. https://www.google.com/books/edition/The_History_of_the_American_Indians/df5SAAAAcAAJ.

Alrutz, Robert W. "The Newark Holy Stones: The History of an Archaeological Tragedy." *Journal of the Scientific Laboratories,* Denison University 57 (1980): 1–57 and 58–72.

Ancient Ohio Trail. "The Octagon's Modern History." Accessed September 21, 2022. https://www.ancientohiotrail.org/sites/newark.

"Annual Report of the Adjutant General to the Governor of the State of Ohio." In *Annual Reports for 1891 Made to the Seventieth General Assembly of the State of Ohio, at the Regular Session, Commencing January 4, 1892.* The Westbote Co., 1892.

Answers in Genesis. "Dinosaurs." Website affiliated with the Creation Museum and the Ark Encounter. Accessed November 24, 2024. https://answersingenesis.org/dinosaurs/.

The Archaeological Conservancy. "Preserving Steel Earthworks." June 19, 2015. https://www.thearchcons.org/steel-earthworks-ohio.

Arizona Museum of Natural History. "Apache Sunrise Dance and Ceremony." October 22, 2020. https://www.arizonamuseumofnaturalhistory.org/explore-the-museum/exhibitions/athapascan-way/apache-sunrise-dance-and-ceremony#ad-image-5.

Associated Press. "Woman arrested while praying pleads innocent." *Marysville (OH) Journal-Tribune,* July 17, 2002.

Atalay, Sonya, Terry Barnhart, Deborah Bolnick, Ken Feder, Alice Kehoe, and Brad Lepper. "Statement About 'The Lost Civilizations of North America' DVD." Ohio History Connection. December 16, 2010. https://www.ohiohistory.org/statement-about-the-lost-civilizations-of-north-america-dvd/.

Aultman, Jennifer. "Aultman: A World Heritage fledgling at the Newark Earthworks." *Newark (OH) Advocate,* April 24, 2022. Accessed October 18, 2024. https://www.newarkadvocate.com/story/news/local/2022/04/24/aultman-world-heritage-fledgling-newark-earthworks/7396423001/.

Aveni, Anthony P. "An Assessment of Studies in Hopewell Astronomy." In *The Fort Ancient Earthworks: Prehistoric Lifeways of the Hopewell Culture in Southwestern Ohio,* edited by Robert P. Connolly and Bradley T. Lepper. Ohio Historical Society, 2004.

Bacon, D. Francis. "The Ohio 'Holy Stone.'" *Harpers Weekly,* vol. IV, no. 192 (Sept. 1, 1860). https://archive.org/details/harpersweeklyv4bonn/page/544/mode/2up.

Bahr, Sarah. "A Push to Move the Golf Course Atop a Native American 'Stonehenge.'" *New York Times,* April 12, 2021. https://www.nytimes.com/2021/04/12/arts/design/octagon-earthworks-newark-ohio-golf-course-native-american.html.

Baity, Elizabeth Chesley "Archaeostronomy and Ethnoastronomy So Far." *Current Anthropology* 14, no. 4 (October 1973): 389–449.

Barnes, Ben, and Brad Lepper. "Drums Along the Scioto: Interpreting Hopewell Material Culture Through the Lens of Contemporary American Indian Ceremonial Practices." *Archaeologies* 14 (2018): 62–84. https://doi.org/10.1007/s11759-018-9334-1.

Beck, Glenn. "Native Americans Wrote in Ancient Hebrew," *Fox News.* August 18, 2010. https://www.youtube.com/watch?v=NgnRN-GOLLI&t=12s.

Bence, Susan. "In Wisconsin, the Menominee Nation reintroducing a sacred animal to the tribe's youth." *Weekend Edition Saturday,* National Public Radio. December 28, 2024. https://www.npr.org/2024/12/28/nx-s1-5224167/in-wisconsin-the-menominee-nation-is-reintroducing-a-sacred-animal-to-the-tribes-youth.

Betz, Eric. "The Wow! Signal: An Alien Missed Connection?" *Astronomy,* September 30, 2020, updated December 27, 2023. https://www.astronomy.com/science/the-wow-signal-alien-missed-connection/.

Black Elk. *Black Elk Speaks.* Edited by John G. Neihardt. University of Nebraska Press, 2014.

Blaisdell, Haku. "Birchbark, the 1893 World's Fair, and Native Resistance." *The Newberry,* November 2, 2021. https://www.newberry.org/blog/birchbark-the-1893-worlds-fair-and-native-resistance.

Boroditsky, Lera. "How Language Shapes the Way We Think." TED, May 2, 2018. https://www.youtube.com/watch?v=RKK7wGAYP6k.

Brewster, Sir David. *Memoirs of the Life, Writings, and Discoveries of Sir Isaac Newton.* Little, Brown, and Co., 1855. https://www.google.com/books/edition/Memoirs_of_the_Life_Writings_and_Discove/Bp8RAAAAYAAJ/.

Buckeye Lake Beacon. "Mound re-blessed," September 4, 2010. https://www.buckeyelakebeacon.net/articles/mound-re-blessed/.

Buckley, Thomas, and Alma Gottlieb. *Blood Magic: The Anthropology of Menstruation.* University of California Press, 1988.

Bush, Jennifer, Reba Kocher, and Bradley Lepper. "The Newark Holy Stones: Touchstones for the Truth." *The Public Historian* 44, issue 1 (February 1, 2022): 78–93. https://doi.org/10.1525/tph.2022.44.1.78.

Byler, William. "The Destruction of American Indian Families," In *The Destruction of American Indian Families,* edited by Steven Unger. Association of American Indian Affairs, 1977.

Carlson, Randall. Interview by Tucker Carlson. Tucker Carlson Today, Fox Nation, December 27, 2022. https://www.bitchute.com/video/24Y2wgIh9mDg/.

Carlson, Wayne. "Grandview Heights Moment in Time." *The Columbus Dispatch*, October 1, 2021. https://www.dispatch.com/story/news/local/communities/grandview-heights/2021/10/01/grandview-heights-moment-time/5913605001/.

Carr, Christopher. "Salient Issues in the Social and Political Organizations of Northern Hopewellian Peoples." In *Gathering Hopewell: Society, Ritual, and Ritual Interaction*, edited by Christopher Carr and D. Troy Case. Kluwer Academic/Plenum Publishers, 2004.

Carr, Christopher. "Scioto Hopewell Ritual Gatherings." In *Gathering Hopewell: Society, Ritual, and Ritual Interaction*," edited by Christopher Carr and D. Troy Case. Kluwer Academic/Plenum Publishers, 2004.

Carr, Christopher and D. Troy Case, eds. *Gathering Hopewell: Society, Ritual, and Ritual Interaction*." Kluwer Academic/Plenum Publishers, 2004.

Carr, Christopher, and Heather Smyth. "1.6 Soul Concepts of Scioto Hopewell Communities: The Ontological Foundation of Their Tripartite Ceremonial Alliance." In *Encountering Hopewell in the Twenty-first Century, Ohio and Beyond*, edited by Jared Burks, Bret Ruby, and Brian Redmond. University of Akron Press, 2020. https://ideaexchange.uakron.edu/encountering_hopewell/6.

Chaatsmith, Marti L. "Singing at a Center of the Indian World: the SAI and Ohio Earthworks." *Studies in American Indian Literatures* 25, no. 2 (Summer 2013): 181–198. https://dx.doi.org/10.5250/studamerindilite.25.2.0181.

Chaudhuri, Jean, and Joytopaul Chaudhuri. *A Sacred Path: The Way of the Muscogee Creeks*. Duane Champagne, UCLA American Indian Studies Center, 2001.

Chicago Tribune. "A Curious Discovery or a Great Hoax." July 10, 1860, 1.

Church of Jesus Christ of Latter-Day Saints. "Lamanite Identity." https://www.churchofjesuschrist.org/study/history/topics/lamanite-identity?lang=eng.

Clarivate, Web of Science Master Journal List. Accessed April 8, 2022. https://mjl.clarivate.com/journal-profile.

Colavito, John. *The Mound Builder Myth: Fake History and the Hunt for a "Lost White Race*." University of Oklahoma Press, 2020.

Cozzens, Peter. *Tecumseh and the Prophet: The Shawnee Brothers Who Defied a Nation*. Alfred A. Knopf, 2020.

"Dache M. Reeves." Military Times Hall of Valor Project. https://valor.militarytimes.com/hero/16202.

The Daily Exchange (Baltimore). "Interesting Discovery—Our Ancient Works Traced Back to the Hebrews—Old Theories Revived." July 12, 1860.

Davies, Keith. "Counting Back to Zero: A Review of Cosmological Models That Begin Under Conditions of Zero Entropy." *The Proceedings of the International Conference on Creationism*, vol. 7, article 41, 2013.

Deloria, Vine, Jr. *Custer Died for Your Sins*. University of Oklahoma Press, 1988.

Deloria, Vine, Jr., and Daniel Wildcat. *Power and Place: Indian Education in America*. American Indian Graduate Center and Fulcrum Resources, 2001.

DeMauro, Susan. "Cherokee wants trial in golf course case," *Newark (OH) Advocate*, July 17, 2002.

Dougherty, Matthew William. "Land of the Jewish Indians: How the Hebrew Bible Made Race and Territory in the Early United States." PhD diss., University of North Carolina at Chapel Hill, 2017. https://doi.org/10.17615/ptyz-8s76.

Eddy, John. "Review of the Paper by Hively and Horn: 'Geometry and Astronomy,'" private correspondence signed by Eddy for publisher considering Hively & Horn paper, dated December 17, 1980. Copy provided by Hively and Horn.

Eddy, John A. Interview by Spencer Weart, April 21, 1999. *Niels Bohr Library & Archives, American Institute of Physics*, College Park, MD. www.aip.org/history-programs/niels-bohr-library/oral-histories/22910.

Ellenberg, Jordon. *Shape: The Hidden Geometry of Information, Biology, Strategy, Democracy, and Everything Else*. Penguin Press, 2021.

Enstad, Robert. "Ex-Nazi leader Collin gets 7 years in child sex case." *Chicago Tribune*, March 15, 1980.

Farrer, Claire. "Star Clocks; Mescalero Apache Ceremonial Timing." *The Canadian Journal of Native Studies* 7, no. 2 (1987): 223–236. https://cjns.brandonu.ca/wp-content/uploads/7-2-farrer.pdf.

Farrer, Claire. *Thunder Rides a Black Horse: Mescalero Apaches and the Mythic Present*. Waveland Press, Inc., 1994.

Feynman, Richard P. *Surely You're Joking, Mr. Feynman!* W. W. Norton & Company, 1985.

Find a Grave. "David Wyrick." Accessed October 24, 2024. https://www.findagrave.com/memorial/15710078/david-wyrick.

Fixico, Donald L. *The American Indian Mind in a Linear World*. Routledge, 2003.

Forbes, Jack K. "Indigenous Americans: Spirituality and Ecos." *Daedelus* 130, no. 4 (Fall 2001): 283–300. https://www.amacad.org/sites/default/files/daedalus/downloads/Daedalus_Fa2001_Religion-and-Ecology-Can-Climate-Change.pdf.

Foster, John Wells. *Pre-historic Races of the United States of America*. 6th ed. S. C. Griggs and Company, 1887.

Friends of Mounds State Park. "Amusing Start." https://friendsofmounds.org/about-the-park.

Gaitten, Chris. "Why the Ohio History Connection and a Golf Course Are Battling Over the Octagon Earthworks." *Columbus Monthly*, October 8, 2019. Accessed October 27, 2024. https://www.columbusmonthly.com/story/lifestyle/2019/10/08/the-battle-over-octagon-earthworks/2528619007/.

Gallatin, A., and American Antiquarian Society. *Map of the Indian Tribes of North America, about 1600 A.D. along the Atlantic & about 1800 A.D. westwardly.* American Antiquarian Society, 1836. https://www.loc.gov/item/2002622260/.

Garcia, Kim, Beci Wright, Sherri Clemons, Chris Houk, Heather Miller, Rebecca S. Wingo, et al. "Wyandot Removal Trail." Partnership of Cultural Division of the Wyandotte Nation, Prof. Rebecca S. Wingo at the University of Cincinnati, and thirteen public history graduate students, supported by a grant from Ohio Humanities Council through September 2022. https://storymaps.arcgis.com/stories/93550d92bf12422b9858b71c19339214.

Gill, Jeff. "Warren King Moorehead at Wounded Knee." *Ohio History Connection,* December 29, 2011. https://www.ohiohistory.org/warren-king-moorehead-at-wounded-knee/.

Golbert, Stefany Anne. "The Face of the Earth." *The Smart Set,* July 30, 2015. https://www.thesmartset.com/the-face-of-the-earth/.

Graeber, David, and David Wengrow. *The Dawn of Everything: A New History of Humanity.* Farrar, Status and Giroux, 2021.

Gravity Research Foundation. "Abstracts of Award Winning and Honorable Mention Essays for 1971." New Boston, NH. https://static1.squarespace.com/static/5852e579be659442a01f27b8/t/5873eb9b15d5db147f3b41d7/1483991964130/1971abstracts.pdf.

Hancock, Graham. *America Before: The Key to Earth's Lost Civilization.* St. Martin's Press, 2019.

Hancock, John. "Ohio's Ancient Earthworks and UNESCO World Heritage." University of Cincinnati School of Architecture and Interior Design Spring 2022 Lecture Series, March 2, 2022. Accessed September 5, 2024. https://www.facebook.com/watch/live/?ref=watch_permalink&v=624688808629891.

Hancock, John E. "On Seeing Fort Ancient." In *The Fort Ancient Earthworks: Prehistoric Lifeways of the Hopewell Culture in Southwestern Ohio,* edited by Robert P. Connolly and Bradley T. Lepper. Ohio Historical Society, 2004.

Harness, Susan Devan. *Mixing Cultural Identities Through Transracial Adoption: Outcomes of the Indian Adoption Project (1958–1967).* The Edwin Mellen Press, 2008.

Hawkins, Gerald. "A Temple or an Observatory—it was both." BBC Archive, #OnThisDay 1966. Accessed May 3, 2025. https://x.com/BBCArchive/status/1161290458070507520.

Hively, Ray, and Robert Horn. "Geometry and Astronomy in Prehistoric Ohio." *Journal for the History of Astronomy, Archaeoastronomy* supplement, 13, no. 4 (1982): S1–S20. https://doi.org/10.1177/002182868201300401.

Hively, Ray, and Robert Horn. "Hopewell Cosmography at Newark and Chillicothe, Ohio." In *Hopewell Settlement Patterns, Subsistence, and Symbolic Landscapes,* edited by Martin Byers and DeeAnne Wymer. University Press of Florida, 2010.

Hively, Ray, and Robert Horn. "A Statistical Study of Lunar Alignments at the Newark Earthworks." *Midcontinental Journal of Archaeology* 31, no. 2 (Fall 2006): 281–321. https://doi.org/10.1179/mca.2006.013.

Hively, Ray, and Robert Horn, "More Topography, Astronomy, and Geometry at the Newark Earthworks." *Midcontinental Journal of Archaeology* 48, no. 1 (2023): 1–45. https://doi.org/10.5406/23274271.48.1.01.

Hively, Ray, and Robert Horn. "The Newark Earthworks: A Grand Unification of Earth, Sky, and Mind." In *The Newark Earthworks: Enduring Monuments, Contested Meanings*, edited by Lindsay Jones and Richard D. Shiels. University of Virginia Press, 2016.

Holden, Richard. "Moon Maze, The Newark Mounds: Native American Earthworks Sculpt Lunar Odyssey." *The Historical Times, the Newsletter of the Granville, Ohio, Historical Society* 9, no. 2 (Spring 1995). Reprint of article originally published in *The Earlhamite* 105, no. 1 (Autumn 1984).

Holt/Smithson Foundation. "Artworks of Nancy Holt." Accessed October 4, 2024. https://holtsmithsonfoundation.org/artworks-nancy-holt.

Howey, Meghan C. L. Comment in response to article, "Ritual, Labor Mobilization, and Monumental Construction in Small-Scale Societies," by G. Logan Miller, *Current Anthropology* 62, no. 2 (April 2021).

Indian Child Welfare Act Law Center. "Understanding the Indian Child Welfare Act." Accessed December 12, 2022. http://www.icwlc.org/education-hub/understanding-the-icwa/.

Johnson, Alan. "Desecration of Serpent Mound appears minor." *Springfield (OH) News-Sun*, November 23, 2012.

Johnson-Humrickhouse Museum. "Newark Holy Stone." https://www.jhmuseum.org/newark-holy-stones.html.

Joseph, Frank [Frank Joseph Collin]. *Advanced Civilizations of Prehistoric America: The Lost Kingdoms of the Adena, Hopewell, Mississippians, and Anasazi.* Bear and Company, 2010.

Kohl, Brianne M. "An Ode to Kent State's Original Bad Ass: Olaf Prufer," on website *Brianne M. Kohl.com* (posted May 26, 2013). https://briannekohl.com/2013/05/26/an-ode-to-kent-states-original-bad-ass-olaf-prufer/#comments.

Knight, Cameron. "Native Americans, prayer group face off at Serpent Mound." *Cincinnati Enquirer*, December 22, 2020.

Kruzman, Diana. "How Ohio's Indigenous Sacred Sites Became a Religious Flashpoint." *Religion News Service/Interfaith America Religion Journalism Fellowship Program*, January 4, 2022. https://religionnews.com/2021/12/21/how-ohios-indigenous-sacred-sites-became-a-religious-flashpoint/.

Kuhn, Thomas. *The Structure of Scientific Revolutions: 50th Anniversary Edition.* The University of Chicago Press, 2012.

LaPier, Rosalyn R. "How a Native American coming-of-age ritual is making a comeback." *The Conversation,* February 10, 2020. https://theconversation.com/how-a-native-american-coming-of-age-ritual-is-making-a-comeback-130524.

Lefgren, John C. "The Newark Earthworks & the Book of Mormon." Book of Mormon Evidence, October 8, 2020. Accessed May 13, 2025. https://bookofmormonevidence.org/the-plan-of-salvation-and-the-newark-earthworks/.

Lepper, Bradley. "Archaeology: Newark 'Holy Stones' are 19th century fake news." *Columbus Dispatch,* May 7, 2017. Accessed August 12, 2022. https://www.dispatch.com/story/news/technology/2017/05/07/archaeology-newark-holy-stones-are/20478640007/.

Lepper, Bradley T. "The Ceremonial Landscape of the Newark Earthworks." In *Hopewell Settlement Patterns, Subsistence, and Symbolic Landscapes,* edited by Martin Byers and DeeAnne Wymer. University Press of Florida, 2010.

Lepper, Bradley. "Conclusive Proof that the Newark Decalogue Stone is a Forgery (and Not a Very Good One at That)." *Archaeology Blog, Ohio History Connection,* December 12, 2014. https://www.ohiohistory.org/conclusive-proof-that-the-newark-decalogue-stone-is-a-forgery-and-not-a-very-good-one-at-that/.

Lepper, Bradley. "Early Historic American Indian Testimony Concerning the Ancient Earthworks of Eastern North America." *Journal of Ohio Archaeology* 3 (2014): 1–11.

Lepper, Bradley T. "Forensic Mystery, The Burning Tree Mastodon." *Timeline, Ohio Historical Society* 23, no. 4 (Oct.–Dec. 2006).

Lepper, Brad, "Lepper: Descendants of builders of the Newark Earthworks are still here," *Newark Advocate,* November 20, 2022. Accessed October 17, 2024. https://www.newarkadvocate.com/story/opinion/columnists/2022/11/20/lepper-descendants-of-builders-of-the-newark-earthworks-are-still-here/69657207007/.

Lepper, Brad. "Newark's Great Circle Becomes Idlewilde Park." *Ohio History Connection* (Sept. 1, 2014). Accessed October 16, 2024. https://www.ohiohistory.org/newarks-great-circle-becomes-idlewilde-park/.

Lepper, Bradley T. *Ohio Archaeology: An Illustrated Chronicle of Ohio's Ancient American Indian Cultures.* Orange Frazer Press, 2005.

Lepper, Bradley T. "A Radiocarbon Date for a Wooden Burial Platform from the Reservoir Stone Mound (33LI20), Licking County, Ohio." *Journal of Ohio Archaeology* 4 (2016): 1–11. https://ohioarchaeology.org/file_download/inline/4cb16ae1-3842-47f4-891b-b7a091938b3d.

Lepper, Bradley, and Jeff Gill, "The Newark Holy Stones." *Timeline: A Publication of the Ohio Historical Society* 17, no. 3 (May–June 2000).

Lewadowski, Tadeusz. *Red Bird, Red Power.* University of Oklahoma Press, 2016.

Lin, Maya. *Boundaries.* Simon & Schuster, 2020.

Lin, Maya. "Making the Memorial." *The New York Review,* November 2, 2000. https://www.nybooks.com/articles/2000/11/02/making-the-memorial/.

Maag, Christopher. "Ohio Indian Mounds: Hallowed Ground and a Nice Par 3." *New York Times*, November 28, 2005. https://www.nytimes.com/2005/11/28/us/ohio-indian-mounds-hallowed-ground-and-a-nice-par-3.html.

Mallett, Kent, "Judge Rules OHC Can Reclaim Octagon Mounds from Moundbuilders." *Newark (OH) Advocate*, May 10, 2019. Accessed October 16, 2024. https://www.newarkadvocate.com/story/news/2019/05/10/judge-rules-ohc-can-reclaim-octagon-mounds-country-cub/1170949001/.

Mallet, Kent. "Moundbuilders Reaches Deal to Buy Trout Club, Allowing State to Control Octagon Earthworks." *Newark (OH) Advocate*, July 24, 2024. Accessed October 19, 2024. https://www.newarkadvocate.com/story/news/local/2024/07/24/moundbuilders-country-club-to-buy-trout-club-sell-its-lease-at-octagon-earthworks-ohio-history/74500220007/.

Malouchos, Elizabeth, Mark R. Schurr, and Edward W. Herrmann. "From the Mound to the Moon: Geophysical Insights into Angel Phase Landscapes." *Journal of Archaeological Science: Reports* 37 (2021): 102886.

Malville, J. McKim. "Chimney Rock and the Moon: The Shrine at the Edge of the World." In *The Chimney Rock Archaeological Symposium*, edited by Malville, J. McKim, and Gary Matlock. USDA Forest Service, General Technical Report, June 1993.

McAlister, Jason. "Mounds' lunar alignment discovered accidentally." *Newark (OH) Advocate*, October 16, 2005, 6.

McCulloch, J. Huston. "The Newark Hebrew Stones: Wyrick's Letter to Joseph Henry." Originally published in *Midwest Epigraphic Journal* 6 (1989): 5–10. Reprinted online at https://www.asc.ohio-state.edu/mcculloch.2/arch/wletter.htm#text1.

McLaird, James D. "The Welsh, the Vikings, and the Lost Tribes of Israel on the Northern Plains: The Legend of the White Mandan." *South Dakota History* 18, no. 4. (1988): 245–273.

Menand, Louis. "Maya Lin, the Reluctant Memorialist." *The New Yorker*, June 20, 2002. https://www.newyorker.com/magazine/2002/07/08/maya-lin-the-reluctant-memorialist.

Miller, G. Logan. "Ritual, Labor Mobilization, and Monumental Construction in Small-Scale Societies." *Current Anthropology* 62, no. 2 (April 2021): 164–197.

Milligan, Susan. "From Embrace to 'Replace.'" *US News & World Report*, May 20, 2022. https://www.usnews.com/news/the-report/articles/2022-05-20/the-republican-embrace-of-the-great-replacement-theory.

Momaday, N. Scott. "A Devine Blindness," in *The Man Made of Words: Essays, Stories, Passages*. St. Martin's Griffin, 1997.

Momaday, N. Scott. *Earth Keeper*. HarperCollins Publishers, 2000.

Moundbuilders Country Club (@Moundbuilders-Country-Club-100063650346075), "Good morning women of MCC." Facebook, May 10, 2021, https://www.facebook.com/permalink.php?story_fbid=pfbid02tbHvGWQjLuJQNwHPNTbfUoSidRVuWPLXMwk9fhYoXtA7Y3CdUqMJf9dXUUJsqH6zl&id=100063650346075.

Murphy, James L. "Ohio National Guard Activities at the Newark Works." Knowledge Bank, The Ohio State University Libraries, undated. https://kb.osu.edu/server/api/core/bitstreams/10bf5a9b-a1ce-5e3b-b779-df4802a3e166/content.

National Park Service. National Register of Historic Places Inventory—Nomination Form for Earlham College Observatory. https://npgallery.nps.gov/GetAsset/fcc0d431-ebb4-4f9c-8763-e261e63fb7d3.

Noodin, Margaret. "Bundling the Day and Unraveling the Night." *American Indian Quarterly* 37, no. 3 (2013): 237–240. https://doi.org/10.5250/amerindiquar.37.3.0237.

Nott, Josiah Clark. *An Essay on the Natural History of Mankind, Viewed in Connection with Negro Slavery: Delivered before the Southern Rights Association 14th December 1850.* Dade, Thompson & Co. Printers, 1851. https://archive.org/details/essayonnaturalhi00nott/mode/2up.

Nott, Josiah Clark, and George R. Gliddon. *Types of Mankind.* Lippincott, Grambo & Co., 1854. https://archive.org/details/typesmankindore01pattgoog/page/n10/mode/2up?q=mounds.

Ohio Hopewell: Ancient Crossroads of the American Midwest. "Excavation of Hopewell Mounds, 1891, Ross County, Ohio," from the collection of The Field Museum, Chicago, on the website of the University of Nebraska Lincoln. http://hopewell.unl.edu/albums/hopewell44/#page/0/mode/1up.

Ohio State Journal. "Columbus Red Men Entertain Indians." October 17, 1911. In the repository of the Columbus Metropolitan Library, Columbus, OH.

The Ohio State Lantern. "A. C. Parker Denies That Indians Are Descended from Ancient Hebrews." October 2, 1912.

Overbye, Dennis. "Philip Morrison, 89, Builder of First Atom Bomb, Dies." *New York Times,* April 26, 2005. https://www.nytimes.com/2005/04/26/science/philip-morrison-89-builder-of-first-atom-bomb-dies.html.

Paper, Jordan. *Native North American Religious Traditions: Dancing for Life.* Praeger Publishers, 2006.

Pauketat, Timothy R. *An Archaeology of the Cosmos: Rethinking Agency and Religion in Ancient America.* Routledge, 2013.

Pauketat, Timothy R. "Lunar Twins: Cahokia's Emerald Acropolis & Chaco's Chimney Rock in 11th Century." Interview by Benjamin Bellorado, *Crow Canyon Archaeological Center,* May 5, 2022. https://www.youtube.com/watch?v=eUI50-AIuCk,l.

PBS (Public Broadcasting Service). "Lost Tribes of Israel, Part 2," from the TV series *Where are the Ten Lost Tribes?* Accessed August 16, 2022. https://www.pbs.org/wgbh/nova/israel/losttribes2.html.

Pickard, Bill. "A View Within the Circle, Part II: Inside Looking Out." *Ohio Historical Society Archaeology Blog,* October 20, 2009. Accessed October 26, 2024. https://ohioarchaeology.wordpress.com/2009/10/20/a-view-within-the-circle-part-ii-inside-looking-out/.

Pratt, Captain R. H. "The Advantages of Mingling Indians with Whites." In *Proceedings of the National Conference of Charities and Correction at the Nineteenth Annual Session*

Held in Denver, Col., June 23–29, 1892, edited by Isabel C. Barrows. Press of Geo. H. Ellis, 1892. https://hdl.handle.net/2027/wu.89030648919.

Prufer, Curt Max. *Rewriting History: The Original and Revised World War II Diaries of Kurt Prufer, Nazi Diplomat.* Translated by Judith M. Melton. Edited by Donald M. McKale. Kent State University Press, 1988.

Redmond, Brian G., Bret J. Ruby, and Jarrod Burks, eds. *Encountering Hopewell in the Twenty-first Century, Ohio and Beyond.* The University of Akron Press, 2019.

Reeves, Dache M. *Aerial Photographs: Characteristics and Military Applications.* The Ronald Press Company, 1927.

Reeves, Dache M. "A Newly Discovered Extension of the Newark Works." *Ohio History Journal* 45, no. 2 (April 1936): 189–193.

Reitz, Elizabeth J. "Minutes of the 1991 Southeastern Archaeological Conference Business Meeting." *Southeastern Archaeological Conference Newsletter* 34, no. 1 (April 1992): 14. https://www.southeasternarchaeology.org/wp-content/uploads/SEAC-Newsletter-Vol.-34-No.-1-April-1992.pdf.

"Remarkable Archaeological Discovery in Ohio." *New York Times,* July 27, 1860. Unattributed account addressed "To the Editor of the New-York Times."

Richmond (IN) Palladium-Item. "Astronomer to help trace comet's trail for readers," November 24, 1985.

Ruby, Bret J., Christopher Carr, and Douglas K. Charles. "Community Organizations in the Scioto, Mann, and Havana Hopewellian Regions." In *Gathering Hopewell: Society, Ritual, and Ritual Interaction,* edited by Christopher Carr and D. Troy Case. Kluwer Academic/Plenum Publishers, 2004.

Schlies, Paula. "Traveling the Road Back to Prehistory." *Magazine of the Akron Beacon Journal,* June 5, 1992.

Schoolcraft, Henry H., letter to the editor, "The 'Hebrew Stone' in Ohio." *New York Times,* August 6, 1860.

Seeman, Erik R. *The Huron-Wendat Feast of the Dead.* The Johns Hopkins University Press, 2011.

Shetrone, Henry C., and Emerson F. Greenman. "Explorations of the Seip Group of Pre-Historic Earthworks." *Ohio History Journal* 40, no. 3 (July 1931): 343–509. https://resources.ohiohistory.org/ohj/search/display.php?page=126&ipp=20&searchterm=Array&vol=40&pages=343-509.

Shiels, Dick, "Shiels: Remembering the Rosa Parks of the Newark Earthworks." *Newark (OH) Advocate,* January 19, 2020. Accessed October 12, 2024. https://www.newarkadvocate.com/story/news/local/2020/01/19/shiels-praying-newark-earthworks-octagon/4487843002/.

Shiels, Dick, "Shiels: The life-changing potential of the Newark Earthworks." *Newark (OH) Advocate,* March 12, 2023. Accessed October 17, 2024. https://www.newarkadvocate.com/story/opinion/columnists/2023/03/12/shiels-the-life-changing-potential-of-the-newark-earthworks/69982920007/.

Silverberg, Robert. *Mound Builders of Ancient America.* New York Graphic Society, Ltd., 1968.

Smithson, Robert. "Cultural Confinement." *Robert Smithson: The Collected Writings.* Edited by Jack Flam. University of California Press. 1996.

Snow, C. P. *The Two Cultures.* Cambridge University Press, 2020.

Sofaer, Anna, Volker Zinser, and Rolf M. Sinclair. "A Unique Solar Marking Construct." *Science* 206, no. 4416 (October 19, 1979): 283–291.

Sofaer, Anna, R. M. Sinclair, and L. E. Doggett. "Lunar Markings on Fajada Butte, Chaco Canyon." In *Archaeoastronomy in the New World,* edited by A. F. Aveni. Cambridge University Press, 1982.

Squier, E. G., and E. H. Davis. *Ancient Monuments of the Mississippi Valley: Comprising the Results of Extensive Original Surveys and Explorations.* Smithsonian Institution, June 1847.

"Summary Records of the 45th Session of the World Heritage Committee (Riyadh, 2023) WHC/23/45 COM/INF.19." UNESCO World Heritage Convention, 2023. https://whc.unesco.org/document/199708.

Thornton, Stuart. "Intriguing Interactions." *National Geographic,* October 1, 2024. https://education.nationalgeographic.org/resource/intriguing-interactions/.

Tribal Law Updates. "Apology from Child Welfare League of America." Website of the Tribal Law and Policy Institute. https://tlpi.wordpress.com/2011/08/11/apology-from-child-welfare-league-of-america/.

Trickey, Erick. "Inside the Story of America's 19th-Century Opiate Addiction." *Smithsonian,* January 4, 2018. https://www.smithsonianmag.com/history/inside-story-americas-19th-century-opiate-addiction-180967673/.

Tuwaletstiwa, Philip, interview. *Written on the Landscape: Mysteries of Chaco Canyon.* Directed and produced by Anna Sofaer. bullfrogfilms, 2024.

UNESCO World Heritage Convention. "Hopewell Ceremonial Earthworks – Nomination." World Heritage Ohio Steering Committee, Ohio History Connection, Hopewell Culture National Historical Park, and the US National Park Service Office of International Affairs, 2023. https://whc.unesco.org/en/list/1689/documents/.

United Kingdom Foreign, Commonwealth & Development Office. "Open Letter to the UNESCO World Heritage Committee," April 8, 2022. Accessed October 17, 2024. https://www.gov.uk/government/publications/open-letter-to-the-unesco-world-heritage-committee-7-april-2022/open-letter-to-the-unesco-world-heritage-committee.

Wallace, Glenna. Speech at Rededication Ceremony, Seip Earthworks. Video by T. Engbert and Brian Knisley / National Park Service. Recorded October 9, 2014.

Warrior, Robert. "The SAI and the End(s) of Intellectual History." *Studies in American Indian Literatures* 25, no. 2 (Summer 2013): 221–235.

Weaver, Al. "Vance Slams 'Poisoning Our blood' Comparisons Between Trump Comments, Nazis." *The Hill*, December 19, 2023. https://thehill.com/homenews/senate/4368234-vance-slams-poisoning-our-blood-comparisons-between-trump-comments-nazis/.

Wesley, Kathy. "Mastodon Unearthed at Golf Course." *Newark (OH) Advocate*, December 13, 1989.

Wilder, Robert. "Interview: Anna Sofaer." *El Palacio: The Magazine of the New Mexico Department of Cultural Affairs* 113, no. 3 (Fall 2008).

Wiles, Laurie. "Maya Ying Lin." *Elysian*, undated. Accessed online October 2, 2024. https://readelysian.com/maya-ying-lin/.

Wilford, John Noble. "Mastodon Yields Living Organisms." *New York Times*, May 4, 1991.

Wilkerson, Isabel. *Caste: The Origin of Our Discontents*. Random House, 2023.

Wimble, Katherine, and Barbara Powers. "Hopewell Earthwork Mounds." *SAH Archipedia, Society of Architectural Historians*. Edited by Gabrielle Esperdy and Karen Kingsley. University of Virginia Press, 2012. https://sah-archipedia.org/buildings/OH-01-141-0003.

Wyandotte Nation. "What History Says." Wyandotte Nation website. https://wyandotte-nation.org/culture/our-history/.

Yerkes, Richard W. "Hopewell Tribes: A Study of Middle Woodland Social Organization in the Ohio Valley." In *The Archaeology of Tribal Societies*, edited by W. A. Parkinson. International Monographs in Prehistory, Archaeological Series 15, 2002. https://doi.org/10.2307/j.ctv8bt29z.16.

Young, Gloria A. "Reconstruction of an Arkansas Hopewellian Panpipe." *Journal of the Arkansas Academy of Science* 24, article 12 (1970).

Zitkala-Ša. *American Indian Stories and Old Indian Legends*. Dover Publications, 2014.

Zitkala-Ša. *Zitkala-Sa: American Indian Stories, Legends, and Other Writings*. Penguin Books, 2003.

Zitkala-Ša. *Zitkala-Sa: Letters, Speeches, and Unpublished Writings, 1898–1929*. Edited by Tadeusz Lewadowski. Brill, 2018.

ABOUT THE AUTHOR

James W. Graham has spent his career working in journalism, public affairs, and nonprofit communications. He is the author of *Victura: The Kennedys, a Sailboat, and the Sea* and has written for *Time, The Huffington Post,* and elsewhere. He lives in suburban Chicago with his wife, Linda Kingman.

www.ingramcontent.com/pod-product-compliance
Lightning Source LLC
LaVergne TN
LVHW081457200826
846010LV00034B/415
9780814259917